CHURCH POTLUCK
❧ SLOW COOKER ❧

Homestyle Recipes for Family and Community Celebrations

LINDA LARSEN

adamsmedia

AVON, MASSACHUSETTS

Published by Adams Media, an F+W Publications Company
57 Littlefield Street
Avon, MA 02322
www.adamsmedia.com

ISBN 13: 978-1-59869-774-2
ISBN 10: 1-59869-774-9

Printed in Canada.

J   I   H   G   F   E   D   C   B   A

Library of Congress Cataloging-in-Publication Data
is available from the publisher.

Unless otherwise noted, the Bible used as a source is the *New Revised Standard Version Bible*, copyright © 1989 by the Division of Christian Education of the National Council of the Churches of Christ in the United States of America.

Many of the designations used by manufacturers and sellers to distinguish their products are claimed as trademarks. Where those designations appear in this book and Adams Media was aware of a trademark claim, the designations have been printed in initial capital letters.

This publication is designed to provide accurate and authoritative information with regard to the subject matter covered. It is sold with the understanding that the publisher is not engaged in rendering legal, accounting, or other professional advice. If legal advice or other expert assistance is required, the services of a competent professional person should be sought.

—From a *Declaration of Principles* jointly adopted by a Committee of the American Bar Association and a Committee of Publishers and Associations

This book is available at quantity discounts for bulk purchases.
For information, please call 1-800-289-0963.

Contents

I will give you your rains in each season, and the land shall yield its produce, and the trees of the field shall yield their fruit. Your threshing shall overtake the vintage, and the vintage shall overtake the sowing; you shall eat your bread to the full, and live securely in your land.

—LEVITICUS 26:4–5

Introduction

You will eat some of the best food anywhere at church potlucks. Everyone brings his or her best recipes, and reputations are made around the communal table. From delicate cakes to rich entrées, crisp salads, decadent desserts, and hot and creamy soups, this food must be the best.

Sharing food in the fellowship of Christ is important in church life. Just as eating dinners as a family is necessary to relationships among family members, so eating breakfast, lunch, or dinner communally as a church family helps build strong bonds. And the people who provide that food are angels in disguise. It takes a lot of talent and knowledge to feed a crowd delicious, healthy, and safe food.

If you're cooking for your church family, you know the challenges and rewards that come with the job. These recipes will help, offering lots of easily prepared and delicious food that caters to a variety of tastes.

The slow cooker can be an assistant in the kitchen, whether you're serving hundreds after Easter services or a small Bible study group that gathers in the evenings after work. You can dou-

ble, triple, or quadruple these recipes, keeping the proportions the same, to fill as many slow cookers as you need and can find. Recipes can also be cut in half, as long as the appliance is filled correctly.

There are quite a few things to think about when you're staging a potluck in your church. The most important is food safety. You will be serving people with varying medical conditions, so the food has to be impeccably safe.

Never let perishable food sit out at room temperature longer than 2 hours. Always wash your hands before (and after) serving or preparing food, and after handling raw dairy or meat products. Keep raw meats away from foods to be served uncooked. Don't cool food in the thick slow cooker liner. Refrigerate cooked food after it's been sitting out for 2 hours (1 hour in hot weather). And always cook eggs and meats to the correct safe, final internal temperature, using a food thermometer to be sure. Each recipe includes the correct final temperature for that particular food.

Not all of the food you serve from the slow cooker has to be hot! You can use this versatile appliance to make fillings for sandwiches, as well as pie fillings. Leftovers of meats like roast beef and poached chicken are ideal for making salads and appetizers.

Newer slow cookers, those which have been manufactured in the last three to four years, cook much hotter than did the slow cookers of ten or fifteen years ago. Many recipes do take this into account. In the newer slow cookers, raw boneless chicken breasts will cook in 5 to 6 hours, as opposed to the 7 to 8 hours called for in older recipes. Use a meat thermometer to check the internal temperature at the minimum cooking time. If it's already done, make a note that your slow cooker cooks at a higher temperature.

When you cook with the slow cooker, you'll get the best results if it is filled between ½ and ¾ full. Because the recipes in this book call for "2 onions, chopped" or "4 carrots, sliced," you may need to alter the amount of food you put in the slow cooker if your vegetables are very large or small. Just adhere to the ½ to ¾ rule and everything will turn out beautifully. You may need to cut large roasts or pieces of meat in half, and do some experimenting to discover which size slow cooker best fits the cut of meat or food you are cooking.

These recipes use the best ingredients—real butter, heavy cream, beef, and fresh vegetables.

For lower-fat versions, you can substitute half-and-half or milk for the cream, or use lower-fat or fat-free dairy products. Please don't use margarine in place of butter; butter adds an important dimension of flavor to many of these recipes.

The slow cookers recommended for these recipes range from 4 to 7 quarts in size. There are a few recipes for the very small slow cooker, usually for sauces or condiments. For cooking large cuts of meat, the oval slow cookers work better. Their shape easily handles the bulk of these foods. Follow directions for cutting and trimming the meat to the letter.

For easy cleanup, spray the slow cooker with nonstick cooking spray before you add the food. You could also use the cooking bags specifically made for the slow cooker (don't use ordinary plastic bags) for no cleanup at all. Soaking the ceramic or glass liners overnight with a little dish soap will help get rid of any food that doesn't come off with gentle scrubbing.

Slow cookers are a great investment for your church kitchen. They cook food perfectly while you work on other tasks, don't heat up the kitchen as much as the oven does, and are portable, too. In addition, a lot of the newer ones are pretty enough to serve from once the food is cooked. Now, collect some slow cookers and let's cook for a crowd!

Appetizers and Beverages

*W*hether you're serving dinner after a wedding or snacks before a hayride, appetizers made in the slow cooker are a great way to save time and effort. Appetizers not only help fill the time and whet the appetite until dinner is ready; they can *be* dinner! A collection of appetizers can be a meal replacement as long as you vary flavors and textures, and include some hearty recipes as well as light ones, with some simple sweets for dessert.

Offer lots of different dippers and bases for these recipes. Baby vegetables, carrot sticks, pepper strips, and cherry tomatoes are obvious choices. Also consider pita breads, cut into wedges; breadsticks; bubble bread; cheese toasts and party rye toast; warmed tortillas; and firm lettuces.

Because these recipes are going to be warm and creamy, think about contrast of texture and temperature in presentation. You can sprinkle a dip with crisp chopped green onions or fresh tomatoes, or use fresh apple or pear slices as dippers. All of these recipes are easily varied to suit your personal and local preferences. You can add or subtract ingredients easily or change the seasonings.

Timing is important when serving these foods. These hot appetizers can be kept warm on the low or warm setting for a few hours. For food safety reasons, remember, when serving a crowd, to start a few batches of a recipe, each an hour apart. Then, every 2 hours, replace each older batch with a fresh one, in its own slow cooker. Do not transfer the fresh batch to the slow cooker that's already been setting out for 2 hours.

Indian Chicken Wings

YIELDS 48

These mildly spicy wings are glazed with a sweet and savory mixture. They are delicious at the start of a barbecue or any meal. Be sure to serve them with lots of napkins!

4 dozen chicken drummies
1 (10-ounce) bottle mango chutney
2 tablespoons lime juice
1 onion, chopped
3 garlic cloves, minced
1 tablespoon grated fresh gingerroot
1 tablespoon curry powder
½ cup honey
2 tablespoons butter, melted
½ teaspoon salt
⅛ teaspoon pepper

1. Preheat broiler. Place the drummies on a broiler pan. Broil 6" from heat, turning once, until browned, about 5–6 minutes. Place in a 4- or 5-quart slow cooker. In a medium bowl, combine remaining ingredients and mix well. Pour over wings.
2. Cover slow cooker and cook on low for 8–9 hours or until chicken is tender and glazed.

Sweet-and-Sour Mini Sausages

SERVES 8–10

The sausages you want for this recipe are called "Little Smokies." Kids and adults alike will gobble up this excellent appetizer.

1 (20-ounce) can pineapple tidbits in juice
2 pounds small fully cooked sausages
1 onion, chopped
¼ cup honey
¼ cup brown sugar
½ cup apple cider vinegar
½ cup applesauce
½ cup ketchup
¼ cup mustard
3 green bell peppers, chopped

1. Drain pineapple, reserving juice. In a 6-quart slow cooker, combine pineapple, sausages, and onion, and mix gently.
2. In medium bowl, combine ¼ cup reserved pineapple juice, honey, brown sugar, vinegar, applesauce, ketchup, and mustard, and mix well. Pour into slow cooker and stir.
3. Cover and cook on low for 4–5 hours until sausages are hot. Add green peppers. Cover and cook on low for 30 minutes longer, until peppers are tender. Stir and serve.

Slow Cooker Reuben Dip

SERVES 10–12

Reuben sandwiches and dip are usually made with sauerkraut. This one is different; red cabbage is cooked until tender, then combined with the dip ingredients. It has less sodium and a fresher taste. You can omit the corned beef for a vegetarian version.

1 red cabbage, chopped

1 red onion, chopped

2 cloves garlic, minced

2 tablespoons apple cider vinegar

2 tablespoons honey

½ teaspoon salt

1 (8-ounce) package cream cheese, cubed

1 cup shredded Gruyère cheese

1 cup shredded Swiss cheese

½ cup Thousand Island dressing

1 (3-ounce) package thinly sliced corned beef, chopped

1. In a 5-quart slow cooker, combine cabbage, onion, garlic, vinegar, honey, and salt. Stir to combine, then cover and cook on low for 7 hours or until cabbage and onions are tender.
2. Drain the cabbage mixture; then return it to the slow cooker. Add remaining ingredients; stir to combine. Cover and cook on low for 2–3 hours longer or until cheeses melt. Stir to blend, and serve with crackers and breadsticks.

Apricot Slow Cooker "Wings"

SERVES 8–10

Cutting dark meat into strips makes an excellent boneless appetizer, glazed with a sweet-and-sour sauce. Serve this recipe with lots of napkins!

3 pounds boneless, skinless chicken thighs

1 onion, chopped

¼ cup apple cider vinegar

½ cup apricot jam

2 tablespoons apple jelly

¼ cup honey

2 tablespoons soy sauce

4 cloves garlic, minced

1. Cut chicken into ½" × 3" strips. Place in 4-quart slow cooker with chopped onion, and stir gently to mix.
2. In small bowl, combine remaining ingredients and mix well. Pour into slow cooker. Cover and cook on low for 6–7 hours or until chicken is thoroughly cooked to an internal temperature of 165°F.

David said to him, "Do not be afraid, for I will show you kindness for the sake of your father Jonathan, I will restore to you all the land of your grandfather Saul, and you yourself shall eat at my table always."

—2 SAMUEL 9:7

Chicken and Artichoke Dip

SERVES 8–10

Slice and toast French bread and rub with cut garlic to make crostini to serve with this fabulous warm and creamy dip.

1 (16-ounce) package frozen cut leaf spinach, thawed

2 (14-ounce) cans marinated artichoke hearts, drained

1 (10-ounce) jar four-cheese Alfredo sauce

½ cup mayonnaise

1 (8-ounce) package cream cheese, cubed

2 cups cubed cooked chicken

3 cloves garlic, minced

2 tablespoons lemon juice

1 cup shredded Monterey jack cheese

1 cup shredded Swiss cheese

½ cup grated Parmesan cheese

½ teaspoon paprika

1. Drain spinach thoroughly, pressing it between kitchen towels to remove as much moisture as possible. Rinse the artichoke hearts and cut into small pieces.
2. Combine all ingredients except Parmesan cheese and paprika in 3½ or 4-quart slow cooker. Cover and cook on low for 3–4 hours, until hot and bubbly. Sprinkle with Parmesan cheese and paprika and serve.

Garlic and Brie Spread

SERVES 10–12

This elegant spread would be delicious for a wedding reception. The garlic and onions become very mellow and sweet, so there's no need to worry about garlic breath!

3 heads garlic

2 onions, chopped

1 tablespoon olive oil

½ teaspoon salt

½ teaspoon dried thyme leaves

2 (8-ounce) wedges Brie cheese, cubed

1. Carefully peel the garlic heads, separating them into cloves, and peel the cloves. Combine the garlic cloves with onion, olive oil, and salt in 2-quart slow cooker.
2. Cover and cook on low for 8–9 hours or until garlic and onion are soft and tender. Using a potato masher, mash the garlic and onion, leaving some pieces whole.
3. Stir in the thyme and cubed Brie. Cover the slow cooker again and cook on low for 30–40 minutes, or until Brie melts. Stir gently and serve.

Slow Cooker Caponata

SERVES 10–12

Caponata can be served as an appetizer with crackers and vegetables, as a sandwich spread, or as a side dish.

1 tablespoon olive oil

1 onion, chopped

3 cloves garlic, minced

1½ pounds plum tomatoes, chopped

2 eggplants, peeled and chopped

1 red bell pepper, chopped

1 cup chopped celery

1 (6-ounce) can tomato paste

1 teaspoon dried basil

½ teaspoon dried oregano

2 tablespoons sugar

1 tablespoon lemon juice

1 teaspoon salt

¼ teaspoon white pepper

2 tablespoons white wine vinegar

½ cup chopped black olives

2 tablespoons capers

½ cup chopped parsley

1 cup chopped smoked mozzarella cheese

1. In 4- or 5-quart slow cooker, combine all ingredients except parsley and cheese; mix well.
2. Cover and cook on low for 7–8 hours until vegetables are tender and mixture blends. Stir in parsley and cheese and place in serving dish. Let cool for 30 minutes. Serve warm or cold.

Blueberry-Raisin Chutney

SERVES 10–12

Serve this chutney hot or cold, plain or poured over Brie or Camembert cheese, along with fruit for dipping. It's also excellent as a sandwich spread or filling.

6 cups fresh blueberries

2 cups golden raisins

1 onion, minced

1 tart apple, cored, peeled and chopped

6 cloves garlic, minced

⅓ cup honey

⅓ cup white wine vinegar

¼ cup orange juice

¾ cup brown sugar

1 tablespoon curry powder

1 teaspoon salt

¼ teaspoon white pepper

2 tablespoons butter

¼ cup cornstarch

½ cup apple cider

1. Combine all ingredients except cornstarch and apple cider in 4-quart slow cooker. Stir to blend. Cover and cook on low for 5–7 hours or until blueberries pop and apple is very tender.
2. In small bowl combine cornstarch and apple cider; stir to blend. Stir into chutney mixture. Cover and cook on high for 20–30 minutes or until chutney has thickened. Serve hot or cold.

Best-Ever Snack Mix

YIELDS 10 CUPS; SERVES 20
Put out small bowls of this snack mix and replace them every hour to keep the mix fresh and crisp. You might want to make another batch of this delicious recipe.

2 cups small square cheese crackers
2 cups square corn cereal
2 cups pecan halves
2 cups cashews
2 cups garlic bagel chips
1 cup butter
¼ cup Worcestershire sauce
1 teaspoon garlic salt
1 teaspoon onion salt
¼ teaspoon pepper
½ cup finely grated Romano cheese

1. In 4-quart slow cooker, combine crackers, cereal, pecans, cashews, and bagel chips. Toss to mix.
2. In small saucepan, melt butter over medium heat. Remove from heat and stir in remaining ingredients except cheese. Drizzle over mixture in slow cooker. Stir gently to coat, then cover and cook on low for 2 hours.
3. Uncover slow cooker and cook for 1 hour, stirring occasionally. Then sprinkle with cheese, turn heat to high, and cook for 15 minutes longer, stirring once during cooking time.
4. Place mixture on cookie sheet to cool. Store covered in airtight container at room temperature.

Toasted Parmesan Nuts

YIELDS 6 CUPS; SERVES 12
You can use any combination of nuts in this simple appetizer. Substitute onion powder for the garlic powder for a slightly different taste.

3 cups small pecan halves
3 cups cashew halves
½ cup butter
½ teaspoon garlic powder
1 teaspoon salt
¼ teaspoon pepper
1½ cups grated Parmesan cheese

1. Combine nuts in a 3-quart slow cooker. In small saucepan, melt butter over low heat. Add garlic powder, salt, and pepper and mix well. Pour over nuts and stir to coat.
2. Cover and cook on low for 2 hours, then uncover slow cooker and turn heat to high. Stir in Parmesan cheese. Cook, uncovered, for 30 minutes, stirring every 10 minutes, until nuts are coated and glazed. Cool on cookie sheet, then store tightly covered in airtight container.

I have been young, and now am old, yet I have not seen the righteous forsaken or their children begging bread. They are ever giving liberally and lending, and their children become a blessing.

—PSALMS 37:25–26

Spicy Meatballs

SERVES 24

You can make this recipe more or less spicy by varying the amounts and types of pepper you use.

1 tablespoon olive oil

2 tablespoons butter

1 onion, finely chopped

4 cloves garlic, minced

1 cup soft bread crumbs

2 eggs

1 tablespoon chili powder

¼ teaspoon hot sauce

1 teaspoon salt

¼ teaspoon pepper

⅛ teaspoon cayenne pepper

1½ pounds lean ground beef

1 pound bulk spicy pork sausage

1 (16-ounce) jar apricot preserves

1 (12-ounce) jar raspberry preserves

2 cups barbecue sauce

1 cup ketchup

1. In skillet, combine olive oil and butter over medium heat. When butter melts, add onion and garlic. Cook and stir until tender, about 6 minutes. Place in large mixing bowl. Add bread crumbs, eggs, chili powder, hot sauce, salt, pepper, and cayenne pepper; mix well. Add ground beef and pork sausage and mix gently until combined.
3. Preheat oven to 350°F. Form meat mixture into 1" meatballs and place on broiler pan. Bake in batches for 30–35 minutes or until meatballs are cooked to 165°F. Drain on paper towels.
4. In bowl, combine apricot preserves, raspberry preserves, barbecue sauce, and ketchup. Mix well. Layer with meatballs in a 5- to 6-quart slow cooker. Cover and cook on low for 5–6 hours or until heated. Provide toothpicks for serving.

Three-Cheese Dip

SERVES 12–14

This creamy, melty cheese dip is delicious with crisp fresh vegetables. You could add meatballs, cooked chicken, or artichoke hearts for more interest.

2 pounds processed cheese, cubed

2 (8-ounce) packages garlic-flavored cream cheese, cubed

2 cups shredded Muenster cheese

1 tablespoon cornstarch

1 cup mayonnaise

½ cup sliced green onions, white and green parts

1. In a 4-quart slow cooker, combine processed cheese and cream cheese. Toss Muenster cheese with cornstarch and add to slow cooker along with mayonnaise; mix gently.
2. Cover and cook on low for 2–3 hours or until cheeses are melted, stirring twice during cooking time. Top with green onions and serve with fresh vegetables, crackers, and tortilla chips.

My soul is satisfied as with a rich feast, and my mouth praises you with joyful lips.

—PSALMS 63:5

Aunt Margaret's Cranberry Meatballs

SERVES 14–16

Two kinds of cranberry sauce make a wonderfully flavored sauce for meatballs in this delicious appetizer. This is a great choice for a Thanksgiving feast.

1 onion, chopped
3 cloves garlic, minced
3 pounds frozen cooked meatballs
1 (16-ounce) can jellied cranberry sauce
1 (16-ounce) can whole berry cranberry sauce
1 cup dried cranberries, chopped
½ cup brown sugar
¼ cup yellow mustard
1 cup chili sauce
1 cup ketchup

1. Layer onions and garlic in bottom of 5-quart slow cooker. Top with meatballs.
2. In large bowl, combine remaining ingredients and mix well, breaking up jellied cranberry sauce. Pour over meatballs.
3. Cover and cook on low for 6–7 hours or until sauce is bubbling and meatballs are hot.

Every moving thing that lives shall be food for you, and just as I gave you the green plants, I give you everything.

—GENESIS 9:3

Cheesy Taco Dip

SERVES 8–10

Place bowls of chopped tomatoes, sour cream, and lettuce around so people can build their own nachos.

1½ pounds pork sausage
2 onions, chopped
4 cloves garlic, minced
2 jalapeño peppers, minced
1 (16-ounce) jar mild salsa
1 pound processed cheese, cubed
2 (8-ounce) cans sliced mushrooms, drained
4 tomatoes, chopped
2 tablespoons chili powder
2 tablespoons cornstarch
½ cup tomato juice
2 cups chopped tomatoes
2 cups shredded lettuce
1 cup sour cream
2 cups shredded CoJack cheese

1. In skillet, cook pork sausage until partially done. Add onions, garlic, and jalapeño pepper; continue cooking until sausage is cooked. Drain.
2. Place in 4-quart slow cooker along with salsa, cheese, mushrooms, tomatoes, and chili powder. Mix well. Cover and cook on low for 6–7 hours, stirring once during cooking time.
3. In small bowl, combine cornstarch and tomato juice. Add to slow cooker; cover and cook on high for 30 minutes. Serve with tortilla chips and the fresh topping ingredients.

Spicy Nuts

YIELDS 8 CUPS; SERVES 18–20

If your crowd likes it spicy, increase the chili powder and cayenne pepper to taste. These nuts are great for snacking after a choir performance.

3 cups small pecan halves

2 cups walnut halves

3 cups salted cashews

½ cup butter, melted

¼ cup brown sugar

3 tablespoons chili powder

½ teaspoon cayenne pepper

1 teaspoon salt

1 teaspoon cinnamon

1. Turn 3½-quart slow cooker to high and let pre-heat for 15 minutes. Add all of the nuts; stir for 4–5 minutes until slightly toasted.
2. Meanwhile, in small bowl combine butter with remaining ingredients; mix well. Spoon mixture over the nuts and stir to coat. Cover and cook on low for 2 hours. Then uncover slow cooker, stir nuts, and cook on high for 20 minutes.
3. Spoon nuts onto a cookie sheet and let cool. Store covered in airtight containers at room temperature.

Sweet-and-Sour Nut Mix

YIELDS 10 CUPS; SERVES 20–30

Snack mixes are easy to make in the slow cooker. Use any combination of nuts and snack foods for a change of pace.

2 cups small pecan halves

2 cups whole almonds

2 cups hazelnuts

2 cups cashew halves

½ cup brown sugar

⅓ cup apple cider vinegar

1 teaspoon salt

3 tablespoons butter, melted

1 to 2 tablespoons curry powder

2 cups small pretzel rods

1. Turn 4-quart slow cooker to high and let preheat for 15 minutes. Add all of the nuts; stir for 4–5 minutes until slightly toasted.
2. Meanwhile, in small bowl combine brown sugar with remaining ingredients; mix well. Spoon mixture over the nuts and stir to coat. Cover and cook on low for 2 hours. Then uncover slow cooker, stir nuts, and cook on high for 1 hour longer, stirring occasionally.
3. Spoon nuts onto a cookie sheet and let cool. Store covered in airtight containers at room temperature.

Onion Chutney over Brie

SERVES 10–12

This chutney can be served warm or cold. If you let it cool for an hour or so, and then spoon it over any type of soft cheese, it will slightly melt the cheese. Yum.

5-pound bag yellow onions
8 cloves garlic, chopped
1 cup butter
1½ teaspoons seasoned salt
¼ teaspoon white pepper
1 cup brown sugar
½ cup apple cider vinegar
3 tablespoons minced fresh gingerroot
2 whole wheels Brie or Camembert cheese

1. Peel onions and coarsely chop. Combine in 5-quart slow cooker with garlic and butter.
2. Cover and cook on low for 8–10 hours, stirring once during cooking time, until onions are browned and caramelized.
3. Stir in seasoned salt, pepper, brown sugar, vinegar, and gingerroot. Cover and cook on high for 1–2 hours or until mixture is blended and hot.
4. Remove mixture from slow cooker to a large bowl. Cover loosely and let cool for 1–2 hours before serving over Brie or Camembert cheese. Serve with crackers and toasts for spreading.

Hot Lemon Cranberry Punch

SERVES 24

If you're having a sleigh ride in the winter for your youth group, serve this hot punch to warm everybody up.

1 (48-ounce) bottle cranberry juice cocktail
1 (12-ounce) can frozen lemonade concentrate
½ cup sugar
1 cup water
1 teaspoon cinnamon
½ teaspoon nutmeg
1 (32-ounce) bottle apple juice

1. In 4- to 5-quart slow cooker, combine cranberry juice, lemonade concentrate, sugar, water, cinnamon, and nutmeg. Stir to blend. Cover and cook on low for 2 hours, stirring once during cooking time.
2. Stir in apple juice. Cover and cook on low for 1–2 hours longer, until hot and blended. Keep warm in slow cooker for 2 hours, stirring occasionally.

Angel Sangria

Angel Sangria gives you the flavor of sangria with no alcohol. It's the perfect punch for an Advent or Christmas gathering.

1 (64-ounce) bottle red grape juice
2 cups pink grapefruit juice
2 tablespoons apple cider vinegar
½ cup sugar
1 teaspoon cinnamon
2 cups fresh cherries, pitted
2 (15-ounce) cans mandarin oranges, chopped

1. In 5-quart slow cooker, combine grape juice with pink grapefruit juice, vinegar, sugar, and cinnamon. Stir well. Cover and cook on high for 1 hour.
2. Stir mixture again, then stir in cherries and undrained mandarin oranges. Cover and cook on low for 1 hour longer. Punch can be kept warm for 2 hours on warm or low.

For the Lord your God is bringing you into a good land, a land with flowing streams, a land of wheat and barley, of vines and fig trees and pomegranates, a land of olive trees and honey, a land where you may eat bread without scarcity, where you will lack nothing, a land whose stones are iron and from whose hills you may mine copper.

—DEUTERONOMY 8:7–10

Pineapple Soother

SERVES 18–20
If you use peach nectar or orange juice, this warm punch can be different, but still delicious. Freeze some pineapple juice in ring molds to add to the punch, so that as the "ice" melts, the mixture isn't diluted.

8 cups pineapple juice
½ cup sugar
1 teaspoon cinnamon
2 cups white grape juice
½ teaspoon nutmeg
⅓ cup lime juice

1. In 3½- or 4-quart slow cooker, combine pineapple juice with sugar and cinnamon. Stir, then cover and cook on low for 1 hour.
2. Stir mixture again and add grape juice, nutmeg, and lime juice. Cover and cook on low for 1 hour longer. Punch can be kept warm on warm or low setting for 2 hours.

Chai Tea

SERVES 16–20

Chai is tea flavored with spices such as cardamom and cinnamon, and mellowed with heavy cream. It's a delicious drink that will warm you up after caroling.

10 cups boiling water
12 tea bags
1 teaspoon ground cardamom
1 teaspoon ground cinnamon
½ teaspoon ground ginger
½ cup sugar
2 cups pineapple juice
2 cups heavy cream

1. Combine boiling water and tea bags in a 5-quart slow cooker. Cover and let stand for 5–7 minutes, until tea is desired strength.
2. Remove tea bags, squeezing each one thoroughly. Stir in spices, sugar, and pineapple juice. Cover and cook on low for 2 hours.
3. Stir tea thoroughly. Add heavy cream. Cover and cook on low for 20 minutes or until hot. Turn slow cooker to warm, or off if not available. Serve from the slow cooker. After 2 hours, discard leftovers.

How does God's love abide in anyone who has the world's goods and sees a brother or sister in need and yet refuses help? Little children, let us love, not in word or speech, but in truth and action.

—1 JOHN 3:17–18

Hot Cider

SERVES 30

Cider is a classic hot drink after winter activities. Is your youth group having a skating party? This recipe will warm them up.

2 oranges
16 whole cloves
2 cinnamon sticks
½ cup sugar
1 gallon apple cider
¼ cup lemon juice

1. Roll the oranges gently on countertop, then stud with the whole cloves. Cut oranges in half and place in 6-quart slow cooker.
2. Add remaining ingredients and stir gently. Cover and cook on low for 2 hours. Remove cinnamon sticks and keep warm on low setting for 1 hour.

One of the scribes came near and heard them disputing with one another, and seeing that he answered them well, he asked him, "Which commandment is the first of all?" Jesus answered, "The first is, 'Hear O Israel: the Lord our God, the Lord is one, you shall love the Lord your God with all your heart, and with all your soul, and with all your mind, and with all your strength.' The second one is this, 'You shall love your neighbor as yourself.' There is no commandment greater than these."

—MARK 12:28–31

Grandpa's Hot Cocoa

SERVES 18–20

Marshmallow crème in the bottom of each cup adds smooth richness to this praline-scented hot chocolate. How deliciously decadent!

½ cup sugar
⅓ cup brown sugar
1 cup unsweetened cocoa powder
½ teaspoon salt
2 tablespoons maple syrup
5 cups boiling water
4 cups nonfat dry milk powder
8 cups water
2 (13-ounce) cans evaporated milk
1 tablespoon vanilla
2 (7-ounce) jars marshmallow crème

1. In 6-quart slow cooker, combine sugar, brown sugar, cocoa powder, salt, maple syrup, and boiling water. Stir until sugar dissolves.
2. Add remaining ingredients except marshmallow crème and stir to blend. Cover and cook on low for 3–4 hours, until blended and hot.
3. Beat mixture with an eggbeater until frothy. Place a spoonful of marshmallow crème in each serving cup, then ladle in hot cocoa.

Spiced Mocha Coffee

SERVES 12

Vary the spices in this easy recipe for a different taste. Multiply the recipe and have it brewing in several slow cookers at the same time.

12 cups brewed coffee
½ cup sugar
¼ cup maple syrup
⅓ cup unsweetened cocoa powder
4 cinnamon sticks
¼ teaspoon cardamom

1. In 4-quart slow cooker, combine all ingredients and mix well. Cover and cook on low for 2–3 hours or until hot and blended.
2. Remove cinnamon sticks and stir well with wire whisk. Serve immediately. Can be kept warm in slow cooker up to 1 hour. Stir occasionally.

I declare that I will bring you up out of the misery of Egypt, to the land of the Canaanites, the Hittites, the Amorites, the Perizzites, the Hivites, and the Jebusites, a land flowing with milk and honey.

—EXODUS 3:17

Breakfast and Brunch

Breakfast is the most important meal of the day. And when parishioners gather together, whether for an Easter service, a brunch on Christmas day, or just regular Sunday morning services, a meal is most welcome.

In college, I always liked attending the sunrise services held before Easter break. There's nothing like welcoming spring in the early morning hours with a worship service. My college had great breakfasts, too; their banana bread was spectacular, and I loved their fluffy and creamy scrambled eggs served with crisp, hot bacon.

With a couple of slow cookers on hand, you can have breakfast ready and waiting for a crowd with very little work. Bread puddings and stratas, which are a combination of bread layered with other ingredients and baked in a custard mixture, are warm and filling, and can even cook overnight while you sleep.

Be sure to follow food safety rules when you're working with eggs in the slow cooker. They should be fully cooked, and reach a temperature of 145°F. Eggs do cook well in the slow cooker, but they won't hold for more than an hour, so be sure to include that information in your planning.

Serve one of the beverages from the Appetizers and Beverages chapter for breakfast. Hot chocolate or a hot punch is welcome on cold mornings. And think about serving these foods with cold foods for contrast. Fresh fruit, in season, is a good choice, as is cold milk for the kids.

Apple Pecan Strata

SERVES 8

This delicious strata is perfect for brunch after morning services. The combination of flavors is perfect, and the aroma that will drift through the sanctuary is tempting. Serve with cold applesauce and heavy cream for a nice contrast.

½ cup light cream

¼ cup orange juice

4 eggs, beaten

3 tablespoons sugar

1 teaspoon cinnamon

1 teaspoon vanilla

6 cups cubed brioche or French bread

2 cups pecan crunch granola

1 cup toasted pecan pieces

2 Granny Smith apples, cored, peeled and cubed

1. To toast nuts, place in a dry skillet over medium heat and toss until fragrant and golden brown. Spray a 4- or 5-quart slow cooker with nonstick cooking spray. In medium bowl, combine cream, orange juice, eggs, sugar, cinnamon, and vanilla and blend well with whisk. Set aside.
2. Place ⅓ of the bread in the bottom of prepared slow cooker and sprinkle with ⅓ of the granola, pecans, and apples. Repeat layers. Pour egg mixture over all.
3. Cover and cook on high for 1½ to 2 hours or until just set. *Do not cook on low.*

Bacon and Waffle Strata

SERVES 8–10

This version of strata uses crisp waffles, which bake into a wonderfully textured casserole in the slow cooker.

8 slices bacon

8 frozen waffles, toasted

2 cups shredded Colby cheese

¼ cup chopped green onions, white and green parts

1 (13-ounce) can evaporated milk

1 (8-ounce) package cream cheese, softened

6 eggs

1 teaspoon dry mustard

½ cup maple syrup

1. In large skillet, cook bacon until crisp. Drain on paper towels, crumble, and set aside. Cut toasted waffles into cubes. Layer bacon and waffle cubes with cheese and green onions in 4- to 5-quart slow cooker.
2. Drain skillet, discarding bacon fat; do not wipe out. Add milk and cream cheese to skillet; cook over low heat, stirring frequently, until cheese melts and mixture is smooth.
3. Remove skillet from heat and beat in eggs, one at a time, until smooth. Stir in dry mustard and pour into slow cooker. Cover and cook on low for about 4–5 hours, until eggs are set. Serve with warmed maple syrup.

Egg and Spinach Casserole

SERVES 12

Topping a hot casserole with a cool, fragrant tomato mixture makes a delicious and hearty egg-and-vegetable breakfast casserole even better.

2 tablespoons butter

2 onions, finely chopped

3 cloves garlic, minced

2 red bell peppers, chopped

1 (16-ounce) package frozen cut leaf spinach, thawed

1 teaspoon dried basil leaves

18 eggs

1 cup sour cream

1 tablespoon flour

1 teaspoon salt

¼ teaspoon white pepper

2 cups grated pepper jack cheese

3 cups chopped grape tomatoes

1 cup sour cream

½ cup torn fresh basil leaves

½ cup grated Parmesan cheese

1. Spray a 5-quart slow cooker with nonstick cooking spray and set aside. In large skillet, melt butter over medium heat. Add onions and garlic; cook and stir until tender, about 6 minutes. Add red bell peppers; cook and stir for 3 minutes longer.

2. Drain spinach well and add to skillet; cook and stir until liquid evaporates. Stir in basil and remove mixture from heat; let stand for 20 minutes.

3. In large bowl, beat eggs with 1 cup sour cream, flour, salt, and pepper. Stir in pepper jack cheese; then stir in vegetable mixture. Pour into prepared slow cooker.

4. Cover and cook on low for 7–8 hours or until set. Meanwhile, in medium bowl combine tomatoes, 1 cup sour cream, basil leaves, and Parmesan cheese. Serve casserole with this sour cream and tomato topping.

Sing to the Lord a new song, his praise from the end of the earth! Let the sea roar and all that fills it, the coastlands and their inhabitants. Let the desert and its town lift up their voice, the villages that Kedar inhabits; let the inhabitants of Sela sing for joy, let them shout from the tops of the mountains. Let them give glory to the Lord, and declare his praise in the coastlands.

—ISAIAH 42:11

Artichoke Tomato Strata

SERVES 8–10

Make sure you purchase regular canned artichoke hearts, not marinated, unless you want a spicy breakfast! I once purchased cocktail onions instead of regular pearl onions for a casserole. Now I read labels very carefully.

8 croissants, cut into cubes

1 (15-ounce) can artichoke hearts, drained

2 tablespoons butter

1 onion, chopped

3 cloves garlic, minced

½ teaspoon salt

1 teaspoon dried marjoram leaves

5 eggs

1 cup light cream

⅛ teaspoon white pepper

6 tomatoes, cubed

1 cup cubed mozzarella cheese

2 cups cubed Colby cheese

1 cup sour cream

1 cup chopped tomatoes

¼ cup chopped fresh chives

1. Preheat oven to 400°F. Place croissant cubes on large cookie sheet. Bake for 10 minutes, turning cubes once, until browned. Set aside. Cut artichoke hearts into small pieces. Spray a 6-quart slow cooker with nonstick cooking spray and set aside.

2. In large skillet, melt butter over medium heat. Add onion and garlic; cook and stir until tender, about 6 minutes. Add artichokes; cook and stir for 2 minutes longer. Set aside.

3. In medium bowl, combine salt, marjoram, eggs, cream, and pepper. Beat until blended.

4. In prepared slow cooker, layer croissant cubes with onion mixture, cubed tomatoes, and cheeses. Pour egg mixture over all; let stand for 15 minutes, pushing bread into the egg mixture as necessary.

5. Cover and cook on low for 4–5 hours or until set. Scoop out of the slow cooker to serve; top with sour cream, tomatoes, and chopped chives.

He brought me to the banqueting house, and his intention toward me was love. Sustain me with raisins, refresh me with apples.

—SONG OF SOLOMON 2:4

Maple Apple Bread Pudding

SERVES 8–10

Serve this dish along with some fresh fruit and scrambled eggs for the perfect brunch after Easter services.

6 apples, cored and chopped

½ cup apple juice

1 cup brown sugar

⅓ cup maple syrup

¼ cup butter, melted

6 eggs, beaten

1 cup whole milk

2 teaspoons vanilla

1 teaspoon cinnamon

10 slices raisin swirl bread

½ (16-ounce) container cream cheese frosting

6 large croissants, cubed

1 cup raisins

1. In saucepan, combine apples with apple juice. Bring to a simmer; simmer for 5 minutes, stirring frequently. Remove from heat and set aside for 10 minutes. Drain apples, reserving juice.
2. In small bowl, combine brown sugar, maple syrup, and butter; mix well and set aside. In large bowl, combine reserved apple juice, eggs, milk, vanilla, and cinnamon; beat well and set aside.
3. Spread one side of the bread slices with the frosting; cut into cubes. In 6-quart slow cooker, layer ⅓ of the bread cubes, croissant cubes, raisins, apples, and the brown sugar mixture. Repeat layers. Pour egg mixture over all.
4. Cover and cook on high for 3½ to 4½ hours, until pudding is set. Turn off slow cooker and let cool for 30 minutes, then serve.

Bacon Sweet Potato Hash

SERVES 8

Hash recipes usually use leftover russet potatoes, but this one is different. Sweet potatoes add great flavor and nutrition to the recipe, and the bacon and pecans are a wonderful touch.

8 slices bacon

1 onion, chopped

4 sweet potatoes, peeled

⅓ cup brown sugar

¼ cup orange juice

⅓ cup applesauce

2 tablespoons butter, melted

½ teaspoon salt

⅛ teaspoon pepper

½ cup chopped pecans, if desired

1. In skillet, cook bacon until crisp; drain on paper towels, crumble, cover, and refrigerate. Drain all but 2 tablespoons drippings from skillet. Add onion; cook and stir for 5 minutes, until onion softens, stirring to loosen brown bits from skillet.
2. Cut sweet potatoes into 1" cubes. Combine potatoes and onions in 4-quart slow cooker; stir to mix.
3. In small bowl, combine all remaining ingredients except pecans and stir well. Pour into slow cooker. Cover and cook on low for 8–9 hours or until potatoes are tender.
4. Stir in reserved bacon and the pecans; cover and cook for 30 minutes longer. If desired, you can place a fried egg on top of each serving of hash.

Apple Pear Bread

SERVES 8

This moist bread can be cooked in a cake or bread insert made to go in the slow cooker, or in a 2-pound coffee can that has been thoroughly cleaned.

⅓ cup butter, softened

⅓ cup sugar

3 tablespoons brown sugar

2 eggs

1¾ cups flour

½ teaspoon baking powder

½ teaspoon baking soda

½ teaspoon cinnamon

pinch cardamom

¼ teaspoon salt

½ cup pear purée

¼ cup applesauce

¼ cup cored, finely chopped apple

1 cup chopped walnuts

1. Spray an 8-cup bread and cake insert for the slow cooker with nonstick baking spray containing flour. Set aside. In large mixing bowl, combine butter, sugar, and brown sugar and beat until light. Add eggs and mix until fluffy.

2. Sift together flour, baking powder, baking soda, cinnamon, cardamom, and salt. Add half of flour mixture to butter mixture and beat. Mix pear purée into butter and flour mixture. Add remaining flour mixture to combined ingredients and beat well. Add applesauce and chopped apple; mix until combined.

3. Stir in walnuts and place batter into prepared insert. Place a rack or trivet or crumpled foil in 3½- or 4-quart slow cooker. Place insert onto rack. Cover and cook on high for 2 to 3½ hours, testing after 2 hours, until bread springs back when lightly touched. Remove insert from slow cooker and place on wire rack; let cool for 10 minutes. Loosen sides of bread and carefully remove from pan; finish cooling on wire rack.

I would feed you with the finest of the wheat, and with honey from the rock I would satisfy you.

—PSALMS 81:16

Dill Cheese Bread

SERVES 8

A non-sweet bread is a nice change for a breakfast or brunch buffet. This tender bread has a nice dill flavor and tender texture.

3 tablespoons butter
1 onion, finely chopped
1 (3-ounce) package cream cheese
¼ cup buttermilk
½ cup small-curd cottage cheese
½ cup ricotta cheese
2 eggs
1½ cups flour
1 cup whole wheat flour
¼ cup sugar
2 teaspoons baking powder
1 teaspoon baking soda
½ teaspoon salt
2 teaspoons dill seed
1 tablespoon butter, melted

1. Spray a 3-quart slow cooker that has a removable liner with nonstick baking spray containing flour and set aside. In small saucepan, melt 3 tablespoons butter over medium heat. Add onion; cook and stir until tender, about 6 minutes.
2. Remove from heat and stir in cream cheese and buttermilk; stir until cream cheese is melted. Pour into medium bowl and add cottage cheese, ricotta cheese, and eggs; beat until combined.
3. In large bowl, combine flour, whole wheat flour, sugar, baking powder, baking soda, salt, and dill seed; mix well. Add cream cheese mixture and stir just until combined. Pour into prepared slow cooker.
4. Cover and cook on high for 1 hour. Put oven mitts on your hands and carefully turn the slow cooker liner ½ turn. Cover and cook for 1 hour to 1 hour 10 minutes longer until bread is golden brown and sounds hollow when gently tapped with fingers. Uncover and let stand for 20 minutes, then turn out onto wire rack and brush with 1 tablespoon melted butter. Let cool.

Can that which is tasteless be eaten without salt, or is there any flavor in the juice of mallows?

—JOB 6:6

Chocolate Pumpkin Bread Pudding

SERVES 8

Serve this wonderful bread casserole with warmed maple syrup, along with a side of crisp bacon and some cold orange juice.

8 cups cubed French bread

1½ cups semisweet chocolate chips

½ cup canned solid-pack pumpkin

½ cup heavy cream

1 cup milk

½ cup brown sugar

3 eggs

¼ cup butter, melted

½ teaspoon salt

1 teaspoon cinnamon

¼ teaspoon cardamom

2 teaspoons vanilla

1. Spray a 3½- to 4-quart slow cooker with nonstick baking spray containing flour. Place bread and chocolate chips in slow cooker; stir gently to mix.
2. In medium bowl, combine pumpkin and heavy cream; stir until combined. Add remaining ingredients and mix until smooth.
3. Pour mixture into slow cooker. Push bread down into the liquid if necessary. Let stand for 15 minutes. Cover and cook on high for about 2 hours or until pudding is set. Turn off slow cooker; remove cover. Loosely cover top of slow cooker with foil and let bread pudding stand for 15 minutes before serving.

Mother's Slow Cooker Oatmeal

SERVES 6–8

Toasting the oats adds a depth of flavor, and helps keep some texture in this easy recipe. You could use chopped apples or strawberries instead of blueberries. If you substitute regular rolled oats for the steel cut oats, the oatmeal will be very soft.

3 tablespoons butter

1½ cups steel cut oats

2 cups water

1 cup milk

1½ cups apple juice

½ teaspoon salt

⅓ cup sugar

1 cup chopped walnuts, toasted

1 cup blueberries

1. Spray a 2-quart slow cooker with nonstick cooking spray and set aside. In skillet, melt butter. Add oats; cook and stir until oats are toasted, about 6–7 minutes. Place in slow cooker and add water, milk, apple juice, salt, and sugar, stirring to mix.
2. Cover and cook on low for 7–8 hours. Stir well, then add walnuts and blueberries; cook for another 30 minutes. Serve with cold cream and brown sugar, if desired.

Feasts are made for laughter, wine gladdens life, and money meets every need.

—ECCLESIASTES 10:19

Apple Oatmeal

SERVES 6

Grated apple helps thicken the oatmeal a bit, and adds great flavor and a bit of texture. Top it with toasted walnuts or pecans for some crunch.

2 tablespoons butter
1½ cups steel cut oats
¼ cup brown sugar
1 cup applesauce
1½ cup apple juice
2 cups water
½ teaspoon salt
1 cup grated peeled apple
⅓ cup heavy cream

1. Spray a 2-quart slow cooker with nonstick cooking spray and set aside. In medium skillet, melt butter. Add oats; cook and stir until toasted, about 5–6 minutes. Combine with brown sugar, applesauce, apple juice, water, and salt in prepared slow cooker.
2. Cover and cook on low for 8–9 hours. Stir well, then add grated apple and cream. Cover and cook on low for 30 minutes longer. Serve with maple syrup and chopped apples, if desired.

Breakfast Casserole

SERVES 10–12

The combination of textures, flavors, and colors in this rich and hearty casserole is just wonderful. Serve with some fresh fruit for a complete breakfast.

1½ pounds breakfast link sausage
10 slices cracked wheat bread, cubed
1 red bell pepper, chopped
1 cup shredded Swiss cheese
1 cup shredded Muenster cheese
8 eggs
1 cup whole milk
1 cup small-curd cottage cheese
2 tablespoons yellow mustard
½ teaspoon salt
⅛ teaspoon white pepper
⅓ cup shredded Romano cheese

1. Cook the link sausage until done in large skillet over medium heat. Drain on paper towels, then cut into 1" pieces. Spray a 5-quart slow cooker with nonstick cooking spray.
2. Layer sausage pieces, bread, bell pepper, and Swiss and Muenster cheeses in slow cooker.
3. In food processor or blender, combine eggs, milk, cottage cheese, mustard, salt, and white pepper. Process or blend until smooth. Pour into slow cooker. Let stand for 20 minutes.
4. Sprinkle with Romano cheese; cover. Cook on high for 2 hours, then reduce heat to low and cook for another 1 to 1½ hours or until casserole is set.

Carrot Bread

SERVES 8–10

A moist carrot bread is a nice change from the usual breakfast quick breads. Serve this with a spread made with 8 ounces cream cheese, ½ cup brown sugar, ⅓ cup toasted chopped walnuts, and 1 teaspoon cinnamon!

1¼ cups flour
½ cup whole wheat flour
1½ teaspoons baking powder
½ teaspoon baking soda
¼ teaspoon salt
¼ cup sugar
⅓ cup brown sugar
1 egg
1 (8-ounce) can crushed pineapple in juice, drained
1 cup finely grated carrots
1 teaspoon vanilla
3 tablespoons butter, melted
1 cup chopped walnuts

1. Spray a baking insert or 2-pound coffee can with nonstick baking spray containing flour; set aside. In large bowl, combine flour, whole wheat flour, baking powder, baking soda, salt, sugar, and brown sugar; mix well.
2. In small bowl, combine egg, drained pineapple, carrots, vanilla, and melted butter. Add to flour mixture and beat until combined. Add walnuts.
3. Pour into prepared pan or can. Place crumpled foil or a wire rack in bottom of 4-quart slow cooker. Place pan in slow cooker, cover, and cook on high for 4–5 hours or until toothpick inserted near center of bread comes out clean. Remove insert from slow cooker and cool on wire rack for 15 minutes. Gently loosen sides of bread and invert onto wire rack; cool completely.

Ho, everyone who thirsts, come to the waters, and you that have no money, come, buy and eat! Come, buy wine and milk without money and without price. Why do you spend your money for that which is not bread, and your labor for that which does not satisfy? Listen carefully to me, and eat what is good, and delight yourselves in rich food.

—ISAIAH 55:1

Dried Fruit Oatmeal

SERVES 8–10

Because the oats aren't toasted, this cereal is creamier than regular oatmeal, even with steel cut oats. Use your favorite combination of dried fruits and nuts.

2 cups steel cut oatmeal (not regular or quick-cooking oatmeal)

2 cups whole milk

3 cups water

2 cups apple juice

1 teaspoon cinnamon

1/3 cup brown sugar

1/8 teaspoon salt

1 cup chopped dried apricots

1/2 cup chopped dried cranberries

1/2 cup dried currants

1 cup chopped pecans

1. Spray 4-quart slow cooker with nonstick baking spray containing flour. Combine all ingredients in slow cooker and stir well.
2. Cover and cook on low for 8–9 hours or until creamy, stirring once during cooking time. Serve immediately with maple syrup, heavy cream, and brown sugar, if desired.

Banana Bread

SERVES 8–10

Banana bread is a classic for breakfast. Made in the slow cooker, it is moist and tender. Let it cool completely on a wire rack before serving.

1¾ cups flour

1 teaspoon baking powder

1/2 teaspoon baking soda

1/4 teaspoon salt

1/4 cup butter, softened

1/4 cup sugar

1/2 cup brown sugar

1 egg

1/3 cup buttermilk

1½ cups mashed bananas (about 3)

1 teaspoon vanilla

1 cup chopped pecans

1. Spray a baking insert or 2-pound coffee can with nonstick baking spray containing flour; set aside. In medium bowl, combine flour, baking powder, baking soda, and salt. Mix well.
2. In large bowl, beat butter with sugar and brown sugar until combined. Add egg, buttermilk, bananas, and vanilla. Add to flour mixture and beat until combined. Add pecans.
3. Pour into prepared pan or can. Place crumpled foil or a wire rack in bottom of 4-quart slow cooker. Place pan in slow cooker, cover, and cook on high for 4–5 hours or until toothpick inserted near center of bread comes out clean. Cool on wire rack for 15 minutes, then loosen edges of bread. Remove from insert and cool completely on wire rack.

Slow Cooker Scrambled Eggs

SERVES 12

Scrambled eggs can be made at your leisure in the slow cooker. Keep them warm for only one hour after cooking time is done. If any are left over at that point (doubtful!), discard them.

¼ cup unsalted butter

18 eggs

1 (16-ounce) jar Alfredo sauce

½ cup heavy cream

1 teaspoon salt

⅛ teaspoon white pepper

2 cups shredded Swiss cheese

¼ cup grated Parmesan cheese

1. Using 1 tablespoon of the butter, grease a 4-quart slow cooker. Melt the rest of the butter and pour into slow cooker.
2. In large bowl, beat eggs with Alfredo sauce, cream, salt, and pepper. Stir in Swiss cheese and pour into slow cooker.
3. Sprinkle with Parmesan cheese, cover, and cook on high for about 2 to 2½ hours, stirring twice during cooking time, until eggs are creamy and reach a temperature of 145°F.

Breakfast Granola Bake

SERVES 8–10

Apples, pears, and granola are a wonderful combination in this casserole. It's a little like hot cereal, but with more texture.

2 apples, peeled, cored, and chopped

3 pears, peeled, cored, and chopped

2 tablespoons lemon juice

4 cups granola

1 cup chopped pecans

⅓ cup maple syrup

1 (4-ounce) jar puréed pears

1 teaspoon cinnamon

⅛ teaspoon salt

3 tablespoons butter, melted

1. Place apples and pears in bottom of a 4-quart slow cooker. Sprinkle with lemon juice. Top with granola and pecans.
2. In medium bowl, combine remaining ingredients and mix well. Pour into slow cooker. Cover and cook on low for 7–9 hours or until apples and pears are tender. Serve with cold maple syrup and heavy cream, if desired.

Then the Lord said to Moses, "I am going to rain bread from heaven for you, and each day the people shall go out and gather enough for that day."

—EXODUS 16:4

Tex-Mex Brunch Bake

SERVES 10–12

Want something spicy for breakfast to wake up your taste buds? This easy casserole fills the bill. Serve it with sour cream and a fruit salad for a cooling contrast.

1 (32-ounce) package frozen hash brown potatoes, thawed and drained

1 (16-ounce) package spicy bulk pork sausage

1 onion, chopped

6 cloves garlic, minced

2 (4-ounce) jars sliced mushrooms, drained

2 jalapeño peppers, minced

14 eggs

½ cup whole milk

½ cup heavy cream

1 tablespoon chili powder

1 teaspoon salt

⅛ teaspoon cayenne pepper

⅛ teaspoon white pepper

2 cups shredded pepper jack cheese

¼ cup grated Parmesan cheese

½ teaspoon smoked paprika

1. Spray 5-quart slow cooker with nonstick cooking spray. Place drained potatoes in slow cooker.
2. In large skillet, cook pork sausage, stirring to break up meat, until almost cooked through. Add onion and garlic; cook and stir until sausage is thoroughly cooked. Drain well and add to slow cooker along with mushrooms and jalapeños.
3. In large bowl, beat eggs with milk, cream, chili powder, salt, cayenne and white pepper until blended. Stir in pepper jack cheese and pour into slow cooker; poke through ingredients with a knife to let egg mixture penetrate.
4. Sprinkle top with Parmesan cheese and paprika. Cover and cook on low for 8–9 hours or until casserole is set and internal temperature reaches 145°F. Serve immediately.

Then God said, "Let the earth put forth vegetation, plants yielding seed, and fruit trees of every kind of earth that bear fruit with the seed in it." And it was so. The earth brought forth vegetation: plants yielding seed of every kind, and trees of every kind bearing fruit with the seed in it. And God saw that it was good.

—GENESIS 1:11–12

Dad's Best Sausage Rolls

SERVES 12

These sausage rolls are like meatballs, but shaped like sausages, and flavored for breakfast. They are slightly spicy and very pleasing.

1½ cups soft bread crumbs

2 eggs, beaten

¼ cup brown sugar

½ cup applesauce

1 teaspoon salt

⅛ teaspoon pepper

2 pounds mild bulk pork sausage

1 pound hot bulk pork sausage

2 tablespoons butter

1 tablespoon olive oil

½ cup maple syrup

½ cup chicken broth

1. In large bowl, combine crumbs, eggs, brown sugar, applesauce, salt, and pepper. Mix well. Stir in both kinds of sausage.
2. Shape into rolls 3" × 1". In large skillet, combine butter and olive oil over medium heat. Add sausage rolls, about 8 at a time, and cook until browned on all sides, about 5–6 minutes. As rolls cook, drain on paper towels, then place into 4-quart slow cooker.
3. In bowl, combine maple syrup and chicken broth and mix well. Pour over sausage rolls in slow cooker.
4. Cover slow cooker and cook on low for 8–9 hours or until sausage rolls are thoroughly cooked, to 165°F on a meat thermometer. Remove from slow cooker with slotted spoon to serve.

Bacon and Potato Strata

SERVES 12

The potatoes have to be evenly and thinly sliced in order to cook thoroughly in this easy and hearty casserole recipe. And the bacon has to be crisp!

1 pound bacon

2 onions, chopped

6 russet potatoes

3 (4-ounce) jars mushrooms, drained

2 cups shredded Cheddar cheese

1 cup shredded Havarti cheese

10 eggs

1 (16-ounce) jar four-cheese Alfredo sauce

¼ teaspoon pepper

1 teaspoon dried thyme leaves

1. In large skillet, cook bacon until crisp. Drain bacon on paper towels, crumble, and set aside. Drain all but 2 tablespoons drippings from skillet. Add onions; cook and stir until tender, about 6 minutes. Set aside.
2. Spray 4- to 5-quart slow cooker with nonstick cooking spray. Thinly sliced unpeeled potatoes (about ⅛" thick). Layer potatoes, crumbled bacon, onions, mushrooms, and cheeses in slow cooker.
3. In large bowl, combine remaining ingredients and beat well. Pour into slow cooker. Cover and cook on low for 8–9 hours or until casserole is set and temperature registers 145°F.

Cornbread Sausage Strata

SERVES 10–12

A bit of corn bread and sausage in the morning is a great way to start the day. This rich strata is delicious served with a fresh fruit salad.

1 pound hot bulk Italian sausage
2 onions, chopped
2 (4-ounce) jars sliced mushrooms, drained
2 cups flour
1 cup yellow cornmeal
¼ cup sugar
3 teaspoons baking powder
1 teaspoon baking soda
1 teaspoon salt
2 eggs
1 cup whole milk
½ cup butter, melted
1½ cups shredded Colby cheese

1. In large skillet, cook sausage with onions over medium heat, stirring to break up sausage, until sausage is cooked. Drain well. Add mushrooms and remove from heat.
2. In large bowl, combine flour, cornmeal, sugar, baking powder, baking soda, and salt. In medium bowl, combine eggs, milk, and butter. Mix well.
3. Add egg mixture to dry ingredients, stirring just until combined.
4. Spray a 4-quart slow cooker with nonstick baking spray containing flour. Place half of the batter in the slow cooker; top with half of the sausage and half of the cheese. Repeat layers.
5. Cover and cook on high for 2½ to 3½ hours or until corn bread tests done when tested with a toothpick. Serve immediately by spooning out of the slow cooker as in spoon bread.

When these days were completed, the king gave for all the people present in the citadel of Susa, both great and small, a banquet lasting for seven days, in the court of the garden of the king's palace.

—ESTHER 1:5

Soups

∾

Soups have been nourishing populations for generations. You can make soup out of practically anything, or almost nothing at all. And soups are really made for the slow cooker. Soup recipes are very tolerant; that is, you can change ingredients, add or subtract just about anything, and they'll still taste wonderful.

Think about using homemade stocks (use the slow cooker!) or boxed broths instead of canned in these recipes. It goes without saying that homemade stocks are richer and more flavorful than canned. Boxed broths are better than canned; they have a smoother and more blended taste. But you can use whatever you have on hand or is available in your local supermarket. Also look for lower-sodium varieties.

When you're serving a crowd, it's easy to set up a soup buffet. Make several different soups and set them up with lots of toppings, including shredded cheese, croutons, flavored popcorn, sour cream, and chopped vegetables, along with accompaniments such as crackers, toasted bread, buns, and breadsticks. For a complete and satisfying meal, all you really need with soup is something crunchy, and either a fruit or green salad.

Have lots of bowls and big spoons on hand, along with lots of napkins. Some of these soups are fun to serve in mugs; then people can just drink them, which is enjoyable and saves you time on cleanup.

Ham and Split Pea Soup

SERVES 10

This velvety and delicious soup is perfect for a cold fall night. Serve it after Advent services, along with a green salad and some homemade biscuits.

2 tablespoons butter

1 tablespoon olive oil

2 onions, chopped

3 cloves garlic, minced

4 carrots, sliced

1½ pounds dried split peas

1 ham hock

3 cups water

8 cups chicken broth

1 teaspoon salt

¼ teaspoon white pepper

1 teaspoon dried marjoram leaves

1 cup heavy cream

1. In large skillet, heat butter and olive oil over medium heat. Add onions and garlic; cook and stir until crisp-tender, about 4 minutes. Place in 5-quart slow cooker and add carrots.
2. Pick over the peas and remove any extraneous material. Rinse peas and drain. Add to slow cooker along with ham hock, water, chicken broth, salt, pepper, and marjoram leaves.
3. Cover and cook on low for 8–9 hours or until peas are tender. Remove ham hock and cut off meat. Return meat to slow cooker. Using a potato masher, mash some of the peas.
4. Stir in cream, cover, and cook on high for 20–30 minutes or until soup is blended. Serve immediately.

Broccoli Cheese Soup

SERVES 10–12

The combination of cream cheese and American cheese makes a mild and creamy soup that everyone will love. The condensed soups add flavor and texture.

2 tablespoons butter

2 tablespoons olive oil

2 onions, chopped

6 cloves garlic, minced

¼ teaspoon pepper

1 teaspoon dried basil leaves

2 (16-ounce) packages frozen cut broccoli

1 (32-ounce) box chicken broth

1 (10-ounce) can condensed cream of broccoli soup

1 (10-ounce) can condensed cheddar cheese soup

2 cups milk

1 cup light cream

1 (8-ounce) package cream cheese, cubed

4 cups diced processed American cheese

1. Turn 6-quart slow cooker to high. Add butter and olive oil and heat until melted. Add onions and garlic. Cook, uncovered, for 30 minutes.
2. Stir onions and garlic. Add pepper, basil, broccoli, broth, and soups. Stir well, then cover and cook on low for 5–6 hours or until broccoli is tender.
3. Turn off slow cooker. Using an immersion blender or potato masher, purée the broccoli in the soup. Stir in remaining ingredients. Cover and cook on low for 1–2 hours or until cheese melts and soup is hot. Stir to combine, then serve.

Ida's Savory Minestrone

SERVES 8–10

Minestrone is a thick vegetable soup that contains pasta. It's hearty and delicious. You can make it vegetarian by using vegetable broth instead of chicken broth.

2 tablespoons olive oil

1 tablespoon butter

2 onions, chopped

6 cloves garlic, minced

6 carrots, sliced

6 cups chicken broth

2 cups tomato juice

2 (15-ounce) cans cannellini beans, drained

3 potatoes, peeled and cubed

1 teaspoon dried basil leaves

1 teaspoon dried oregano leaves

1 teaspoon salt

¼ teaspoon white pepper

2 (14-ounce) cans diced tomatoes, undrained

1 (6-ounce) can tomato paste

1 cup orzo pasta

½ cup grated Parmesan cheese

1. In large skillet, combine olive oil and butter over medium heat. When butter melts, add onions and garlic; cook and stir for 5 minutes.

2. Pour into 6- to 7-quart slow cooker. Add carrots, chicken broth, tomato juice, beans, potatoes, basil, oregano, salt, and pepper. Mix well. Cover and cook on low for 7–8 hours or until potatoes are tender.

3. In large bowl, combine diced tomatoes with tomato paste until paste dissolves. Stir into slow cooker along with orzo. Cover and cook on high for 30–40 minutes or until soup is hot and orzo is tender.

4. Top each serving with cheese.

Yet he commanded the skies above, and opened the doors of heaven; he rained down on them manna to eat, and gave them the grain of heaven. Mortals ate of the bread of angels; he sent them food in abundance.

—PSALMS 78:23–25

Meatball Veggie Soup

SERVES 12–14

There are many varieties of frozen meatballs available, from Italian flavored to wild rice. Use your favorites in this hearty stew.

2 tablespoons olive oil

1 tablespoon butter

2 onions, chopped

5 cloves garlic, minced

2 (8-ounce) jars sliced mushrooms, undrained

2 (14-ounce) cans diced tomatoes, undrained

2 (16-ounce) packages frozen small meatballs

3 cups frozen corn

1 (16-ounce) bag baby carrots

2 (32-ounce) boxes beef broth

2 cups water

¼ teaspoon pepper

1 teaspoon dried oregano leaves

1 teaspoon dried thyme leaves

1 (12-ounce) package orzo pasta

1 cup grated Parmesan cheese

1. In large skillet, combine olive oil and butter over medium heat. Add onions and garlic; cook and stir until tender, about 5 minutes. Place in 6- to 7-quart slow cooker.
2. Add all remaining ingredients except pasta and cheese. Cover and cook on low for 7–8 hours or until meatballs are hot and vegetables are tender.
3. Stir in pasta. Cover and cook on high for 20–30 minutes or until pasta is tender, stirring twice during cooking time. Top with cheese and serve.

Black Bean Soup

SERVES 8

This spicy soup is delicious when served with a cool tomato and sour cream mixture and crisp tortilla chips. It's a meal in itself!

1 tablespoon butter

1 tablespoon olive oil

1 onion, chopped

4 cloves garlic, minced

4 large carrots, sliced

1 (32-ounce) box vegetable stock

1 (16-ounce) jar chunky medium salsa

3 (15-ounce) cans black beans, drained

1 teaspoon cumin

¾ cup sour cream

3 tablespoons minced green onions, white and green parts

1 tablespoon minced chives

½ cup chopped tomatoes

2 tablespoons lime juice

2 cups crushed blue corn tortilla chips

1. In medium skillet, melt butter and olive oil over medium heat. Add onion and garlic; cook and stir until tender, about 5 minutes. Place in 5-quart slow cooker along with carrots, vegetable stock, salsa, black beans, and cumin.
2. Cover slow cooker and cook on low for 7–8 hours. Meanwhile, in serving bowl combine sour cream, green onion, chives, and tomatoes; refrigerate.
3. When soup is done, stir in lime juice. Serve with sour cream mixture and tortilla chips as topping.

Rich Vegetable Soup

SERVES 8

Buying a wedge of real Parmesan cheese may seem expensive, but for a special occasion the flavor just can't be beat. And the rind adds incredible flavor to this soup.

2 tablespoons butter

2 onions, chopped

4 cloves garlic, minced

1 cup water

1 (32-ounce) box vegetable broth

1 (4-inch) wedge of Parmesan cheese

3 (14-ounce) cans diced tomatoes, undrained

1 (16-ounce) package baby carrots

1 teaspoon dried basil leaves

1 teaspoon dried oregano leaves

½ teaspoon salt

⅛ teaspoon white pepper

2 (6-inch) yellow summer squash, sliced

½ cup grated Parmesan cheese

¼ cup minced fresh chives

2 tablespoons grated lemon zest

1. In large skillet, melt butter over medium heat. Add onions and garlic; cook and stir until onions start to brown, about 9–11 minutes. Carefully add water and broth to skillet; cook and stir until mixture boils.

2. Pour into 5-quart slow cooker. Grate cheese from the wedge, reserving cheese. Add cheese rind along remaining ingredients except for squash, grated Parmesan cheese, chives, and lemon zest to slow cooker. Cover and cook on low for 8–9 hours or until vegetables are tender.

3. Remove Parmesan rind from soup and discard. Add squash to soup and cook on high for 20–30 minutes or until squash is crisp-tender.

4. In medium bowl, combine grated Parmesan cheese, chives, and lemon zest. Serve soup in bowls and top with chive mixture.

So Laban gathered together all the people of the plate, and made a feast.

—GENESIS 29:22

Creamy Ginger-Pumpkin Soup

SERVES 8–10

Pumpkin soup is creamy, velvety, hearty, and delicious. Choose garlic or plain croutons to top this wonder.

2 (15-ounce) cans solid-pack pumpkin

2 onions, chopped

5 cloves garlic, minced

2 tablespoons minced fresh gingerroot

1 (32-ounce) box chicken broth

2 cups water

1 teaspoon salt

¼ teaspoon white pepper

½ teaspoon ground ginger

1 cup heavy cream

½ cup sour cream

2 tablespoons cornstarch

1½ cups croutons

1. In 5-quart slow cooker, combine pumpkin with onions, garlic, and gingerroot; mash to combine. Gradually stir in chicken broth, stirring with wire whisk until blended.
2. Add water, salt, pepper, and ground ginger. Stir to combine. Cover and cook on low for 5–6 hours or until soup is hot and blended.
3. In medium bowl combine heavy cream, sour cream, and cornstarch; mix well. Stir into soup, cover, and cook on high for 30 minutes or until soup is hot. Top with croutons and serve.

Ham and Bean Soup

SERVES 10–12

Ham hocks add incredible flavor to this easy soup. Serve it with toasted cheese bread and coleslaw.

1½ pounds dried great
   Northern beans

2 onions, chopped

5 cloves garlic, minced

4 carrots, sliced

⅓ cup brown sugar

2 (32-ounce) boxes
   chicken broth

2 cups water

2 ham hocks

1 bay leaf

¼ teaspoon white pepper

½ cup heavy cream

1. Sort and pick over beans to remove stones or extraneous material; rinse and drain. Place beans in a soup pot. Cover with water and bring to a boil over high heat. Boil for 2 minutes, then cover, remove from heat, and let stand for 2 hours.
2. Drain beans, then place in 6-quart slow cooker. Add onions, garlic, and carrots. In small bowl, dissolve brown sugar in 1 cup chicken broth. Add it and the rest of the chicken broth and 2 cups water to the slow cooker.
3. Add ham hocks, bay leaf, and pepper to the slow cooker. Cover and cook on low for 8–10 hours or until beans are tender.
4. Remove ham hocks from slow cooker and cut off meat. Meanwhile, mash some of the beans in slow cooker with a potato masher. Discard ham bones.
5. Return meat to slow cooker along with cream. Cover and cook on low for 30–40 minutes or until soup is hot. Remove bay leaf and serve.

Sweet Potato Bacon Soup

SERVES 10–12

Two kinds of bacon make this creamy soup very rich and hearty. You can serve it as part of a soup course, or in smaller portions as an appetizer.

8 slices bacon

2 onions, chopped

3 pounds sweet potatoes

1 pound Yukon Gold potatoes

1 russet potato

1 (8-ounce) package sliced Canadian bacon, chopped

1 (32-ounce) box chicken broth

1 (32-ounce) box vegetable broth

2 teaspoons dried thyme leaves

1 teaspoon dried oregano leaves

1 teaspoon salt

¼ teaspoon white pepper

2 tablespoons cornstarch

½ cup apple juice

1. In large skillet, cook bacon until crisp. Drain on paper towels, crumble, and set aside in refrigerator. Add onions to drippings remaining in skillet and cook for 4 minutes.
2. Peel all the potatoes and cut into 1" cubes. Combine in 5- to 6-quart slow cooker with Canadian bacon, broths, thyme, oregano, salt, and pepper.
3. Cover and cook on low for 8–9 hours or until potatoes are tender. Turn off slow cooker. Using an immersion blender or potato masher, blend or mash potatoes, leaving some chunks.
4. In small bowl, combine cornstarch and apple juice and blend well. Stir into soup along with reserved crisp bacon. Cover and cook on high for 30 minutes. Stir well before serving.

Chicken Corn Soup

SERVES 10–12

This delicious soup is slightly creamy and perfect with the Havarti cheese melting into each spoonful. You can use the technique of topping hot soup with a cheese and vegetable mixture with many other recipes.

2 tablespoons butter

1 tablespoon olive oil

1 onion, chopped

3 cloves garlic, minced

8 boneless, skinless chicken breasts, cubed

1 (10.75-ounce) can cream of chicken soup

1 (32-ounce) box chicken broth

4 cups water

1 teaspoon dried basil leaves

¼ teaspoon white pepper

1 teaspoon dried marjoram

3 cups frozen corn

2 (15-ounce) cans cream-style corn

1 cup chopped tomatoes

⅓ cup chopped fresh basil

1 cup diced Havarti cheese

1. In large skillet, melt butter and olive oil over medium heat. Add onion and garlic; cook and stir until crisp-tender, about 5 minutes. Place in 6- to 7-quart slow cooker.
2. Add remaining ingredients except tomatoes, basil, and cheese to slow cooker. Keep cheese refrigerated until ready to serve. Stir to blend. Cover and cook on low for 7–8 hours or until chicken is thoroughly cooked and soup is blended.
3. In small bowl, combine chopped tomatoes, basil, and cheese. Top each serving of soup with the tomato mixture.

Tomato Chicken Bisque

SERVES 12

A bisque is a soup that has cream or milk added. Cream adds a wonderful richness and mouthfeel that you just can't get with anything else.

2 tablespoons butter

2 onions, chopped

4 cloves garlic, minced

1 (6-ounce) can tomato paste

2 (14-ounce) cans diced tomatoes, undrained

1 (28-ounce) can puréed tomatoes

2 pounds boneless, skinless chicken breasts, cubed

2 (14-ounce) cans chicken broth

1 teaspoon dried basil

½ teaspoon salt

⅛ teaspoon white pepper

⅓ cup butter

⅓ cup flour

2 cups heavy cream

1. In large skillet, melt 2 tablespoons butter over medium heat. Add onions and garlic; cook and stir for 8 minutes, until translucent and beginning to brown. Add tomato paste. Stir, then let cook for 4–5 minutes until tomato paste starts to brown in spots.

2. Add diced tomatoes; cook and stir until bubbly. Pour into 5- to 6-quart slow cooker. Add puréed tomatoes, cubed chicken breasts, chicken broth, basil, salt, and white pepper; stir well.

3. Cover and cook on low for 7–8 hours or until chicken is thoroughly cooked.

4. In medium saucepan, melt ⅓ cup butter over medium heat. Add flour; cook and stir until bubbly. Stir in heavy cream and cook until thickened. Stir this mixture into the slow cooker.

5. Cover and cook on high for 20–30 minutes or until soup is steaming. Serve immediately.

For he did not despise or abhor the affliction of the afflicted; he did not hide his face from me, but heard when I cried to him. From you comes my praise in the great congregation; my vows I will pay before those who fear him. The poor shall eat and be satisfied.

—PSALMS 22:24–26

Curried Chicken Noodle Soup

SERVES 10–12

Coconut milk and curry powder add great flavor and a touch of the exotic near East to this classic soup.

2 tablespoons butter

1 tablespoon olive oil

6 boneless, skinless chicken breasts

1½ teaspoons salt

¼ teaspoon pepper

1 tablespoon curry powder

2 onions, chopped

2 green bell peppers, chopped

1 (16-ounce) bag baby carrots

1 tablespoon curry powder

2 (32-ounce) boxes chicken broth

3 cups egg noodles

1 (13-ounce) can coconut milk

1. In large skillet, heat butter and olive oil over medium heat. Sprinkle chicken with salt, pepper, and 1 tablespoon curry powder. Add to skillet; cook, turning once, for 4–5 minutes or until chicken begins to brown.
2. Remove chicken from skillet. Add onions to skillet; cook and stir until crisp-tender, about 5 minutes; remove from heat.
3. Place bell peppers and baby carrots in 6-quart slow cooker. Add onions and chicken to slow cooker along with 1 tablespoon curry powder. Pour broth over all.
4. Cover and cook on low for 5–6 hours or until chicken and vegetables are tender. Remove chicken from slow cooker and shred. Return chicken to slow cooker; add noodles and coconut milk.
5. Turn heat to high and cook for 15–20 minutes or until noodles are tender. Serve in warmed bowls, topped with minced green onion if desired.

The sated appetite spurns honey, but to a ravenous appetite even the bitter is sweet.

—PROVERBS 27:7

Albondigas

SERVES 8–10

This classic Mexican soup is filling and hearty. You can increase the spice level by adding some jalapeño peppers, or using more chili powder.

2 tablespoons butter
1 onion, chopped
4 cloves garlic, minced
1 (32-ounce) box beef broth
2 cups chicken broth
2 cups water
1 teaspoon salt
¼ teaspoon pepper
1 tablespoon chili powder
½ teaspoon cumin
1 (16-ounce) bag baby carrots
1 (16-ounce) jar medium salsa
3 cups frozen green beans
1 (16-ounce) package small frozen precooked meatballs
½ cup chopped cilantro
1 cup sour cream

1. In large skillet, melt butter over medium heat. Add onions and garlic; cook and stir until tender, about 6–7 minutes. Place in 6-quart slow cooker along with all remaining ingredients except cilantro and sour cream.
2. Cover and cook on low for 8–9 hours or until vegetables are tender and meatballs are hot. Combine cilantro and sour cream in small bowl and serve with soup.

Chicken Wild Rice Soup

SERVES 12–14

Wild rice and chicken cook together beautifully in this excellent soup recipe. The slow cooker is the perfect environment for cooking wild rice.

2 tablespoons butter
1 tablespoon olive oil
2 onions, chopped
5 cloves garlic, minced
1½ cups wild rice
1 (16-ounce) bag baby carrots
3 cups frozen corn
5 boneless, skinless chicken breasts, cubed
2 (32-ounce) boxes chicken broth
1½ teaspoons seasoned salt
¼ teaspoon pepper
1 teaspoon dried thyme leaves
1 bay leaf
2 cups water

1. In large skillet, heat butter and olive oil over medium heat. Add onions and garlic; cook and stir until crisp-tender, about 5 minutes.
2. Place wild rice in bottom of 6- or 7-quart slow cooker and top with carrots, corn, and onion mixture. Add chicken breasts; do not stir.
3. Pour one box of the chicken broth into slow cooker. Sprinkle food with seasoned salt, pepper, thyme, and add bay leaf. Pour second box of broth and water into slow cooker over seasonings.
4. Cover and cook on low for 5 hours; then remove bay leaf, and stir soup. Cover and cook on low for 1–2 hours longer or until wild rice is tender and chicken is thoroughly cooked at 165°F.

Black-Eyed Pea Soup

SERVES 12

In the South, eating black-eyed peas on New Year's Day is a guarantee of good luck in the New Year. It's delicious anytime.

1 (16-ounce) bag black-eyed peas

1 ham hock

2 onions, chopped

6 cloves garlic, minced

1 (32-ounce) box chicken stock

6 cups water

1 teaspoon salt

½ teaspoon pepper

1 teaspoon dried tarragon leaves

2 (14-ounce) cans diced tomatoes, undrained

½ cup instant brown rice

1. Sort and rinse black-eyed peas to remove any extraneous material. Place in large saucepan and cover with water. Bring to a boil; boil hard for 2 minutes. Cover pan, remove from heat, and let stand for 2 hours.
2. Drain peas and place in 6-quart slow cooker with ham hock, onions, and garlic. Pour stock and water over; sprinkle with salt, pepper, and tarragon.
3. Cover and cook on low for 8–9 hours until peas are tender. Remove ham hock from slow cooker; cut off meat, dice, and return to slow cooker. Discard ham bone.
4. Stir in tomatoes and instant rice. Cover and cook on high for 20–30 minutes or until rice is tender.

Tomato Bean Soup

SERVES 12–14

You must use canned beans in this recipe, because the acid in the tomato will slow down the softening of dried beans.

2 (10-ounce) cans condensed tomato soup

2 (14-ounce) cans diced tomatoes, undrained

3 (15-ounce) cans navy beans, drained

8 plum tomatoes, chopped

2 onions, chopped

4 cups tomato juice

2 cups water

1 tablespoon sugar

1 teaspoon dried basil leaves

¼ teaspoon pepper

Combine all ingredients in 6-quart slow cooker. Cover and cook on low for 8–9 hours or until soup is hot and blended. Stir and serve immediately.

Speak out for those who cannot, for the rights of the destitute. Speak out, judge righteously, defend the rights of the poor and needy.

—PROVERBS 31:8–9

Lentil Soup

SERVES 12

Lentils cook better when the broth is low in salt and acid. Acidic ingredients include tomatoes, lemon juice, and vinegar. Be sure to follow the directions for this recipe closely; the tomato purée and vinegar called for are not to be added until the cooking is nearly complete. This hearty soup is inexpensive and filling.

2 onions, chopped
5 cloves garlic, minced
5 carrots, cut into chunks
2 cups lentils, rinsed
1 (32-ounce) box vegetable broth
4 cups water
1 teaspoon dried oregano leaves
2 bay leaves
1 teaspoon salt
¼ teaspoon pepper
1 (15-ounce) can tomato purée
3 tablespoons balsamic vinegar

1. Combine all ingredients except tomato purée and vinegar in 6-quart slow cooker. Cover and cook on low for 8–9 hours or until lentils and vegetables are tender.
2. Stir in tomato purée and vinegar. Cover and cook on high for 20–30 minutes longer or until soup is hot. Stir and serve immediately.

Carrot Potato Bisque

SERVES 18

This rich and elegant soup is inexpensive to make, and it serves a crowd. Pair it with a simple green salad and some crisp breadsticks.

2 onions, chopped
4 cloves garlic, minced
6 carrots, sliced
6 russet potatoes, peeled and cubed
3 (32-ounce) boxes vegetable broth
¼ teaspoon white pepper
2 teaspoons dried marjoram
1 teaspoon dried oregano
¼ cup cornstarch
1 cup heavy cream
1 cup light cream

1. Combine all ingredients except cornstarch and both kinds of cream in 6-quart slow cooker. Cover and cook on low for 7–8 hours or until vegetables are very tender.
2. Turn off slow cooker. Using a potato masher or immersion blender, mash or purée the vegetables right in the slow cooker.
3. In large bowl, combine cornstarch with both kinds of cream; mix well with wire whisk. Stir into slow cooker, cover, and cook on high for 20–30 minutes or until soup is slightly thickened and creamy.

Creamy Onion Soup

SERVES 12–14

This rich soup is usually made with beef broth, but chicken broth makes a lighter taste. You can serve this one in mugs for people to sip slowly as they mingle.

3 tablespoons butter
6 onions, chopped
6 cloves garlic, minced
1 teaspoon salt
1 tablespoon sugar
¼ cup flour
2 (32-ounce) boxes chicken broth
1 teaspoon dried marjoram leaves
1 teaspoon dried thyme leaves
1½ cups heavy cream
2 cups shredded Gruyère cheese

1. Place butter in 5-quart slow cooker and turn to high. When butter melts, add onions and garlic. Sprinkle with salt and sugar. Cover and cook on low for 6–7 hours, stirring twice during cooking time, until onions are golden brown.
2. Turn off slow cooker. Using a potato masher or immersion blender, purée the onions. Add flour. Cover and cook on high for 30 minutes.
3. Gradually stir in 2 cups of the chicken broth. Add remaining broth along with marjoram and thyme. Cover and cook on low for 2–3 hours.
4. Stir in heavy cream and shredded cheese; cook and stir on high until cheese melts and soup is creamy, about 10–15 minutes. Serve immediately.

Chicken Bisque

SERVES 12–14

This super-rich and creamy soup is filling and satisfying on a cold winter day. Serve it with crisp breadsticks and a baby spinach salad with tomatoes and celery.

6 boneless, skinless chicken breasts, chopped
2 (32-ounce) boxes chicken broth
2 cups water
2 onions, chopped
1 cup chopped celery with leaves
½ cup butter
½ cup flour
1 teaspoon salt
¼ teaspoon white pepper
2 teaspoons dried thyme leaves
1 cup light cream
2 cups heavy cream

1. In 6-quart slow cooker, combine chicken, broth, water, onions, and celery. Cover and cook on low for 6–7 hours or until chicken is cooked and vegetables are tender.
2. At this point, melt butter in a medium saucepan over medium heat. Add flour, salt, pepper, and thyme; cook and stir until bubbly, about 5 minutes. Stir in both kinds of cream and bring to a simmer.
3. Stir this mixture into the slow cooker. Cover and cook on high for 20–30 minutes or until soup is hot and blended.

Stews, Chowders, and Chilies

What's the difference between stews, chilies, and chowders? It's really just semantics, although traditionally stews are heavy on the vegetables, chilies have lots of meat and beans, and chowders have some kind of dairy product such as milk or cream added. They're all thick and delicious.

Stews, chilies, and chowders are more than just thick soups. Each is a meal in itself, and can be used in other ways. Chili can be served as part of a Mexican salad or served over spaghetti for Tex-Mex pasta, while chowder can be the sauce for filled crepes.

Stews are among the most tolerant of all recipes. You can change the vegetables, the meat, the seasonings, and the liquid you use, and it will still be delicious. Remember, the slow cooker doesn't evaporate liquid as it cooks, and the ingredients will release water as they cook, so don't add too much liquid at first. Keep an eye on the stew, and add more liquid if needed after about half of the cooking time has passed.

Slow cooker stews are thickened with flour or cornstarch, or sometimes with mashed vegetables. One method is to dredge the meat in flour, then sauté until brown to add flavor and color and help thicken the mixture. Another is to stir a cornstarch slurry into the stew at the end of cooking time.

Sausage and Potato Stew

SERVES 8

Boxes of chicken stock are not only easier to store, but they taste better than canned broths. You don't have to decant leftovers into another container; just close the box and pop it in the fridge.

4 slices bacon

1 pound Polish sausage

1 onion, chopped

3 cloves garlic, minced

4 potatoes, peeled and cubed

1 (32-ounce) box chicken broth

2 cups water

2 cups frozen corn

1 red bell pepper, chopped

1 (13-ounce) can evaporated milk

2 tablespoons cornstarch

1 (15-ounce) can creamed corn

¼ cup chopped chives

1. In large skillet, cook bacon until crisp. Drain on paper towels, crumble, and refrigerate. Cut sausage into 1" links and cook for 2–3 minutes in bacon drippings. Remove and place in 4-quart slow cooker.
2. Add onion and garlic to skillet; cook and stir for 4 minutes. Pour all ingredients from skillet into slow cooker. Add potatoes, chicken broth, water, and frozen corn.
3. Cover and cook on low for 8 hours. Add red bell pepper and evaporated milk to slow cooker. In small bowl, combine cornstarch and creamed corn; mix well. Add to slow cooker along with reserved bacon.
4. Cover and cook on high for 30 minutes, or until soup is thickened. Sprinkle with chives. Serve.

Turkey Wild Rice Chowder

SERVES 10–12

Buy the mushrooms already sliced to save time.

¼ cup butter

2 onions, chopped

6 cloves garlic, minced

⅓ cup flour

1 teaspoon salt

¼ teaspoon pepper

1 tablespoon fresh thyme leaves or 1 teaspoon dried thyme leaves

1 tablespoon chopped fresh rosemary

2 (1-pound) turkey tenderloins, cubed

2 cups water

1½ cups wild rice, rinsed

4 carrots, sliced

1 (8-ounce) packages sliced mushrooms

3 cups frozen corn

2 (32-ounce) boxes chicken broth

1 cup heavy whipping cream

1. In large skillet, melt butter over medium heat, then add onions and garlic; cook and stir for 4 minutes. Remove onions and garlic with slotted spoon to 5-quart slow cooker.
2. On shallow plate, combine flour, salt, pepper, thyme, and fresh rosemary. Toss cubed turkey in this mixture. Brown turkey in remaining drippings in skillet, stirring frequently, about 4–5 minutes total. Add water to skillet and bring to a boil, stirring to loosen drippings.
3. Place wild rice, carrots, and mushrooms in slow cooker. Add mixture from skillet along with frozen corn and chicken broth. Stir to combine.
4. Cover and cook on low for 8 hours or until turkey is cooked and rice and vegetables are tender. Stir in cream; cover and cook for 20 minutes longer until hot. Serve topped with croutons, if desired.

Curried Chicken Stew

SERVES 8–10

Dark meat chicken cooks beautifully in the slow cooker for longer periods of time. This exotic stew is a real treat.

1½ teaspoons salt

¼ teaspoon pepper

2 tablespoons curry powder

⅓ cup flour

8 chicken thighs, cubed

¼ cup butter

1 tablespoon olive oil

2 cups apple juice

4 sweet potatoes, peeled and cubed

1 cup golden raisins

1 (16-ounce) bag baby carrots

2 onions, chopped

2 (32-ounce) boxes chicken broth

1 (10-ounce) can coconut milk

1 (16-ounce) bottle mango chutney

1. On plate, combine salt, pepper, curry powder, and flour. Dredge cubed chicken in this mixture.
2. Heat butter and olive oil in large skillet over medium heat. Add chicken; cook and stir until browned, about 4–5 minutes. Remove chicken from skillet to a 6-quart slow cooker using a slotted spoon.
3. If there is any flour mixture left, add it to the skillet; cook and stir for 2 minutes. Add apple juice; cook and stir to loosen pan drippings. Bring to a boil.
4. Combine mixture in skillet and all other ingredients except coconut milk and chutney in 6-quart slow cooker. Cover and cook on low for 8–9 hours or until chicken is thoroughly cooked and vegetables are tender.
5. Stir in coconut milk and chutney. Cover and cook on low for another 20–30 minutes or until stew is hot and blended.

For the Lord your God is God of gods and Lord of lords, the great god, mighty and awesome, who is not partial and takes no bribe, who executes justice for the orphan and the widow, and who loves the strangers, providing them with food and clothing.

—DEUTERONOMY 10:17–18

Beef Burgundy Stew

SERVES 10–12

This stew comes from the Burgundy region of France. If you choose to use the wine, be aware that not all of the alcohol will cook out.

2 pounds beef sirloin steak

¼ cup flour

1 teaspoon salt

⅛ teaspoon pepper

1 tablespoon oil

2 tablespoons butter

2 onions, chopped

½ pound portobello mushrooms, chopped

½ pound button mushrooms, sliced

1 (16-ounce) bag baby carrots

1 (32-ounce) box beef broth

1 (14-ounce) can diced tomatoes, undrained

1 (10-ounce) can condensed tomato soup

1 cup Burgundy wine, or apple juice

1 teaspoon dried marjoram

2 tablespoons balsamic vinegar

2 tablespoons cornstarch

⅓ cup water

1. Trim excess fat from steak and cut into 1½" cubes. On shallow plate, combine flour, salt, and pepper. Dredge beef in this mixture.
2. Combine oil and butter in large skillet over medium heat. Add beef; cook and stir until browned, about 4 minutes. As beef browns, remove to 4- to 5-quart slow cooker with a slotted spoon.
3. Add onions to skillet and cook and stir until tender, about 5 minutes. Add to slow cooker along with mushrooms and carrots; stir gently.
4. Add broth, tomatoes, soup, wine or apple juice, and marjoram. Cover and cook on low for 8–9 hours or until beef and vegetables are very tender.
5. In small bowl, combine vinegar, cornstarch, and water. Mix well. Stir into slow cooker. Cover and cook on high for 15–20 minutes or until stew thickens. Serve immediately.

Just before daybreak, Paul urged all of them to take some food, saying, "Today is the fourteenth day that you have been in suspense and remaining without food, having eaten nothing. Therefore I urge you to take some food, for it will help you survive; for none of you will lose a hair from your heads."

—ACTS 27:33

French Chicken Stew

SERVES 10–12

Thyme and tarragon give this stew a French flair. Serve with breadsticks and a fruit salad.

4 slices bacon

2 tablespoons butter

2 onions, chopped

6 cloves garlic, minced

6 boneless, skinless chicken breasts, sliced

1 teaspoon salt

½ teaspoon pepper

2 teaspoons dried thyme leaves

1 teaspoon dried tarragon leaves

1 (28-ounce) can stewed tomatoes, chopped

1 cup dry white wine or apple juice

1 (32-ounce) box chicken broth

2 cups water

5 carrots, cut into chunks

18 tiny whole new red potatoes

¼ cup cornstarch

1 cup heavy cream

1. In large skillet, cook bacon until crisp. Drain on paper towels, crumble, and set aside in refrigerator. Drain all but 2 tablespoons drippings from skillet. Add butter. When butter melts, add onions and garlic; cook and stir over medium heat until crisp-tender, about 5 minutes.
2. In 6-quart slow cooker, combine onion mixture with chicken breasts, salt, pepper, thyme, tarragon, tomatoes, wine or apple juice, chicken broth, water, carrots, and potatoes.
3. Cover and cook on low for 7 hours or until vegetables are tender. In bowl combine cornstarch with cream; mix well. Stir into slow cooker along with reserved bacon. Cover and cook on high for 30 minutes or until stew is thickened. Serve.

Chicken Waldorf Stew

SERVES 8–10

This thick stew is a nice twist on the classic Waldorf salad, with the same flavors and textures. It's rich and creamy, perfect for a cold fall day.

6 boneless, skinless chicken breasts, cubed

2 onions, chopped

4 tart apples, cored, peeled and chopped

2 tablespoons lemon juice

6 stalks celery, sliced

1 teaspoon celery seed

1 teaspoon salt

¼ teaspoon pepper

1 (32-ounce) box chicken broth

3 cups apple juice

1 cup white grape juice

3 tablespoons cornstarch

1 cup heavy cream

2 cups purchased croutons

1 cup chopped walnuts, toasted

1. In 6-quart slow cooker, combine all ingredients except cornstarch, cream, croutons, and walnuts. Cover and cook on low for 5–7 hours or until chicken is thoroughly cooked and apples are tender.
2. In small bowl, combine cornstarch and cream and mix well. Stir into slow cooker. Cover and cook on high for 20–25 minutes or until stew is thickened.
3. Serve topped with croutons and toasted walnuts.

Four-Bean Chili

SERVES 18–20
Serve this hearty chili with sour cream, chopped avocados, chopped tomatoes, and more salsa.

1 pound spicy bulk pork sausage

1 pound lean ground beef

2 onions, chopped

5 cloves garlic, minced

1 (6-ounce) can tomato paste

2 cups tomato juice

1 (16-ounce) jar mild or medium salsa

1 green bell pepper, chopped

2 (32-ounce) boxes beef broth

2 tablespoons chili powder

1 teaspoon cumin

¼ teaspoon pepper

⅛ teaspoon cayenne pepper

1 (15-ounce) can black beans, drained

1 (15-ounce) can kidney beans, drained

1 (15-ounce) can pinto beans, drained

1 (15-ounce) can lima beans, drained

1 (4-ounce) can chopped green chiles, drained

1. In large skillet, brown pork sausage and ground beef until done, stirring to break up meat. Drain well and place in 6- to 7-quart slow cooker. Add onions and garlic; cook and stir until tender.

2. Add tomato paste to skillet; cook and stir over medium heat until paste begins to brown in spots. Add tomato juice to skillet; cook and stir to loosen pan drippings. Pour into slow cooker.

3. Add all remaining ingredients. Cover and cook on low for 7–9 hours or until chili is blended and thick.

Is there anyone among you who, if your child asks for a fish, will give a snack instead? Or if the child asks for an egg, will give a scorpion? If you then, who are evil, know how to give good gifts to your children, know much more will the heavenly Father give the Holy Spirit to those who ask Him!

—LUKE 11:11–13

Ribollita

SERVES 14–16

Ribollita means "re-boiled" in Italian. It's usually made with the leftovers of a vegetable soup, layered with bread and baked in the oven. This version is easier, and sublime.

6 slices bacon

3 tablespoons olive oil

2 onions, chopped

6 cloves garlic, minced

1 (6-ounce) can tomato paste

2 cups water

1½ teaspoons dried Italian seasoning

½ teaspoon pepper

4 carrots, sliced

4 russet potatoes, peeled and cubed

2 (15-ounce) cans cannellini beans, drained

2 (14-ounce) cans diced tomatoes, undrained

2 (32-ounce) boxes beef broth

8 (1-inch) thick slices Italian bread

¼ cup olive oil

1½ cups grated Parmesan cheese, divided

1 (16-ounce) bag frozen cut leaf spinach, thawed

1. In large skillet cook bacon until crisp. Remove bacon from skillet, drain on paper towels, crumble, and refrigerate. Remove all but 2 tablespoons drippings from skillet. Add olive oil.

2. Cook onions and garlic in drippings and olive oil until crisp-tender, about 5 minutes. Add tomato paste, stir, and then let cook until tomato paste begins to brown in spots. Add 2 cups water, Italian seasoning, and pepper; cook and stir to loosen drippings from pan.

3. In 7-quart slow cooker, layer carrots, potatoes, and beans. Add mixture from skillet along with canned tomatoes and beef broth. Cover and cook on low for 8–9 hours or until potatoes and carrots are tender.

4. Preheat oven to 400°F. Cut bread into 1" cubes and place on cookie sheet. Drizzle with ¼ cup olive oil and ½ cup Parmesan cheese; toss to coat. Toast bread in the oven until golden brown, about 10–15 minutes.

5. Stir spinach and bread cubes into soup. Cover and cook on high for 25–35 minutes or until bread dissolves into the soup. Serve with remaining Parmesan cheese.

Wild Rice Cheese Chowder

SERVES 12–14

Bacon flavors this delicious and thick stew, which features tender wild rice. It's a meal all in one pot.

6 slices bacon

2 tablespoons butter

2 onions, chopped

6 cloves garlic, minced

3 tablespoons flour

1 teaspoon salt

¼ teaspoon pepper

1 teaspoon dried tarragon leaves

4 cups water

2 cups wild rice

1 (16-ounce) bag baby carrots

1 (32-ounce) box beef broth

2 cups frozen corn

2 cups apple juice

3 cups shredded Swiss cheese

2 tablespoons cornstarch

1½ cups light cream

⅓ cup chopped flat-leaf parsley

1. In large skillet, cook bacon until crisp. Drain bacon on paper towels, crumble, and set aside in refrigerator. Add butter to skillet; cook onion and garlic until crisp-tender, about 5–6 minutes.

2. Add flour, salt, pepper, and tarragon to skillet; cook and stir until bubbly. Add water and bring to a simmer, stirring frequently.

3. Place wild rice in 6-quart slow cooker. Top with baby carrots and onion mixture. Pour in beef broth, corn, and apple juice.

4. Cover and cook on low for 7–8 hours or until rice is tender. In large bowl, toss cheese with cornstarch. Stir into slow cooker along with cream and reserved bacon.

5. Cover and cook on high for 20–30 minutes or until cheese is melted and chowder is thick. Sprinkle with parsley and serve.

Yet he commanded the skies above, and opened the doors of heaven; he rained down on them manna to eat, and gave them the grain of heaven. Mortals ate of the bread of angels; he sent them food in abundance.

—PSALMS 78:23–25

Classic Beef Barley Stew

SERVES 10–12

Barley is a wonderful grain; it's chewy and nutty tasting. In this hearty stew, with beef and vegetables, it's filling and warming.

2 pounds beef stew meat, cubed

¼ cup flour

2 teaspoons paprika

1 teaspoon salt

¼ teaspoon pepper

2 tablespoons olive oil

1 tablespoon butter

2 onions, chopped

4 cloves garlic, minced

1 (16-ounce) bag baby carrots

1 (8-ounce) package sliced fresh mushrooms

1 cup medium pearl barley

1 (32-ounce) box beef broth

4 cups water

2 bay leaves

1. Trim excess fat from stew meat. On large plate, combine flour, paprika, salt, and pepper; mix well. Toss beef in this mixture to coat.
2. Heat olive oil and butter in large skillet. Add beef cubes; brown, stirring, on all sides, about 5–6 minutes.
3. Remove beef from skillet and place in 6-quart slow cooker. Add onions and garlic to skillet; cook and stir until crisp-tender, about 5 minutes, stirring to loosen pan drippings.
4. Add onions and garlic to slow cooker. Add all remaining ingredients. Cover and cook on low for 7–9 hours or until barley and vegetables are tender. Remove bay leaves and serve.

Mexican Stew

SERVES 18–20

The heat in jalapeños is contained in the seeds and membranes. If you remove those, the stew will be milder. Top with guacamole and sour cream for a cooling contrast.

1 pound ground beef

1 pound spicy bulk pork sausage

2 cups chopped chorizo sausage

2 onions, chopped

6 cloves garlic, minced

2 or 3 jalapeño peppers, minced

1 (15-ounce) can tomato sauce

3 cups tomato juice

3 cups beef broth

3 (14-ounce) cans diced tomatoes

2 tablespoons chili powder

1 teaspoon cumin

1 teaspoon salt

¼ teaspoon pepper

⅛ teaspoon cayenne pepper

2 (15-ounce) can chili beans, undrained

1. In skillet, cook ground beef and pork sausage until done, stirring to break up meat. Drain well.
2. Meanwhile, combine chorizo, onions, garlic, and jalapeño peppers in 6- or 7-quart slow cooker. Add meat mixture from skillet; then add remaining ingredients.
3. Cover and cook on low for 7–9 hours or until soup is blended and thick. Serve with guacamole and sour cream for toppings.

Oyster Stew

SERVES 10–14

Oyster stew is traditional for Christmas Eve in the eastern United States. This version is rich and creamy, and so easily made in the slow cooker. The combination of smoked and canned oysters adds a great depth of flavor.

½ cup butter

2 onions, chopped

6 cloves garlic, minced

4 (8-ounce) cans whole oysters

6 stalks celery, sliced

3 potatoes, peeled and cubed

1 teaspoon salt

¼ teaspoon white pepper

1 (32-ounce) box chicken stock

2 cups water

3 (12-ounce) cans evaporated milk

3 (3-ounce) packages smoked oysters

¼ cup cornstarch

1 cup heavy cream

1 (8-ounce) package cream cheese, cubed

⅓ cup minced chives

1. In large skillet melt butter over medium heat. Add onions and garlic; cook and stir until crisp-tender, about 5 minutes.
2. Meanwhile, drain oysters, reserving juice. Cover oysters and refrigerate. Pour juice into skillet; cook and stir until mixture bubbles.
3. Place celery and potatoes in a 6- to 7-quart slow cooker. Top with salt, pepper, onion mixture, chicken stock, water, and evaporated milk.
4. Cover and cook on low for 7–9 hours or until potatoes are tender. Stir in both types of oysters. In medium bowl, combine cornstarch and cream and mix well. Stir into slow cooker along with cubed cream cheese.
5. Cover and cook on high for 20–30 minutes or until stew is thickened and oysters are hot. Stir to blend. Serve with chives and oyster crackers.

On the fourth day they got up early in the morning, and he prepared to go, but the girl's father said to his son-in-law, "Fortify yourself with a bit of food, and after that you may go."

—JUDGES 19:5

Shrimp and Corn Chowder

SERVES 10–12

This thick and creamy chowder should be served in small portions. It's delicious as the meal starter for a more formal dinner.

6 slices bacon

2 tablespoons butter

2 onions, chopped

6 cloves garlic, minced

2 leeks, sliced

4 potatoes, peeled and cubed

1½ teaspoons seasoned salt

¼ teaspoon white pepper

1 teaspoon Old Bay Seasoning

1 (32-ounce) box chicken broth

3 cups water

1 (16-ounce) package frozen corn

¼ cup cornstarch

1 cup heavy cream

2 pounds frozen cooked shrimp, thawed

⅓ cup chopped flat-leaf parsley

1. In large skillet, cook bacon until crisp. Drain bacon on paper towels, crumble, and set aside in refrigerator.
2. Add butter to skillet; cook onions, garlic, and leeks for 4–5 minutes to loosen pan drippings. Place in 5- or 6-quart slow cooker along with potatoes.
3. Add salt, pepper, Old Bay, chicken broth, water, and corn. Stir gently, then cover and cook on low for 7–9 hours or until potatoes are tender.
4. In bowl, combine cornstarch with cream; mix well. Stir into slow cooker along with shrimp. Cover and cook on high for 20–30 minutes or until stew is thick and shrimp is hot and tender. Sprinkle with reserved bacon and parsley and serve.

Spicy Black Bean Chili

SERVES 12–14

Chipotles are smoked jalapeño peppers canned in adobo sauce. Serve with chopped tomatoes, sour cream, Cheddar cheese, and corn chips.

1½ pounds spicy bulk pork sausage

2 onions, chopped

6 cloves garlic, minced

2 jalapeño peppers, minced

1 tablespoon chopped chipotle peppers

1 (4-ounce) can chopped green chiles, undrained

4 (15-ounce) cans black beans

2 (14-ounce) cans diced tomatoes

2 cups frozen corn

2 (32-ounce) boxes beef broth

2 tablespoons chili powder

1 teaspoon cumin

1 teaspoon salt

¼ teaspoon pepper

¼ teaspoon cayenne pepper

3 tablespoons cornstarch

1 cup apple juice

1. Cook sausage until done, stirring to break up meat. Place in 6- or 7-quart slow cooker along with onions, garlic, jalapeño peppers, chipotle peppers, and green chiles.
2. Drain two cans of the beans and add to slow cooker. Add the other two cans of beans, including liquid. Stir in tomatoes, corn, beef broth, and seasonings.
3. Cover and cook on low for 8 hours or until chili is blended. In bowl, combine cornstarch and apple juice and stir well. Stir into slow cooker.
4. Cover and cook on high for 20–30 minutes. Stir well and serve with toppings.

Split Pea Chowder

SERVES 12–14

This soup is puréed right in the slow cooker. Be sure to use an immersion blender approved for use with stoneware. If you can't find one, just mash the ingredients before stirring in the cream and Canadian bacon.

2 onions, chopped

6 cloves garlic, minced

1 pound green split peas, rinsed

4 potatoes, peeled and cubed

1 ham hock

1 teaspoon salt

¼ teaspoon pepper

1 teaspoon dried tarragon leaves

4 cups water

1 (32-ounce) box chicken broth

1½ cups heavy cream

¼ cup cornstarch

2 cups cubed Canadian bacon

1. Combine onions, garlic, split peas, potatoes, and ham hock in 6- or 7-quart slow cooker. Sprinkle with salt, pepper, and tarragon. Pour water and chicken broth over all.
2. Cover and cook on low for 7–9 hours or until potatoes and peas are tender. Remove ham hock and cut off meat; reserve. Discard ham bone.
3. Turn off slow cooker. Using an immersion blender or potato masher, mash the ingredients in the slow cooker until desired consistency.
4. In small bowl, combine cream with cornstarch; stir into slow cooker along with Canadian bacon and meat from ham hock. Cover and cook on high for 20–30 minutes longer or until chowder is thick and meat is hot.

Cowboy Chili

SERVES 12–14

True Texas chili doesn't contain tomatoes, onions, or beans, but I don't think it's chili without them. Serve with sour cream and shredded cheese for toppings.

3 pounds beef chuck steak

2 teaspoons salt

¼ teaspoon pepper

⅓ cup flour

1 teaspoon dried oregano leaves

3 tablespoons olive oil

3 cups water

2 onions, chopped

4 cloves garlic, minced

2 tablespoons chili powder

1 (32-ounce) box beef broth

1 (15-ounce) can chili beans, undrained

2 (15-ounce) cans kidney beans, drained

1. Trim excess fat from steak and cut into 2" cubes. On shallow plate, combine salt, pepper, flour, and oregano; mix well. Toss steak cubes in flour mixture.
2. In skillet, heat olive oil over medium heat. Brown steak cubes in oil for 5–6 minutes, stirring occasionally. Place meat in 5- or 6-quart slow cooker.
3. Add water to skillet; cook and stir until mixture boils, stirring to loosen pan drippings. Pour into slow cooker.
4. Add all remaining ingredients. Cover and cook on low for 8–9 hours or until steak is very tender.

Lamb Sweet Potato Stew

SERVES 12–14

Fresh rosemary is really essential to this stew. Dried rosemary tends to be very spiky and hard, with a more subtle flavor; don't substitute it for fresh in this recipe.

3 pounds boneless lamb stew meat, cubed

1½ teaspoons seasoned salt

½ teaspoon pepper

⅓ cup flour

2 tablespoons butter

2 tablespoons olive oil

3 cups water

4 sweet potatoes, peeled and cubed

2 (16-ounce) packages baby carrots

2 onions, sliced

1 (32-ounce) box beef broth

2 fresh rosemary sprigs

2 fresh thyme sprigs

¼ cup cornstarch

1 cup apple cider

3 cups frozen cut green beans, thawed

1. Trim excess fat from lamb. On shallow plate, combine salt, pepper, and flour; mix well. Dredge lamb cubes in this mixture to coat.
2. In large skillet, heat butter and olive oil over medium heat. Add lamb; cook and stir until browned, about 5–6 minutes. Remove lamb to 7-quart slow cooker.
3. Add water to skillet; cook and stir to loosen pan drippings. Pour over lamb. Add sweet potatoes, carrots, and onions to slow cooker. Pour in broth and bury rosemary and thyme sprigs in broth.
4. Cover and cook on low for 8–9 hours or until potatoes are tender and lamb registers 160°F. In small bowl combine cornstarch and cider; stir into stew along with green beans. Cover and cook on high for 20–30 minutes or until stew is thickened and hot. Remove rosemary and thyme stems, stir, and serve immediately.

Then Abigail hurried and took two hundred loaves, two skins of wine, five sheep ready dressed, five measures of parched grain, one hundred clusters of raisins, and two hundred cakes of figs.

—1 SAMUEL 25:18

Pork and Cabbage Stew

SERVES 12–14

Cabbage adds great flavor and nutrition to this hearty stew, which is full of vegetables. Using red and green cabbage also adds color!

2 pounds bulk pork sausage

3 cups water

3 onions, chopped

5 carrots, sliced

4 potatoes, sliced

2 cups chopped green cabbage

2 cups chopped red cabbage

1 (32-ounce) box chicken broth

3 tablespoons apple cider vinegar

3 tablespoons brown sugar

1 teaspoon salt

¼ teaspoon pepper

1 teaspoon dried marjoram leaves

1 teaspoon dried basil leaves

2 (14-ounce) cans diced tomatoes, undrained

½ cup potato flakes

1. In large skillet, cook pork sausage until done, stirring to break up meat. Drain pork well and place in 7-quart slow cooker. Do not wipe out skillet.
2. Add water to skillet and bring to a boil, stirring to loosen pan drippings. Remove from heat.
3. Layer onions, carrots, potatoes, and both kinds of cabbage in slow cooker. Pour skillet mixture over vegetables, along with chicken broth and all remaining ingredients except potato flakes.
4. Cover and cook on low for 7–9 hours or until potatoes and cabbage are tender. Stir in potato flakes; cover and cook on high for 30 minutes longer until mixture is thickened. Serve immediately.

Salmon Chowder

SERVES 12–14

Salmon packaged in a pouch already has the skin and bones removed, saving you a lot of work. This creamy chowder is a great way to showcase this fish.

6 slices bacon

2 onions, chopped

4 cloves garlic, minced

4 potatoes, peeled and cubed

4 cups frozen corn

1 (32-ounce) box chicken broth

2 cups water

1 teaspoon dried thyme leaves

½ teaspoon dried dill weed

1 teaspoon salt

¼ teaspoon white pepper

1½ cups heavy cream

½ cup whole milk

⅓ cup potato flakes

4 (7.1-ounce) pouches salmon, drained

1. In large skillet, cook bacon until crisp. Drain bacon on paper towel, crumble, and refrigerate. Add onions and garlic to skillet; cook and stir for 5 minutes to loosen pan drippings.
2. Place potatoes and corn in 6- or 7-quart slow cooker. Add onion mixture to slow cooker along with broth, water, thyme, dill weed, salt, and pepper. Cover and cook on low for 7–9 hours or until potatoes are tender.
3. Stir in cream, milk, potato flakes, salmon, and reserved bacon. Cover and cook on high for 20–30 minutes or until chowder is thick and hot. Serve immediately.

Curried Turkey and Squash Bisque

SERVES 12–14

Apples and squash combine beautifully; they are both sweet and become very tender when cooked in the slow cooker. Add ground turkey and some curry for a hearty bisque.

1 (2-pound) butternut squash

1 (1-pound) acorn squash

1 (16-ounce) bag baby carrots

2 pounds ground turkey

2 onions, chopped

3 tart apples, cored, peeled and chopped

2 tablespoons curry powder

1 teaspoon salt

¼ teaspoon white pepper

2 (32-ounce) boxes chicken broth

3 tablespoons cornstarch

1 cup heavy whipping cream

1. Peel butternut squash and remove seeds and membranes. Cut into 1" pieces. Do the same with acorn squash. Place in 6- to 7-quart slow cooker along with baby carrots.
2. In large skillet, cook turkey until done, stirring to break up meat. Remove turkey to slow cooker. Add onions to skillet; cook and stir to loosen pan drippings. Add onions to slow cooker along with apples.
3. Sprinkle contents of slow cooker with curry powder, salt, and pepper. Pour chicken broth into slow cooker. Cover and cook on low for 8–9 hours or until squash is tender.
4. In small bowl, combine cornstarch with cream and mix well. Stir into slow cooker. Cover and cook on high for 20–30 minutes or until bisque is thickened. Serve immediately.

But the father said to his slaves, "Quickly, bring out a robe—the best one—and put it on him; put a ring on his finger and sandals on his feet. And get the fatted calf and kill it, and let us eat and celebrate; for this son of mine was dead and is alive again; he was lost and is found!" And they began to celebrate.

—LUKE 15:22–24

Beef Entrées

*B*eef is one of the most popular meats today, and with good reason. It's tender, filling, and hearty. And you can prepare it in so many ways! My paternal grandmother made the best pot roast in the world, and no one ever got her recipe. There's a good idea for a fundraiser—collect heirloom recipes and make a cookbook.

One of the best things about the slow cooker is that it lets you use less expensive cuts of beef; in fact, those cuts are preferred for this type of cooking. The long, slow cooking in moist heat tenderizes tough cuts of beef so they literally fall apart on your fork.

When you're cooking ground beef in the slow cooker, you must first brown the beef in a skillet for best results, cooking it thoroughly and draining off any fat before it goes into the slow cooker. The beef will not overcook in the appliance; it will be tender and moist.

Many other cuts of beef are browned before cooking because this step adds flavor and improves the appearance of the final dish. If the beef is first dredged in seasoned flour, that can help thicken the final dish.

Beef roasts and steaks should be cooked to an internal temperature of 145°F; this is considered rare. Ground beef must be cooked to 165°F. Use your imagination when thinking about beef; consider ethnic cuisines and the preferences of the crowd you're serving.

Sweet-and-Sour Meatball Casserole

SERVES 8

This is a great hot dish for an evening Bible study. There are many varieties and types of frozen fully cooked meatballs. A favorite, especially in this recipe, are ground beef meatballs made with wild rice.

1 onion, chopped

3 cloves garlic, minced

1 cup wild rice, rinsed

1 (14-ounce) can ready-to-serve beef broth

1½ cups water

3 tablespoons sugar

¼ cup apple cider vinegar

1 (8-ounce) can pineapple tidbits in juice, undrained

1 (1-pound) package frozen meatballs

1 red bell pepper, chopped

1 green bell pepper, chopped

2 tablespoons cornstarch

5 tablespoons ketchup

2 tablespoons water

1. In 4- or 5-quart slow cooker, combine onions, garlic, and rice. Pour broth and water over all. Add sugar, cider vinegar, and pineapple tidbits; stir to combine. Then add meatballs. Cover and cook on low for 7–8 hours.
2. Add red and green bell peppers; stir. Cover and cook on low for 45 minutes.
3. Turn heat to high. In small bowl, combine cornstarch, ketchup, and water; mix well. Add to slow cooker and stir. Cook on high for 15–20 minutes or until liquid is thickened and bell peppers are tender. Serve immediately.

Spaghetti Sauce

SERVES 10–12

Spaghetti sauce that cooks slowly in a slow cooker has the best flavor. Enjoy this one with some buttery toasted garlic bread.

2 pounds 90% lean ground beef

2 onions, chopped

3 cloves garlic, minced

1 (8-ounce) package sliced mushrooms

2 (14-ounce) cans diced tomatoes, undrained

1 (6-ounce) can tomato paste

1 (8-ounce) can tomato sauce

1 (10-ounce) can condensed tomato soup

1 cup tomato juice

1 tablespoon sugar

1 teaspoon salt

1½ teaspoons dried basil

1½ teaspoons dried oregano

¼ teaspoon pepper

2 (12-ounce) packages spaghetti pasta, cooked and drained

1 cup grated Parmesan or Romano cheese

1. In large skillet, cook ground beef until done; drain well and place in 5-quart slow cooker. Add remaining ingredients except pasta and cheese, stirring to mix.
2. Cover and cook on low for 8–9 hours, until sauce is blended and vegetables are tender. Serve over cooked spaghetti and top with grated Parmesan or Romano cheese.

Tender Pot Roast

SERVES 12–14

There's nothing better than the aroma of pot roast in the kitchen on a cold winter's day.

4-pound beef chuck roast
1 teaspoon salt
¼ teaspoon pepper
2 teaspoons paprika
2 tablespoons olive oil
2 onions, chopped
3 carrots, chopped
3 cloves garlic, minced
1 (14-ounce) can ready-to-serve beef broth
1 (6-ounce) can tomato paste
2 tablespoons balsamic vinegar
1 tablespoon sugar

1. Sprinkle roast with salt, pepper, and paprika. In large skillet, heat olive oil over medium heat. Add roast; brown on all sides, turning frequently, about 10 minutes total. Remove from heat.
2. In 6- to 7-quart slow cooker, combine onions, carrots, and garlic. Top with roast. Add broth, tomato paste, vinegar, and sugar to skillet; mix until paste dissolves. Pour over roast.
3. Cover and cook on low for 8–10 hours or until beef is tender and registers at least 155°F. Remove beef from slow cooker and cover to keep warm. Turn off slow cooker; using an immersion blender, purée the mixture in the slow cooker. Serve sauce along with the roast.

Beefy Baked Beans

SERVES 12

Canned beans are an inexpensive and nutritious way to feed a crowd. Serve this over hot cooked rice for a hearty and filling dinner.

2 pounds 90% lean ground beef
3 onions, chopped
6 cloves garlic, minced
3 (16-ounce) cans baked beans, drained
2 (15-ounce) can black beans, drained
2 (15-ounce) cans lima beans, drained
½ cup brown sugar
¼ cup apple cider vinegar
1 cup ketchup
1 cup barbecue sauce

1. In large skillet, brown ground beef, stirring to break up meat. Drain well and place in 5- to 6-quart slow cooker.
2. Add all remaining ingredients and stir gently. Cover and cook on low for 8–9 hours. If sauce needs thickening, remove cover and cook on high for 20–30 minutes.

Solomon's provision for one day was ten fat oxen, twenty pasture-fed oxen, a hundred sheep besides deer, gazelles, roebucks, and fattened fowl.

—1 KINGS 4:22–23

Picadillo

SERVES 8

Picadillo can be served as a stew, over rice, as a taco or burrito filling, or as part of a taco salad. This versatile dish is bursting with flavor.

1 tablespoon olive oil

1 tablespoon butter

3 potatoes, peeled and chopped

1½ pounds ground beef

2 onions, chopped

4 cloves garlic, minced

½ teaspoon salt

¼ teaspoon pepper

¼ teaspoon ground cloves

1 teaspoon cumin

1 cup sliced green pimento-stuffed olives

1 cup raisins

2 (14-ounce) cans diced tomatoes, undrained

1 (6-ounce) can tomato paste

2 tablespoons apple cider vinegar

4 tomatoes, chopped

1. In large skillet, heat olive oil and butter together. Add chopped potatoes; cook and stir for 5 minutes. Place potatoes in 5-quart slow cooker and set aside.
2. In same skillet, cook ground beef with onions and garlic until beef is browned, stirring to break up meat. Drain well, then add salt, pepper, cloves, and cumin to meat.
3. Place olives and raisins in slow cooker over potatoes. Add tomatoes, tomato paste, and vinegar to beef mixture; bring to a simmer. Simmer for 10 minutes, stirring frequently.
4. Layer beef mixture with chopped tomatoes in slow cooker. Cover and cook on low for 8–9 hours or until potatoes are tender. Stir and serve immediately.

He asked for water and she gave him milk; in a magnificent bowl she brought him curds.

—JUDGES 5:25

Italian Roast Beef

SERVES 12–14

Italian seasonings add great flavor to a simple rump roast in this easy recipe. Leftovers (if there are any!) are great in sandwiches.

1 (4-pound) boneless beef rump roast

1 teaspoon salt

¼ teaspoon pepper

¼ cup flour

2 tablespoons butter

1 tablespoon olive oil

2 onions, chopped

1 (8-ounce) package sliced mushrooms

½ teaspoon dried oregano

1 teaspoon dried basil

1 teaspoon dried Italian seasoning

2 cups spaghetti sauce

1. Trim excess fat from roast and sprinkle with salt, pepper, and flour. In large skillet, combine butter and olive oil over medium heat. When butter melts, brown beef on all sides, about 10 minutes total. Place beef in 6- to 7-quart slow cooker.
2. Add onions and mushrooms to skillet. Cook and stir until tender, about 6–7 minutes. Add to beef in slow cooker.
3. Add oregano, basil, Italian seasoning, and spaghetti sauce to skillet and stir. Pour into slow cooker. Cover and cook on low for 8–9 hours or until beef is tender.

Tangy Apricot Cube Steaks

SERVES 8–10

Sweet fruit and tangy onions are always a good combination. Add that to tender cube steaks and you have a feast!

2½ pounds cube steak

1 teaspoon salt

¼ teaspoon pepper

⅓ cup flour

1 teaspoon paprika

2 tablespoons oil

1 tablespoon butter

1½ cups beef broth

1 (16-ounce) jar apricot preserves

2 (1-ounce) envelopes dry onion soup mix

1 cup chopped dried apricots

1. Cut steak into serving-sized pieces. On shallow plate, combine salt, pepper, flour, and paprika; stir to blend. Dredge steaks in this mixture.
2. In large skillet, combine oil and butter over medium heat. Brown steaks on both sides, turning once, about 3–4 minutes.
3. As steaks brown, place in 4-quart slow cooker. When all the steaks are cooked, add beef broth to skillet. Cook and stir over medium heat to loosen drippings. Remove from heat and add remaining ingredients to skillet.
4. Pour contents of skillet into slow cooker. Cover and cook on low for 7–8 hours or until meat is very tender. Serve meat with sauce.

Tex-Mex Steak and Potato Salad

SERVES 12–14

Cooking sirloin tip and potatoes together until tender is a wonderful way to make a lot of salad with ease. This is a good choice for a summer picnic.

3 pounds sirloin tip

2 tablespoons chili powder

1½ teaspoons salt

½ teaspoon pepper

6–8 potatoes, peeled and cubed

2 onions, chopped

5 cloves garlic, minced

2 jalapeño peppers, minced

1 (16-ounce) jar mild or medium salsa

1½ cups mayonnaise

1½ cups plain yogurt

1 (16-ounce) jar mild or medium salsa

2 green bell peppers, chopped

2 red bell peppers, chopped

2 cups cubed pepper jack cheese

⅓ cup chopped fresh cilantro

1. Cut sirloin into 1" pieces. Sprinkle with chili powder, salt, and pepper. Place potatoes, onions, garlic, and jalapeños in bottom of 6-quart slow cooker. Top with beef. Pour one jar salsa over all.
2. Cover and cook on low for 8–9 hours or until beef and potatoes are tender.
3. In large bowl, combine mayonnaise, yogurt, second jar of salsa, green and red bell peppers, and cheese; mix well. Remove hot beef mixture from slow cooker with large slotted spoon or sieve and add to mixture in bowl. Discard liquid left in slow cooker. Stir gently to coat.
4. Cover and refrigerate for 4–5 hours until cold. Stir gently before serving, and top with cilantro.

Spend the money for whatever you wish—oxen, sheep, wine, strong drink, or whatever you desire. And you shall eat here in the presence of the Lord your God, you and your household rejoicing together.

—GENESIS 14:26

Mom's Meatloaf

SERVES 8

Potatoes add moisture and flavor to this comforting, hearty meatloaf recipe. Everyone will ask how you did it, and then ask for seconds.

2 tablespoons olive oil

1 onion, chopped

3 cloves garlic, minced

1 cup chopped mushrooms

½ cup refrigerated mashed potatoes from package

1 egg

¼ cup heavy cream

¼ cup yellow mustard

¼ cup ketchup

¼ cup beef broth

1 tablespoon Worcestershire sauce

¼ teaspoon pepper

1½ pounds lean ground beef

1 pound lean ground pork

2 tablespoons honey

2 tablespoons mustard

½ teaspoon paprika

1. In large skillet, heat olive oil over medium heat. Add onion, garlic, and mushrooms. Cook and stir until mushrooms give up their liquid and that liquid evaporates, about 10 minutes.

2. Remove skillet from heat and transfer onion mixture to a large bowl. Add potatoes, egg, and cream; mix well. Stir in mustard, ketchup, beef broth, Worcestershire sauce, and pepper; mix well.

3. Stir in beef and pork, and mix gently with your hands. Form into an 8" ball. Tear off two 24" sheets of heavy-duty foil and fold into thirds lengthwise. Place crosswise in bottom of 5-quart slow cooker. Place meatloaf on top.

4. In small bowl, combine honey, mustard, and paprika. Spread over meatloaf. Cover slow cooker. Cook on low for 7–8 hours or until meat thermometer registers 165°F.

5. Using the foil, carefully lift the meatloaf out of the slow cooker. Drain on paper towels for 5 minutes, then slice to serve.

In those days when there was again a great crowd without anything to eat, Jesus called his disciples and said to them, "I have compassion for the crowd, because they have been with me now for three days and have nothing to eat. If I send them away hungry to their homes, they will faint on the way—and some of them have come from a great distance."

—MARK 8:1–3

Ranchero Beef Roast

SERVES 12–14

There's nothing better than Tex-Mex seasonings with beef. The spices blend together in the long cooking time to turn mild and savory.

1 (4-pound) boneless beef rump roast

1 teaspoon salt

¼ teaspoon pepper

1 tablespoon chili powder

¼ cup flour

2 tablespoons butter

1 tablespoon olive oil

2 onions, chopped

5 cloves garlic, minced

2 jalapeño peppers, chopped

1 teaspoon cumin

1 teaspoon dried oregano leaves

1 (16-ounce) jar chunky mild or medium salsa

1. Trim excess fat from roast. In small bowl combine salt, pepper, chili powder, and flour. Sprinkle over roast. In large skillet, combine butter and olive oil over medium heat. When butter melts, brown beef on all sides, about 10 minutes total. Place beef in 6- to 7-quart slow cooker.
2. Add onions, garlic, and jalapeños to skillet. Cook and stir until tender, about 6–7 minutes. Add to beef in slow cooker.
3. In bowl, combine cumin, oregano, and salsa and mix well. Pour into slow cooker. Cover and cook on low for 8–9 hours or until beef is tender.

Shepherd's Pie

SERVES 8

This flavorful pie full of beef and vegetables is topped with creamy and cheesy mashed potatoes.

1½ pounds ground beef

2 onions, chopped

1 leek, chopped

5 cloves garlic, minced

1 teaspoon salt

¼ teaspoon pepper

1 teaspoon dried thyme leaves

4 carrots, sliced

1 (8-ounce) package sliced mushrooms

1 (14-ounce) can diced tomatoes, undrained

1 (6-ounce) can tomato paste

½ cup ketchup

¼ cup yellow or Dijon mustard

2 tablespoons Worcestershire sauce

1 (24-ounce) package refrigerated mashed potatoes

½ cup sour cream

½ cup grated Parmesan cheese

1. In large skillet, brown ground beef with onions, leek, and garlic, stirring to break up meat. When beef is thoroughly cooked, drain well.
2. Add salt, pepper, and thyme; mix well. Pour mixture into 5 quart slow cooker. Stir in carrots, mushrooms, tomatoes, tomato paste, ketchup, mustard, and Worcestershire sauce. Mix well.
3. Prepare mashed potatoes as directed on package. Stir in sour cream and Parmesan cheese. Spoon on top of meat mixture in slow cooker.
4. Cover and cook on low for 6–7 hours or until mixture is hot and bubbling.

Beef and Bean Potpie

SERVES 8

This mild pie is comforting and rich. The corn bread topping stays moist and tender when cooked in the slow cooker. This recipe could also be made with ground turkey or pork.

1½ pounds ground beef

2 onions, chopped

6 cloves garlic, minced

½ teaspoon salt

⅛ teaspoon pepper

1 teaspoon dried marjoram

2 (15-ounce) cans kidney beans

2 (4-ounce) jars sliced mushrooms, drained

4 carrots, sliced

1 (10-ounce) can condensed tomato soup

1 (8-ounce) can tomato sauce

1 (8-ounce) package corn muffin mix

1 egg

½ cup sour cream

2 tablespoons oil

⅓ cup grated Parmesan cheese

1. In large skillet, cook ground beef with onions and garlic until ground beef is done, stirring to break up meat. Drain well. Add salt, pepper, and marjoram; stir.
2. Stir in kidney beans and mushrooms with their liquid, carrots, soup, and tomato sauce; bring to a simmer.
3. Spray a 5-quart slow cooker with nonstick cooking spray. Pour beef mixture into slow cooker.
4. In medium bowl, combine remaining ingredients and stir just until combined. Spoon by tablespoons over beef mixture in slow cooker.
5. Cover and cook on low for 6–8 hours or until corn bread is set and toothpick inserted in center of topping comes out clean.

But when you give a banquet, invite the poor, the crippled, the lame, and the blind. And you will be blessed, because they cannot repay you, for you will be repaid at the resurrection of the righteous.

—LUKE 14:13–14

Pesto Beef Strata

SERVES 8–10

Pesto is a paste or sauce made of basil leaves, Parmesan cheese, garlic, pine nuts, and olive oil. It's flavorful and delicious used in this easy recipe.

2 pounds lean ground beef

2 onions, chopped

4 cloves garlic, minced

1 (14-ounce) can diced tomatoes, undrained

1 (10-ounce) can condensed tomato soup

1 teaspoon dried basil

½ teaspoon salt

⅛ teaspoon pepper

6 potatoes, peeled and sliced

1 (16-ounce) jar Alfredo sauce

2 (7-ounce) containers refrigerated pesto

½ cup grated Parmesan cheese

1. In large skillet, cook ground beef with onions and garlic, stirring to break up beef, until beef is thoroughly cooked. Drain well. Add tomatoes, tomato soup, basil, salt, and pepper. Bring to a simmer.
2. Slice potatoes ⅛" thick. In medium bowl, combine Alfredo sauce, pesto, and Parmesan cheese. Layer ¼ of beef mixture, ¼ of potatoes, and ¼ of pesto mixture in 5-quart slow cooker. Continue until all ingredients are used.
3. Cover and cook on low for 7–9 hours or until potatoes are tender.

Spicy Steak Bake

SERVES 8

Serve this delicious mixture over hot cooked pasta or hot mashed potatoes for a homey meal.

2 pounds beef sirloin tip steak

⅓ cup flour

1 teaspoon seasoned salt

⅛ teaspoon pepper

⅛ teaspoon cayenne pepper

2 tablespoons olive oil

2 onions, chopped

4 cloves garlic, minced

2 green bell peppers, chopped

2 tablespoons Worcestershire sauce

¼ cup honey

2 (14-ounce) cans diced tomatoes, undrained

1 (6-ounce) can tomato paste

1 cup beef broth

2 tablespoons yellow mustard

1. Trim excess fat from steak and cut into 1½" cubes. On shallow plate, combine flour, seasoned salt, pepper, and cayenne pepper; mix well. Toss steak in this mixture to coat.
2. Heat olive oil in large skillet over medium heat. Add steak; cook and stir until browned, about 4–5 minutes. Remove meat to 4-quart slow cooker.
3. Add onions and garlic to skillet; cook and stir for 4–5 minutes, scraping pan to remove drippings. Pour into slow cooker along with bell peppers.
4. Add Worcestershire sauce, honey, undrained tomatoes, tomato paste, beef broth, and mustard to skillet. Bring to a simmer, then pour into slow cooker.
5. Cover and cook on low for 8–9 hours or until beef is very tender. Serve mixture over hot cooked pasta or rice.

Orange Beef with Broccoli

SERVES 10–12

Orange marmalade, juice, and zest add fresh flavor to this dish, which is usually made as a stir-fry.

3½ pounds round steak

⅓ cup flour

1 teaspoon salt

1 teaspoon paprika

¼ teaspoon pepper

2 tablespoons butter

2 tablespoons olive oil

2 cups beef broth

4 shallots, peeled and chopped

6 cloves garlic, minced

1 cup orange marmalade

1 teaspoon dried thyme leaves

1 tablespoon grated orange zest

¼ cup soy sauce

3 tablespoons cornstarch

½ cup orange juice

2 (16-ounce) packages frozen broccoli florets, thawed

6 cups hot cooked rice

1. Trim excess fat from steak and cut into 1½" cubes. On shallow plate, combine flour, salt, paprika, and pepper; mix well. Toss steak in flour mixture to coat.

2. In large saucepan, melt butter and olive oil over medium heat. Add steak; cook and stir until browned, about 5–7 minutes total. Remove beef from skillet with slotted spoon and place in 5-6 quart slow cooker.

3. Add beef broth to saucepan and cook until mixture bubbles, stirring to remove drippings. Pour into slow cooker. Add remaining ingredients except for cornstarch, orange juice, broccoli, and rice. Cover and cook for 7–8 hours or until beef is very tender.

4. In small bowl, combine cornstarch and orange juice and mix well. Stir into slow cooker along with thawed and drained broccoli. Turn slow cooker to high and cook for 20–30 minutes until sauce is thickened and broccoli is hot and tender. Serve over hot cooked rice.

When the Lord your God enlarges your territory, as he has promised you, and you say, "I am going to eat some meat," because you wish to eat meat, you may eat meat whenever you have the desire.

—GENESIS 12:20

Beef with Root Vegetables

SERVES 10

You can thicken the sauce with a slurry of 2 table-spoons cornstarch and ¼ cup water at the end of cooking time; cook on high for 20 minutes longer after adding this mixture.

2½ pounds bottom round steak

⅓ cup flour

1 teaspoon salt

1 teaspoon dried Italian seasoning

⅛ teaspoon pepper

2 tablespoons butter

2 tablespoons olive oil

1 cup water

2 onions, chopped

5 cloves garlic, minced

4 carrots, sliced

3 russet potatoes, peeled

2 sweet potatoes, peeled

2 cups cubed rutabaga

2 cups beef broth

1. Trim excess fat from steak and cut into 2" cubes. On shallow plate, combine flour, salt, Italian seasoning, and pepper; sprinkle over beef. In large skillet, combine butter and olive oil over medium heat.

2. Add beef to skillet; cook and stir until browned, about 6–7 minutes. Remove beef cubes from skillet and set aside. Add water to skillet; cook and stir until mixture comes to a boil, stirring to release drippings.

3. In 6-quart slow cooker, combine onions, garlic, carrots, both kinds of potatoes, and rutabaga. Place browned beef on top.

4. Add beef broth to skillet. Pour into slow cooker. Cover and cook on low for 9–10 hours or until vegetables are tender.

For the whole law is summed up in a single commandment, "You shall love your neighbor as yourself."

—GALATIANS 5:14

Classic Swiss Steak

SERVES 8

What's a church dinner without Swiss steak? This classic is updated with lots of vegetables and made easily in the slow cooker.

2½ pounds beef round steak

5 tablespoons flour

1 teaspoon salt

½ teaspoon garlic salt

1 teaspoon paprika

½ teaspoon pepper

2 teaspoons steak seasoning

2 tablespoons butter

3 tablespoons olive oil

4 carrots, cut into chunks

2 onions, sliced

1 (8-ounce) package sliced mushrooms

6 cloves garlic, minced

4 stalks celery, sliced

2 cups beef broth

1 (14-ounce) can diced tomatoes, undrained

1 cup chili sauce

1 (6-ounce) can tomato paste

1. Cut steak into 8 portions and trim off excess fat. On shallow plate, combine flour, salt, garlic salt, paprika, pepper, and steak seasoning; mix well. Dredge steaks in this mixture. Place steaks between two sheets of waxed paper, and pound to tenderize.

2. In large skillet, heat butter and olive oil over medium heat. Add steaks; brown on both sides, turning once, about 4–5 minutes total. Remove from heat.

3. Combine carrots, onions, mushrooms, garlic, and celery in 6-quart slow cooker. Top with steaks.

4. Add beef broth, tomatoes, chili sauce, and tomato paste to skillet; cook and stir over high heat until mixture simmers. Pour into slow cooker.

5. Cover and cook on low for 7–8 hours or until beef and vegetables are very tender. Serve steak with vegetables and sauce over mashed potatoes or cooked pasta.

Bring me game, and prepare for me savory food to eat, that I may bless you before the Lord before I die.

—GENESIS 27:7

Beef à la King

SERVES 14

Chicken à la King may be a lunchroom staple, but using beef instead elevates this dish to a new level. You could add sliced carrots if you'd like.

3 pounds sirloin tip
⅓ cup flour
2 teaspoons steak seasoning
½ teaspoon salt
⅛ teaspoon pepper
2 tablespoons butter
2 tablespoons olive oil
2 onions, chopped
4 cloves garlic, minced
2 (8-ounce) packages sliced mushrooms
1 (32-ounce) box beef broth
1 cup heavy cream
3 tablespoons cornstarch
3 cups frozen baby peas
14 frozen puff pastry shells

1. Trim excess fat from beef and cut into 1" cubes. On shallow plate, combine flour, steak seasoning, salt, and pepper; mix well. Dredge beef in flour mixture to coat.
2. In large skillet, heat butter with olive oil over medium heat. Add steak; brown cubes, stirring frequently, for about 6 minutes. Place in 6-quart slow cooker.
3. Add onions and garlic to skillet. Cook and stir to loosen pan drippings; cook for 4 minutes. Add to slow cooker along with mushrooms and beef broth.
4. Cover and cook on low for 7–8 hours or until beef and vegetables are tender. In small bowl, combine cream and cornstarch; stir into slow cooker along with peas. Turn to high; cook for 20–25 minutes until sauce thickens.
5. Prepare puff pastry shells as directed on package. Serve beef mixture over the hot baked shells.

However, there should be no poor among you, for in the land the Lord your God is giving you to possess as your inheritance, he will richly bless you.

—DEUTERONOMY 15:4

Cajun Beef

SERVES 12–14

You can find Cajun seasoning and steak seasoning in the spice aisle of any supermarket. They add a sweet heat to this wonderful recipe.

3 pounds bottom round steak

⅓ cup flour

2 tablespoons Cajun seasoning

2 teaspoons steak seasoning

¼ teaspoon pepper

2 tablespoons butter

2 tablespoons olive oil

2 onions, chopped

8 cloves garlic, minced

2 poblano peppers, chopped

1 yellow bell pepper, chopped

1 orange bell pepper, chopped

1 red bell pepper, chopped

1 (14-ounce) can diced tomatoes, undrained

1 (6-ounce) can tomato paste

1 (8-ounce) can tomato sauce

3 cups beef broth

1½ cups instant brown rice

1. Trim excess fat from beef. Cut into 2" cubes. On shallow plate, combine flour, Cajun seasoning, steak seasoning, and pepper; mix well. Dredge beef cubes in this mixture.

2. In large skillet, heat butter and olive oil over medium heat. Brown beef, stirring occasionally, about 5–6 minutes total.

3. Remove beef from skillet and place in 6- to 7-quart slow cooker. Add onions and garlic to skillet; cook and stir to release drippings. Add to slow cooker along with remaining ingredients except rice; stir.

4. Cover and cook on low for 8–9 hours or until beef is cooked and vegetables are tender.

5. Turn heat to high. Stir in brown rice, making sure rice is submerged in liquid. Cover and cook for 25 minutes. Stir and serve.

They shall eat the lamb that same night;
they shall eat it roasted over the fire with
unleavened bread and bitter herbs.

—EXODUS 12:8

Beef Curry

SERVES 12–14

Balsamic vinegar adds a nice tang to this dish. You could stir in frozen peas at the end of cooking time just to warm through to stretch the dish and add color.

3 pounds beef stew meat	3 tablespoons minced fresh gingerroot
1/3 cup flour	1 (28-ounce) can tomato purée
2 tablespoons curry powder	
1 teaspoon salt	1 (6-ounce) can tomato paste
1/2 teaspoon pepper	
1/4 cup butter	1 cup beef broth
3 onions, chopped	3 tablespoons balsamic vinegar
6 cloves garlic, minced	
3 green bell peppers, chopped	Cooked rice, mashed potatoes, or cooked noodles

1. Trim excess fat from beef and cut into 2" cubes. On shallow plate, combine flour, curry powder, salt, and pepper. Dredge meat in flour mixture.
2. Melt butter in large skillet over medium heat. Brown beef in batches, stirring occasionally, until browned, about 5–6 minutes per batch. Place beef in 6-quart slow cooker.
3. Add onions and garlic to skillet; cook and stir to loosen pan drippings. Cook for 4 minutes until crisp-tender. Add to slow cooker along with bell peppers and gingerroot.
4. Add tomato purée, tomato paste, and beef broth to skillet; cook and stir until mixture bubbles. Pour into slow cooker. Cover and cook on low for 7 hours or until beef is tender. Stir in balsamic vinegar and serve over rice, mashed potatoes, or noodles.

Slow Cooker Stuffed Cabbage

SERVES 12–14

This easy layered casserole tastes like stuffed cabbage, but with much less work. The gingersnaps add a layer of flavor to the sauce.

1 cup pearl barley	1 teaspoon salt
2 cups beef broth	1/4 teaspoon pepper
2 1/2 pounds ground beef	1/4 cup brown sugar
2 onions, chopped	1/4 cup red wine vinegar
6 cloves garlic, minced	6 gingersnaps, crumbled
1 (14-ounce) can diced tomatoes, undrained	9 cups shredded red cabbage
2 (8-ounce) cans tomato sauce	1 (8-ounce) can tomato sauce
1 (6-ounce) can tomato paste	

1. In large saucepan, combine barley and broth and bring to a boil. Reduce heat to low, cover, and simmer for 30–35 minutes or until barley is almost tender. Drain well, if necessary; set aside.
2. In large skillet, brown ground beef with onions and garlic, stirring to break up beef. When beef is almost cooked, drain well. Add tomatoes, 2 cans tomato sauce, tomato paste, salt, pepper, brown sugar, vinegar, and gingersnaps. Simmer until gingersnaps dissolve.
3. Stir barley into beef mixture. In 7-quart slow cooker, place a layer of 1/3 (3 cups) of the cabbage, then top with half of the beef mixture. Repeat layers, ending with cabbage. Pour 1 can tomato sauce over all.
4. Cover and cook on low for 8–9 hours or until cabbage is tender.

Tropical Breeze Pot Roast

SERVES 12–14

This flavorful roast offers a taste of the islands! Beef with fruit is a wonderful combination, and some ginger and spice will really wake up your taste buds.

4 pound beef chuck roast

⅓ cup flour

1 teaspoon salt

1 teaspoon cumin

½ teaspoon cinnamon

¼ teaspoon cayenne pepper

3 tablespoons olive oil

3 onions, chopped

4 cloves garlic, minced

½ cup beef broth

2 jalapeño peppers, minced

3 tablespoons minced fresh gingerroot

1 (20-ounce) can pineapple tidbits in juice, undrained

1 (8-ounce) can crushed pineapple in juice, undrained

1 (20-ounce) can tropical fruit salad in juice, drained

½ cup orange juice

3 tablespoons cornstarch

8 cups hot cooked rice

1. Trim excess fat from roast. On shallow plate, combine flour, salt, cumin, cinnamon, and cayenne pepper. Dredge meat in this mixture.

2. In large skillet, heat olive oil over medium heat. Brown roast on both sides, turning once, for about 7–8 minutes. Transfer to 6- to 7-quart slow cooker.

3. Add onions and garlic to skillet; cook and stir about 4–5 minutes, stirring to loosen pan drippings. Add beef broth and bring to a simmer. Pour into slow cooker.

4. Add jalapeño peppers, gingerroot, pineapple tidbits, and crushed pineapple to slow cooker. Cover and cook on low for 8–9 hours or until beef is very tender.

5. Remove beef from slow cooker and cover to keep warm. Add tropical fruit salad to slow cooker. In small bowl, combine orange juice with cornstarch and stir into slow cooker. Cover and cook on high for 20 minutes until thickened.

6. Slice beef and serve with fruit sauce over the hot cooked rice.

The house of Israel called it manna; it was like coriander seed, white, and the taste of it was like wafers made with honey.

—EXODUS 16:31

Fish and Seafood Entrées

I've always loved seafood. In fact, when I was small and we ate out in restaurants (which didn't happen very often), my parents would let us order whatever we wanted; then they would order the most inexpensive thing on the menu in order to balance the budget. I, of course, always ordered shrimp. I love it to this day; it's sweet and tender and tastes of the sea. The best shrimp I ever had was in a restaurant in Florida. I ordered a shrimp cocktail to start. The shrimp was caught that day, and it came to the table still warm inside. Instead of ordering a main course, I got another shrimp cocktail! The chef peered around the door of the kitchen to see who was doing such a strange thing.

Seafood and the slow cooker don't automatically mix. Since fish fillets, shrimp, and other seafood cooks in such a short time, the long, slow cooking time usually results in overcooked, rubbery fish. But there are some tricks you can use!

Use the slow cooker to make a side dish: anything from potatoes to rice to vegetables. Then add the seafood during the last 30 to 60 minutes of cooking time. Voilà! Perfectly cooked seafood with very little work.

Mom's Tuna Casserole

SERVES 8

What's better than tuna casserole, especially Mom's version? Yes, you can cook pasta in the slow cooker; it just needs to be added at the very end of the cooking time.

2 onions, chopped
2 cloves garlic, minced
1 (8-ounce) package sliced mushrooms
2 (12-ounce) cans chunk white tuna, drained
1 (16-ounce) jar Alfredo sauce
½ cup milk
½ cup sour cream
2 cups shredded Colby cheese
1 pound green beans, trimmed
1 (12-ounce) package egg noodles
1 cup crushed sour cream and onion potato chips

1. In 5-quart slow cooker, combine onion, garlic, mushrooms, and tuna. Pour Alfredo sauce into slow cooker. Pour milk into the Alfredo sauce jar, close tightly, and shake. Pour this mixture into the slow cooker along with sour cream. Cover and cook on low for 7 hours.
2. Cut green beans in half and add to slow cooker along with the cheese. Cook on low for 1 hour. Then add the noodles and stir well. Cover and cook on low for 45 minutes to 1 hour or until noodles are tender. Top each serving of the casserole with a sprinkling of crushed potato chips.

Orange Ginger Fish and Sweet Potatoes

SERVES 8

Sweet potatoes and onions form the base to cook tender and moist fish fillets in this wonderful recipe. It's a meal in one dish!

6 sweet potatoes, peeled
2 onions, chopped
3 cloves garlic, minced
1 tablespoon minced gingerroot
½ cup brown sugar
½ cup orange juice
3 tablespoons butter
½ teaspoon salt
⅛ teaspoon pepper
2 pounds fish fillets
1 cup sour cream
¼ cup orange marmalade
2 tablespoons orange juice concentrate, thawed
¼ teaspoon ground ginger

1. Cut sweet potatoes into 1" cubes and combine in oval 5-quart slow cooker with onions, garlic, and gingerroot. In small bowl, combine brown sugar, orange juice, butter, salt, and pepper; mix well. Spoon over potatoes.
2. Cover and cook on low for 7–8 hours or until potatoes are tender when pierced with fork.
3. Place fish fillets on top of potatoes. Cover and cook on low for 1 to 1½ hours, or until fish flakes when tested with fork.
4. Meanwhile, in small bowl combine sour cream, marmalade, thawed concentrate, and ground ginger; mix well. Serve along with fish and potatoes.

Red Snapper and Succotash

SERVES 8–10

Succotash is a combination of lima beans and corn. Ginger and sour cream add fabulous flavor. The fish cooks perfectly in the moist heat of the slow cooker.

2 onions, chopped

3 (10-ounce) packages frozen lima beans

6 stalks celery, chopped

4 cups frozen corn kernels

1 teaspoon salt

1 teaspoon ground ginger

¼ teaspoon pepper

½ cup apple cider vinegar

½ cup sugar

2 tablespoons butter

½ cup sour cream

8–10 (6-ounce) red snapper fillets

Salt and pepper to taste

1 teaspoon paprika

1. In 6-quart oval slow cooker, combine onions, lima beans, celery, corn, salt, ginger, and pepper; mix gently. In small bowl, combine vinegar and sugar; blend well. Pour into slow cooker.
2. Cover and cook on low for 7–8 hours or until succotash is blended and hot. Stir in butter and sour cream.
3. Sprinkle fillets with salt and pepper to taste, along with paprika. Spoon some of the succotash out of the slow cooker. Layer fish and succotash in slow cooker, making sure no fillets are touching.
4. Cover and cook on low for 1 to 1½ hours or until fish flakes when tested with fork. Serve immediately.

Shrimp and Potato Tacos

SERVES 8–10

Potatoes add a wonderful texture and flavor and stretch shrimp to serve many people. This can be made spicier with more chili powder and cayenne pepper.

6 potatoes, peeled and cubed

3 onions, chopped

5 cloves garlic, minced

3 tablespoons butter, melted

1 teaspoon salt

1 tablespoon chili powder

1 teaspoon cumin

1 teaspoon dried oregano leaves

¼ teaspoon cayenne pepper

1½ pounds frozen cooked medium shrimp, thawed

10–12 taco shells

2 cups chopped tomatoes

2 avocados, peeled and diced

1 tablespoon lemon juice

2 cups shredded pepper jack cheese

1. In 4-quart slow cooker, combine potatoes, onions, garlic, butter, salt, chili powder, cumin, oregano, and cayenne pepper; mix well. Cover and cook on low for 8–9 hours or until potatoes are very tender.
2. Stir in shrimp, increase heat to high, and cook for 20–30 minutes or until shrimp are hot, pink, and curled.
3. Heat taco shells according to package directions. In medium bowl combine chopped tomatoes, avocados, and lemon juice; mix well. Serve the shrimp mixture with tomato mixture and cheese, and let everyone make their own tacos.

Jambalaya

SERVES 8–10

Jambalaya traditionally contains chicken, sausage, and seafood. This one leaves out the sausage to cut down on the fat. It's delicious, hearty, and flavorful.

2 onions, chopped

1 green bell pepper, chopped

1 red bell pepper, chopped

4 stalks celery, chopped

3 cloves garlic, minced

2 (14.5-ounce) cans diced tomatoes, undrained

4 boneless, skinless chicken breasts, cubed

1 teaspoon salt

¼ teaspoon pepper

1 teaspoon dried oregano leaves

1 teaspoon dried basil leaves

3 cups chicken broth

5 tablespoons cornstarch

¾ cup apple juice

1½ pounds frozen cooked shrimp, thawed

4–5 cups cooked rice

1. In 5-quart slow cooker, combine onions, green and red bell peppers, celery, garlic, and tomatoes; mix well. Sprinkle chicken with salt and pepper and place on top of vegetables in slow cooker.

2. Sprinkle contents of slow cooker with oregano and basil; pour chicken broth over all. Cover and cook on low for 7–8 hours or until chicken is thoroughly cooked.

3. In small bowl, combine cornstarch and apple juice; mix well. Stir into slow cooker along with shrimp. Cook on high for 20–30 minutes or until sauce is thickened and shrimp is hot.

4. Stir in rice and cook for 10 minutes longer. Serve immediately.

You shall not deprive a resident alien or an orphan of justice; you shall not take a widow's garment in pledge . . . When you reap your harvest in your field and forget a sheaf in the field, you shall not go back to get it; it shall be left for the alien, the orphan, and the widow, so that the Lord your God may bless you in all your undertakings.

—DEUTERONOMY 24:17–20

Fish Dumplings in Spicy Broth

SERVES 8

This unusual recipe has the flavors of the Orient. To serve, the tender dumplings are placed in bowls, and the broth with carrots and celery is spooned on top.

2 (32-ounce) boxes chicken broth

1 cup dry white wine or white grape juice

¼ teaspoon cayenne pepper

½ teaspoon crushed red pepper flakes

6 cloves garlic, minced

4 carrots, sliced

4 stalks celery, sliced

1½ pounds red snapper fillets, cubed

3 tablespoons flour

1 onion, finely chopped

1 teaspoon salt

⅛ teaspoon white pepper

1 teaspoon paprika

3 eggs

1 cup dried bread crumbs

2 tablespoons lemon juice

1. In 5-quart slow cooker, combine chicken broth, wine or grape juice, cayenne pepper, red pepper flakes, garlic, carrots, and celery. Cover and cook on low for 5–6 hours or until vegetables are tender.

2. Meanwhile, place fish and flour in food processor. Process, using the pulse feature, until fish is ground. Remove fish from food processor and place in large bowl.

3. Add onion, salt, pepper, paprika, eggs, bread crumbs, and lemon juice to fish; mix well. Using a small ice cream scoop, shape mixture into thirty-six 1½" dumplings and place on waxed paper. Cover and refrigerate.

4. When vegetables in broth are tender, bring a large pot of salted water to a boil. Cook the dumplings in salted water, about 8 at a time, until cooked through, to an internal temperature of 160°F.

5. Turn slow cooker to warm. As dumplings finish cooking, drop them into the slow cooker. To serve, place 3 or 4 dumplings in a serving bowl and top with some of the broth and vegetables.

You shall eat in plenty and be satisfied,
and praise the name of the Lord your God,
who has dealt wondrously with you. And my people
shall never again be put to shame.

—JOEL 2:26

Curried Tuna and Potato Casserole

SERVES 8–10

Tuna and potatoes are a nice comforting combination. Add some curry powder and suddenly you have a gourmet dish!

8 potatoes, peeled
3 tablespoons butter
2 onions, chopped
4 cloves garlic, minced
5 tablespoons flour
1 tablespoon curry powder
1 teaspoon salt
1/8 teaspoon pepper
1 1/2 cups heavy cream
1/2 cup milk
1 (16-ounce) jar Alfredo sauce
2 (12-ounce) cans chunk tuna, drained
1 (6-ounce) can chunk tuna, drained

1. Slice potatoes 1/8" thick and place in cold water. In large skillet, melt butter over medium heat. Add onions and garlic; cook and stir for 5 minutes. Add flour, curry powder, salt, and pepper; cook until bubbly.
2. Add heavy cream, milk, and Alfredo sauce and bring to a simmer. Drain potatoes thoroughly. Layer potatoes and both cans of tuna in 5-quart slow cooker. Pour cream mixture over all.
3. Cover and cook on low for 7–9 hours, or until potatoes are tender and casserole is bubbling.

Sweet-and-Sour Shrimp

SERVES 12

You have to serve this fresh-tasting, well-seasoned recipe over lots of hot cooked rice or pasta. Serve it with a green salad and some homemade rolls.

2 onions, chopped
4 cloves garlic, minced
2 tablespoons minced fresh gingerroot
1 (20-ounce) can pineapple tidbits in juice, undrained
5 carrots, sliced
2 cups water
1 (32-ounce) box chicken broth
1/3 cup sugar
1/4 cup low-sodium soy sauce
1/4 teaspoon white pepper
2 green bell peppers, chopped
1/4 cup cornstarch
1/2 cup apple cider vinegar
2 pounds frozen cooked shrimp, thawed

1. Combine onions, garlic, gingerroot, undrained pineapple, carrots, water, chicken broth, sugar, soy sauce, and pepper in 5-quart slow cooker.
2. Cover and cook on low for 7–8 hours or until vegetables are tender.
3. Stir green bell peppers into slow cooker. In small bowl, combine cornstarch and vinegar and mix well. Stir into slow cooker along with shrimp.
4. Cover and cook on high for 20–30 minutes or until sauce is thickened and shrimp is hot. Serve over hot cooked rice.

Salmon with Rice Pilaf

SERVES 8

Rice pilaf cooks to perfection, and then salmon fillets coated with a dill sauce are placed on top to steam until flaky. Yum!

3 tablespoons butter

2 onions, chopped

4 cloves garlic, minced

1½ cups long grain brown rice

4 carrots, sliced

1 (8-ounce) package sliced mushrooms

4 cups chicken broth

1 teaspoon dried dill weed

2 pounds salmon fillets

1 teaspoon salt

⅛ teaspoon pepper

1 cup sour cream

2 tablespoons mustard

½ teaspoon dried dill weed

1. In large skillet, melt butter over medium heat. Add onion and garlic; cook and stir until tender, about 5 minutes.
2. Add rice; cook and stir until coated, about 3–4 minutes longer. Transfer to 4-quart slow cooker. Add carrots, mushrooms, chicken broth, and dill weed.
3. Cover and cook on low for 5 hours or until rice is almost tender. Sprinkle salmon with salt and pepper.
4. In small bowl, combine sour cream, mustard, and dill weed. Spread over salmon fillets. Place salmon in slow cooker on top of rice.
5. Cover slow cooker and cook on low for 1 to 1½ hours or until salmon flakes when tested with a fork. Serve fish with the rice pilaf.

I was hungry and you gave me food,
I was thirsty and you gave me drink,
I was a stranger and you welcomed me.

—MATTHEW 25:35

Slow Cooker Shrimp Gumbo

SERVES 10–12

Gumbo is a recipe for a celebration! Serve this in large bowls with big spoons and lots of napkins and lemonade.

½ cup olive oil

½ cup flour

2 cups water

3 cups chicken broth

2 onions, chopped

5 stalks celery, chopped

2 green bell peppers, chopped

6 cloves garlic, minced

2 teaspoons Cajun seasoning

1 teaspoon smoked paprika

1 teaspoon dried oregano leaves

1 teaspoon salt

¼ teaspoon cayenne pepper

2 (14-ounce) cans diced tomatoes, undrained

2 pounds frozen cooked shrimp, thawed

1½ cups instant white rice

1. In heavy saucepan, combine oil and flour over medium heat. Cook and stir for 12–15 minutes until mixture turns golden brown. Carefully add water and chicken broth; cook and stir with wire whisk until flour mixture (called *roux*, pronounced roo) dissolves.

2. Pour contents of skillet into 6-quart slow cooker. Add all remaining ingredients except for shrimp and rice. Cover and cook on low for 7–8 hours or until vegetables are tender.

3. Turn slow cooker to high; stir in shrimp and rice. Cover and cook for another 15–20 minutes or until shrimp is hot and rice is tender. Serve immediately.

For he delivers the needy when they call, the poor and those who have no helper. He has pity on the weak and the needy, and saves the lives of the needy.

—PSALMS 72:12–13

Scallop Wild Rice Casserole

SERVES 12

This rich and comforting casserole is a slight twist on the traditional, using cream of mushroom soup, wild rice, and creamy scallops.

3 cups wild rice

1 (32-ounce) box chicken broth

3 cups water

1 (10-ounce) can cream of mushroom soup

2 onions, chopped

1 (8-ounce) package sliced fresh mushrooms

1 teaspoon salt

¼ teaspoon pepper

1½ teaspoons dried tarragon leaves

3 pounds bay scallops

1 (12-ounce) package frozen cut green beans, thawed

1 cup sliced almonds, toasted

1. Put wild rice into 6-quart slow cooker. Pour chicken broth and 2 cups of the water over the rice.
2. In medium bowl, combine soup and remaining 1 cup water; mix well with wire whisk until smooth. Add to slow cooker along with onions, mushrooms, salt, pepper, and tarragon.
3. Cover and cook on low for 7–8 hours or until wild rice and vegetables are tender. Stir in scallops and green beans.
4. Cover and cook on high for 30–40 minutes or until scallops are opaque and green beans are hot and tender. To toast almonds, place in dry pan over medium heat; toast, shaking pan frequently, until nuts are fragrant. Stir food in slow cooker, sprinkle with almonds, and serve.

When you beat your olive trees, do not strip what is left; it shall be for the alien, the orphan, and the widow. When you gather the grapes of your vineyard, do not glean what is left; it shall be for the alien, the orphan, and the widow.

—DEUTERONOMY 24:21

Fisherman's Chowder

SERVES 12–14

A chowder is a soup that has been thickened with cornstarch or flour and made richer with some cream. This version is hearty and simple.

2 onions, chopped

4 cloves garlic, minced

4 carrots, cut into chunks

4 potatoes, peeled and cubed

1 sweet potato, peeled and cubed

6 cups water

2 cups clam juice

1½ teaspoons salt

¼ teaspoon white pepper

2 teaspoons dried thyme leaves

1 teaspoon dried basil leaves

1 cup heavy cream

3 tablespoons cornstarch

2 pounds halibut or haddock fillets, cubed

1 pound frozen cooked shrimp, thawed

2 cups shredded Swiss cheese

⅓ cup chopped fresh flat-leaf parsley

1. In 7-quart slow cooker, combine onions, garlic, carrots, potatoes, sweet potato, water, clam juice, salt, pepper, thyme, and basil; mix well.
2. Cover and cook on low for 7–8 hours or until vegetables are tender. In medium bowl, combine cream with cornstarch and mix with wire whisk. Stir into slow cooker along with cubed fish fillets. Cover and cook on high for 15 minutes or until fish is almost opaque.
3. Stir in shrimp and cheese. Cover and cook on high for 8–10 minutes longer or until chowder is thickened and fish is done. Sprinkle with parsley and serve immediately.

Clam Linguine

SERVES 12

This is an easy method for cooking lots of linguine in clam sauce. You could add more vegetables to the original mixture, to stretch the clams and add nutrition.

2 onions, chopped

1 leek, chopped

1 (8-ounce) package sliced fresh mushrooms

6 cloves garlic, minced

1 teaspoon salt

½ teaspoon pepper

2 (14-ounce) cans diced tomatoes with herbs, undrained

1 (28-ounce) can tomato purée

2 cups water

4 (6-ounce) cans clams, undrained

2 tablespoons lemon juice

2 (12-ounce) packages linguine pasta

¼ cup butter

½ cup chopped fresh flat-leaf parsley

1 cup grated Parmesan cheese

1. In 5-quart slow cooker, combine onions, leek, mushrooms, garlic, salt, pepper, diced tomatoes, tomato purée, and water.
2. Cover and cook on low for 7–8 hours or until vegetables are tender. Stir in clams with their juice and lemon juice. Cover and cook on low for 20–30 minutes longer or until clams are hot.
3. 30 minutes before clam mixture is done, heat two large pots of salted water to boiling. Add linguine; cook according to package directions until almost tender. Drain and toss with butter.
4. Transfer linguine to three serving bowls. Ladle ⅓ of clam mixture into each bowl, and then top each with ⅓ of parsley and cheese. Serve.

Seafood Enchiladas

SERVES 12–14

Here the slow cooker is just used to heat the mixture through, so everything has to be cooked beforehand.

3 tablespoons butter

2 onions, chopped

6 cloves garlic, minced

2 green bell peppers, chopped

1 teaspoon salt

¼ teaspoon white pepper

1 tablespoon chili powder

2 (16-ounce) jars four-cheese Alfredo sauce

1 cup heavy cream

1 cup sour cream

2 tablespoons cornstarch

1 pound imitation crab, flaked

1 (16-ounce) bag frozen cooked shrimp, thawed

12 (6-inch) corn tortillas, cut into 4 wedges each

4 cups shredded pepper jack cheese

½ cup grated Parmesan cheese

1 teaspoon paprika

1. In large saucepan, melt butter over medium heat. Add onions and garlic; cook and stir until crisp-tender, about 5 minutes. Add green bell peppers; cook and stir for another 4 minutes. Sprinkle with salt, pepper, and chili powder; set aside.
2. In large bowl, combine Alfredo sauce, cream, sour cream, and cornstarch; mix well. Stir in imitation crab, shrimp, and the vegetable mixture.
3. Spray a 6-quart slow cooker with nonstick cooking spray. Place a couple of spoonfuls of the seafood sauce in the bottom. Layer tortillas over that, and then sprinkle on some cheese. Repeat layers, ending with seafood mixture. Sprinkle top with Parmesan cheese and paprika. Cover and cook on low for 4 hours or until casserole is hot. Serve.

Tuna Dumpling Casserole

SERVES 12–14

This meal-in-one is comforting and rich. You could use cooked chicken or ham instead of the tuna.

1 (16-ounce) bag baby carrots

2 onions, chopped

4 stalks celery, chopped

2 sweet potatoes, peeled and cubed

1 (32-ounce) box chicken broth

1 (10-ounce) can cream of celery soup

1 teaspoon dried oregano

1 teaspoon dried marjoram

1 teaspoon salt

¼ teaspoon pepper

2 (12-ounce) cans chunk tuna, drained

3 tablespoons cornstarch

⅓ cup apple juice

2 cups biscuit mix

½ cup grated Parmesan cheese

1 teaspoon dried marjoram

⅓ cup milk

⅓ cup light cream

2 tablespoons butter, melted

1. In 5-quart slow cooker, combine carrots, onions, celery, sweet potatoes, chicken broth, soup, oregano, 1 teaspoon marjoram, salt, and pepper. Cover and cook on low for 7–8 hours or until vegetables are tender.
2. Stir in drained tuna. In small bowl, combine cornstarch with apple juice and mix well; stir into slow cooker. Turn heat to high.
3. In medium bowl combine biscuit mix, cheese, and 1 teaspoon marjoram; mix well. Stir in milk, light cream, and melted butter just until blended.
4. Drop biscuit mixture by spoonfuls into slow cooker. Cover and cook on high for 30 minutes or until dumplings are cooked through. Serve.

Sweet-and-Sour Cabbage and Salmon

SERVES 10–12

The cabbage will cook down as it simmers. The combination of colors, textures, and flavors in this dish is wonderful.

14 cups chopped red cabbage

2 large red onions, chopped

6 cloves garlic, minced

⅓ cup brown sugar

⅓ cup apple cider vinegar

1 cup chicken broth

2 teaspoons dried thyme leaves

1 teaspoon salt

¼ teaspoon white pepper

3 pounds salmon fillets

½ teaspoon salt

⅛ teaspoon cayenne pepper

2 tablespoons lemon juice

1. In 6-quart oval slow cooker, combine cabbage, red onions, and garlic; mix well. In medium bowl, combine brown sugar, vinegar, broth, thyme, 1 teaspoon salt, and white pepper; mix well. Pour into slow cooker. Cover and cook on low for 7–8 hours or until cabbage is tender.
2. Drain cabbage mixture. Sprinkle salmon with ½ teaspoon salt, cayenne pepper, and lemon juice. Arrange salmon on the cabbage mixture in slow cooker.
3. Cover and cook on low for 1 to 1½ hours or until salmon flakes when tested with fork. Serve salmon with cabbage mixture.

Shrimp with Apricot Rice

SERVES 8

To toast almonds, place them in a dry skillet over medium heat and toss until fragrant and golden brown. They add wonderful crunch and flavor to this special dish.

1 onion, chopped

1 leek, chopped

3 carrots, sliced

2½ cups long-grain brown rice

2 cups chicken broth

2 cups apricot nectar

1 cup water

1 teaspoon salt

¼ teaspoon white pepper

1 teaspoon dried thyme leaves

1 cup finely chopped dried apricots

1 (16-ounce) jar apricot preserves

2 pounds frozen cooked shrimp, thawed

⅓ cup sliced almonds, toasted

1. In 6-quart slow cooker, combine onion, leek, carrots, and brown rice. Add chicken broth, nectar, water, salt, pepper, thyme, and apricots. Stir well, then cover and cook on low for 6–8 hours or until rice and vegetables are tender.
2. Stir in apricot preserves and shrimp. Cover and cook on low for 1 hour or until casserole is hot and shrimp is hot and tender. Stir again, top with almonds, and serve immediately.

Aunt Bessie's Salmon Meatloaf

SERVES 10–12

The foil method lets you remove these meatloaves from the slow cookers with ease. Serve this classic with peas and carrots.

2 tablespoons butter

1 onion, finely chopped

4 cloves garlic, minced

1 green bell pepper, finely chopped

4 eggs

¾ cup heavy cream

¾ cup clam juice

2 cups crushed saltine crackers

½ cup dry bread crumbs

¼ teaspoon pepper

1 teaspoon dried thyme leaves

1 teaspoon dried basil leaves

3 (14-ounce) cans salmon, drained

1½ cups shredded Havarti cheese

½ cup grated Parmesan cheese

1. In large skillet, melt butter over medium heat. Add onions and garlic; cook and stir until crisp-tender, about 5 minutes. Add green bell pepper; cook and stir for another 3–4 minutes. Remove from heat.

2. In large bowl, combine eggs, cream, clam juice, crushed crackers, bread crumbs, pepper, thyme, and basil; mix well. Stir in onion mixture; then add all of the salmon and the Havarti cheese.

3. Spray two 4-quart slow cookers with nonstick cooking spray. Tear off four 24" sheets of heavy-duty foil. Fold each in thirds lengthwise; then place two in each slow cooker, forming an X.

4. Divide the salmon mixture in half. Place half in each slow cooker; form into a loaf shape as much as you can. Sprinkle each with half of the Parmesan cheese.

5. Cover and cook on high for 1 hour, then turn slow cookers to low and cook for 3–4 hours longer or until meat thermometer registers 160°F.

6. Turn off slow cookers and let stand, uncovered, for 15 minutes. Gently loosen loaves, using an offset spatula, and then lift the foil and loaves out of the slow cooker. Slice to serve.

For if you forgive men their trespasses, your heavenly Father will also forgive you; but if you do not forgive men their trespasses, neither will your Father forgive your trespasses.

—MATTHEW 6:14–15

Clam Chowder

SERVES 12–14
This rich and thick chowder is perfect for a gathering after singing Christmas carols. Serve it with tiny oyster crackers and a wilted spinach salad.

8 slices bacon

2 tablespoons butter

2 onions, chopped

4 cloves garlic, minced

4 (6-ounce) cans minced clams

4 carrots, sliced

5 stalks celery, chopped

¼ cup chopped celery leaves

5 potatoes, peeled and cubed

1½ teaspoons salt

¼ teaspoon white pepper

2 cups clam juice

2 cups chicken broth

4 cups water

¼ cup cornstarch

2 cups light cream

1 cup heavy cream

1. In large saucepan, cook bacon until crisp. Drain bacon on paper towels, crumble, and refrigerate. Drain all but 2 tablespoons drippings from saucepan and add butter. When butter melts, add onion and garlic; cook and stir until crisp-tender, about 5 minutes.

2. Drain clams, reserving liquid. Place clams in a bowl, cover, and refrigerate. Combine onion mixture, carrots, celery, celery leaves, potatoes, salt, pepper, clam juice, chicken broth, water, and reserved clam liquid in 7-quart slow cooker.

3. Cover and cook on low for 7–8 hours or until vegetables are tender. In medium bowl combine cornstarch with light cream; stir with wire whisk until smooth. Stir into slow cooker along with heavy cream; cover and cook on high for 15 minutes.

4. Stir in reserved bacon and clams. Cover and cook on high for 15–20 minutes or until soup is thoroughly heated. Serve immediately.

From everyone to whom much has been given, much will be required; and from the one to whom much has been entrusted, even more will be demanded.

—LUKE 12:48

Potato Seafood Salad

You could add even more seafood to this recipe if you'd like, stirring in drained canned crab or salmon with the potato mixture.

5 pounds russet potatoes

2 onions, chopped

4 cloves garlic, minced

1½ teaspoons salt

¼ teaspoon white pepper

2 cups water

2 pounds red snapper fish fillets

1 pound frozen small cooked shrimp, thawed

3 cups frozen peas, thawed and drained

1½ cups mayonnaise

1 cup whipped salad dressing

½ cup plain yogurt

½ cup seafood cocktail sauce

⅓ cup whole milk

1. Peel potatoes and cut into cubes. Combine in 6-7 quart slow cooker with onions and garlic. Sprinkle with salt and pepper, then pour water over all.
2. Cover and cook on low for 8–9 hours or until potatoes are tender.
3. Turn heat to high. Place red snapper fillets on potato mixture. Cover and cook on high for 30 minutes or until fish flakes easily with fork.
4. In large bowl, combine remaining ingredients and mix well. Remove fish and potato mixture from slow cooker with large slotted spoon or sieve and add to mixture in bowl. Stir gently to coat. Cover and chill for 4–5 hours until cold. Stir gently before serving.

And the crowds asked him, "What then should we do?" In reply Jesus said to them, "Whoever has two coats must share with anyone who has none; and whoever has food must do likewise."

—LUKE 3:10–11

Chicken and Turkey Entrées

*C*hicken is inexpensive, satisfying, and adapts to any cuisine. My mother makes the best fried chicken, but she never used the slow cooker. I use the slow cooker all the time for moist and tender chicken, flavored in umpteen ways. Any of the following recipes could be easily changed to suit local flavors or produce.

Some of these recipes call for chicken that has already been cooked. The slow cooker is the ideal way to cook plain chicken. For boneless, skinless chicken breasts, follow instructions for Poached Chicken and Broth (page 208). For bone-in, skin on chicken breasts, place in slow cooker and add a cup of chicken broth or water. Cover and cook on low for 7–9 hours until 170°F. Boneless chicken thighs and legs should cook for 7–9 hours; bone-in thighs and legs for 8–9 hours.

Remove the cooked chicken from the slow cooker and let cool for 10–15 minutes until cool enough to handle. Then pull or cut meat from bones and shred by hand or chop with a knife. Refrigerate or freeze promptly.

Make sure that when you cook chicken it is cooked thoroughly, to the proper temperature. A food thermometer is necessary. Chicken breasts should be cooked to 165°F, dark meat chicken to 170°F, and whole chickens to 180°F. Also be careful handling raw chicken. Be sure to wash your hands, countertops, and utensils thoroughly with hot soapy water after contact with raw poultry.

Everyone has his or her own favorite family holiday recipes for turkey and stuffing. You can make them together in the slow cooker for real ease. If you want to roast a turkey or two in the oven for a Christmas or Thanksgiving banquet, think about making some slow cooker dressings from Chapter 10 (Side Dishes), not only for food safety reasons, but because that will allow you to offer a selection of dressings for everyone's tastes!

Honey Mustard Turkey Roast

SERVES 12

A turkey roast is a nice entrée to serve after a Bible study gathering on Sunday afternoon. Round out this meal with cooked carrots, a green salad, and crisp breadsticks.

1 (3-pound) turkey roast, thawed if frozen

3 onions, sliced

4 cloves garlic, minced

¼ cup honey

3 tablespoons Dijon mustard

1 teaspoon dried thyme leaves

½ teaspoon salt

¼ teaspoon pepper

1 cup chicken broth

½ cup apple cider

2 tablespoons cornstarch

1. Cut the turkey in half lengthwise to make two equal pieces. Place onions in bottom of 4- or 5-quart slow cooker and top with turkey.
2. In a bowl, combine garlic, honey, mustard, thyme, salt, and pepper. Rub over turkey. Pour chicken broth into slow cooker, cover, and cook on low for 6 hours or until meat thermometer registers 170°F.
3. Remove turkey and onions from slow cooker. In small bowl, combine cider and cornstarch; mix well. Add to liquid remaining in slow cooker; cook on high for 15 minutes or until thickened.
4. Meanwhile, slice the turkey. Return turkey and onions to slow cooker; cook for 10–15 minutes longer until hot. Serve immediately.

Chicken and Potato Hot Dish

SERVES 8–10

The easiest way to thaw the potatoes is to let the package stand in the refrigerator overnight. Then drain and mix with the other ingredients.

12 boneless, skinless chicken thighs, cubed

2 onions, chopped

3 cloves garlic, minced

2 (4-ounce) jars sliced mushrooms, undrained

2 green bell peppers, chopped

2 cups frozen corn kernels

1 (32-ounce) package frozen hash brown potatoes, thawed

2 (10.75-ounce) cans cream of chicken soup

1 cup chicken broth

1 cup barbecue sauce

½ cup grated Parmesan cheese

1. In 6-quart slow cooker, combine chicken, onions, garlic, mushrooms, bell peppers, corn, and potatoes; mix well.
2. In medium bowl, combine remaining ingredients except cheese; mix well. Pour into slow cooker. Cover and cook on low for 9–10 hours or until chicken is thoroughly cooked. Stir once during cooking time. Add cheese, stir again, and serve immediately.

Slow Cooker Chicken and Cheese Soufflé

SERVES 8

This recipe is like a cross between a soufflé and a strata. It's hearty and comforting and mildly flavored.

8 cups cubed French bread

2 cups shredded Cheddar cheese

1 cup cubed Havarti cheese

3 cups cubed cooked chicken

1 tablespoon olive oil

1 onion, chopped

1 red bell pepper, chopped

1 (3-ounce) package cream cheese

1 (13-ounce) can evaporated milk

½ cup whole milk

½ teaspoon dried thyme leaves

½ teaspoon salt

⅛ teaspoon white pepper

6 eggs, beaten

2 tablespoons grated Parmesan cheese

½ teaspoon paprika

1. In 5-quart slow cooker, combine bread with Cheddar, Havarti, and cubed cooked chicken; set aside.
2. In medium saucepan, heat olive oil over medium heat. Add onion; cook and stir for 3 minutes. Add red bell pepper; cook and stir for 2 minutes longer. Add to slow cooker and toss gently to combine with bread mixture.
3. Mix cream cheese and evaporated milk in saucepan; cook and stir over low heat until cheese melts. Remove from heat and beat in whole milk, thyme, salt, and pepper. Beat in eggs until smooth.
4. Pour into slow cooker and let stand for 15 minutes. Sprinkle with Parmesan cheese and paprika. Cover and cook on low for 3½ to 4½ hours or until soufflé is set. Serve immediately.

Scalloped Chicken

SERVES 8

This hearty casserole is a combination of stuffing, gravy, and chicken, all in one! Serve with a fruit salad for a complete meal for a Ladies Aid meeting.

3 tablespoons butter

1 onion, chopped

1 cup chopped, cored apple

3 cups soft bread crumbs

½ cup coarsely chopped pecans

½ cup raisins

¼ cup butter

¼ cup flour

1 teaspoon salt

⅛ teaspoon pepper

3 cups chicken stock

1 cup light cream

4 cups chopped cooked chicken

1. Spray a 4-quart slow cooker with nonstick cooking spray and set aside. In large skillet, melt 3 tablespoons butter over medium heat. Add onion; cook and stir until tender, about 5 minutes. Add apple; cook and stir for 2 minutes longer.
2. Add bread crumbs to skillet, and toss to coat. Stir in pecans and raisins; set aside.
3. In large saucepan, melt ¼ cup butter over medium heat. Add flour, salt, and pepper. Cook and stir until flour begins to brown, about 8–10 minutes. Stir in chicken stock and cream; cook and stir until sauce bubbles and thickens.
4. Layer half of bread crumb mixture, half of cooked chicken, and half of sauce in prepared slow cooker. Repeat layers.
5. Cover and cook on low for 7–9 hours or until casserole is set and bubbling. Serve immediately.

Slow Cooker Chicken à la King

SERVES 8–10

Chicken à la King is a classic recipe that's comforting and easy to make. And everybody loves it!

3 pounds chicken tenders, cut in half
1 (16-ounce) package baby carrots
2 red bell peppers, chopped
2 onions, chopped
3 cloves garlic, minced
1 (8-ounce) package cream cheese, cut into cubes
2 (16-ounce) jars four-cheese Alfredo sauce
1 cup milk
1 (10-ounce) can cream of chicken soup
1 teaspoon dried basil leaves
1/8 teaspoon pepper
Hot cooked noodles, mashed potatoes, biscuits, or baked
   puff pastry shells

1. Place chicken tenders in 5–6-quart slow cooker. Add carrots, bell peppers, onions, and garlic; mix gently.
2. In food processor or blender, combine cream cheese with Alfredo sauce and milk; process or blend until combined. Pour into large bowl and add cream of chicken soup, basil, and pepper. Mix well.
3. Pour sauce into slow cooker. Cover and cook on low for 7–9 hours or until chicken and vegetables are tender. Serve over hot cooked noodles, mashed potatoes, biscuits, or baked puff pastry shells.

Slow Cooker Chicken Divan

SERVES 8

Mushrooms and bell pepper add color, texture, and flavor to this easy recipe. It's a delicious casserole that will please adults and kids alike.

4 cups fresh broccoli florets
2 tablespoons lemon juice
2 onions, chopped
1 (8-ounce) package sliced mushrooms
2 red bell peppers, chopped
5 cups chopped cooked chicken
2 (10-ounce) cans cream of broccoli soup
1 cup light cream
2 cups shredded Swiss cheese

1. Toss broccoli with lemon juice. Place in bottom of 6-quart slow cooker. Top with onions, mushrooms, bell peppers, and chicken.
2. In medium bowl, combine soup with cream and cheese; mix until blended. Pour into slow cooker.
3. Cover and cook on low for 5–6 hours or until thoroughly heated. Stir well, then serve.

When the poor and needy seek water, and their tongue is parched with thirst, I the Lord will answer them, I will not forsake them.

—ISAIAH 41:17

Corn Bread and Cranberry–Stuffed Turkey Breast

SERVES 8

Corn bread and cranberries make an all-American stuffing for a moist turkey breast in this twist on a classic recipe.

3 cups cubed corn bread
3 shallots, minced
1 leek, rinsed and chopped
¾ cup chopped fresh cranberries
½ cup dried cranberries
2 pears, peeled, cored, and chopped
⅓ cup butter, melted
½ cup mayonnaise
1 teaspoon dried thyme leaves
1 teaspoon salt
¼ teaspoon white pepper
1 (4-pound) boneless turkey breast, thawed
¼ cup fresh sage leaves
2 tablespoons butter, melted

1. Preheat oven to 350°F. Place cubed corn bread on a baking sheet in a single layer. Bake for 15–25 minutes or until crisp. Place in large bowl.
2. Add shallots, leek, fresh and dried cranberries, and pears; mix gently. Add ⅓ cup melted butter, mayonnaise, thyme, salt, and pepper. Mix to coat.
3. Place stuffing in a 6- to 7-quart slow cooker. Loosen skin from turkey breast. Place sage leaves in a decorative pattern on the turkey flesh; smooth skin back into place. Brush with 2 tablespoons melted butter. Place turkey on stuffing.
4. Cover slow cooker and cook on low for 8–10 hours or until turkey registers 170°F on a meat thermometer. Turn off slow cooker and let stand for 10 minutes; then slice turkey to serve. Serve with stuffing.

Give, and it will be given to you. A good measure, pressed down, shaken together, running over, will be put into your lap; for the measure you give will be the measure you get back.

—LUKE 6:38

Glazed Chicken with Blueberry Chutney

SERVES 8

Make the chutney at the same time you're making the chicken if you wish to serve it as a warm sauce, or make it ahead of time and refrigerate for the contrast of a cold sauce.

2 onions, chopped

4 cloves garlic, minced

8 boneless, skinless chicken breasts

1 (6-ounce) container frozen lemonade concentrate, thawed

½ cup honey

1 teaspoon salt

⅛ teaspoon pepper

1 teaspoon ground ginger

2 cups Blueberry-Raisin Chutney (page 6)

1. Place onions and garlic in bottom of 5–6-quart slow cooker. Top with chicken breasts.
2. In small bowl combine lemonade concentrate, honey, salt, pepper, and ginger; mix well. Pour into slow cooker.
3. Cover and cook on low for 5–7 hours or until chicken is thoroughly cooked. Drain chicken, slice, and serve with Blueberry-Raisin Chutney.

Sell all that you have and distribute it
to the poor, and you will have treasure in heaven;
and come, follow me.

—LUKE 18:22

Updated Chicken Cordon Bleu

SERVES 8

Instead of being stuffed with ham and cheese, this tender chicken is wrapped in ham and served with a flavorful cheese sauce. Yum.

8 boneless, skinless chicken breasts

1 teaspoon salt

⅛ teaspoon white pepper

1 teaspoon dried thyme leaves

8 thin slices boiled ham

2 onions, chopped

4 cloves garlic, minced

1 (16-ounce) bag baby carrots

1 (16-ounce) jar Alfredo sauce

1 (10-ounce) can condensed chicken soup

2 cups shredded Swiss cheese

1. Sprinkle chicken breasts with salt, pepper, and thyme. Wrap a slice of ham around each breast and secure with toothpicks.
2. Place onion, garlic, and carrots in a 5- to 6-quart slow cooker. Top with wrapped chicken breasts.
3. In medium bowl, combine remaining ingredients. Pour into slow cooker. Cover and cook on low for 6–8 hours or until chicken is thoroughly cooked. Serve chicken and carrots with sauce.

The Lord Jesus himself said:
"it is more blessed to give than to receive."

—ACTS 20:35

Thai Chicken Drumsticks

SERVES 12

For crisp skin, you have to brown these drumsticks after they are cooked. But that's easy to do under the broiler, and that step adds wonderful caramelized flavor to the finished dish.

4 pounds chicken drumsticks
2 onions, chopped
6 cloves garlic, minced
½ cup peanut butter
1 (14-ounce) can diced tomatoes, undrained
1 (6-ounce) can tomato paste
⅓ cup low-sodium soy sauce
1 cup chunky mild or medium salsa
2 tablespoons minced gingerroot
¼ teaspoon pepper
½ teaspoon hot pepper sauce
2 cups chopped peanuts

1. Place drumsticks in a 6- to 7-quart slow cooker. Add onions and garlic. In medium bowl, stir together remaining ingredients except peanuts. Pour into slow cooker.
2. Cover and cook for 6–8 hours on low, or until internal temperature reaches 170°F. Remove chicken from slow cooker and roll each piece in the chopped peanuts. Arrange on broiler pan. Preheat broiler.
3. Broil chicken 6" from heat source, turning frequently, until browned, about 6–8 minutes. Serve immediately.

Turkey Tenderloin Curry

SERVES 8–10

Turkey tenderloin is delicious when cooked with curry and chutney. Serve over lots of hot cooked rice.

2½ pounds turkey tenderloins
2 onions, chopped
1 (16-ounce) bag baby carrots
1 (16-ounce) can crushed pineapple, undrained
5 cloves garlic, minced
4 cups chicken broth
2 tablespoons curry powder
1 tablespoon grated gingerroot
½ teaspoon turmeric
1 teaspoon salt
¼ teaspoon pepper
1 (12-ounce) jar mango chutney
3 tablespoons cornstarch
½ cup apple juice

1. Cut turkey into 2" pieces. Place onions, carrots, pineapple, and garlic in a 5-quart slow cooker. Top with turkey pieces.
2. In medium bowl, combine chicken broth, curry powder, gingerroot, turmeric, salt, and pepper; mix well. Pour into slow cooker.
3. Cover and cook on low for 6–8 hours or until vegetables are tender and turkey is thoroughly cooked. In bowl, combine chutney, cornstarch, and apple juice; mix well. Stir into slow cooker.
4. Cover and cook on high for 20–30 minutes. Stir thoroughly, then serve over hot cooked rice.

Apple-Stuffed Chicken Rolls

SERVES 8

Tender chicken stuffed with an apple-and-raisin mixture will be incredibly popular at your next potluck.

4 slices oatmeal bread
¾ cup finely chopped, cored, peeled apple
½ cup raisins
1 tablespoon lemon juice
2 tablespoons butter, melted
2 tablespoons sugar
½ teaspoon salt
8 boneless, skinless chicken breasts
2 onions, chopped
⅓ cup apple juice
½ teaspoon cinnamon

1. Toast bread until golden brown, then cut into cubes. In medium bowl, combine apple, raisins, lemon juice, melted butter, sugar, and salt; mix well. Stir in bread cubes.
2. Arrange chicken breasts on work surface. Pound gently with a meat mallet or rolling pin until ⅓" thick. Divide bread mixture among chicken breasts. Roll up chicken and secure with a toothpick.
3. Place onions in bottom of 6-quart slow cooker. Top with filled chicken rolls. In bowl, combine apple juice and cinnamon; spoon over chicken.
4. Cover and cook on low for 5 to 6 hours, or until chicken registers 165°F on food thermometer. Remove toothpicks and serve chicken with the cooked onions.

Chicken and Wild Rice Salad

SERVES 12

This easy recipe cooks the chicken and wild rice together, so all you have to do is add a dressing and a few more ingredients and then chill the salad.

2 cups wild rice
2 onions, chopped
8 boneless, skinless chicken breasts, cubed
4 cups chicken broth
2 cups apple juice
1 teaspoon salt
¼ teaspoon pepper
2 teaspoons dried thyme leaves
2 cups mayonnaise
1 cup yogurt
½ cup apple juice
2 cups small pecans
3 cups seedless red grapes
6 stalks celery, chopped

1. In 5-quart slow cooker, combine wild rice and onion. Place chicken on top. Sprinkle with salt, pepper, and thyme, then pour chicken broth and apple juice over all. Cover and cook on low for 6 hours or until wild rice is tender and chicken is cooked.
3. In large bowl, combine mayonnaise, yogurt, and apple juice. Remove chicken mixture from slow cooker using large slotted spoon or sieve and stir into mayonnaise mixture along with remaining ingredients. Cover and chill for 3–4 hours until cold. Stir gently before serving.

Chicken Tacos

SERVES 8–10
Tacos are always fun, and when made with chicken they are delightfully different. Use your community's favorite toppings in this easy recipe.

2 onions, chopped
4 cloves garlic, minced
1 jalapeño pepper, minced
8 boneless, skinless chicken breasts
2 tablespoons chili powder
1 teaspoon cumin
1 teaspoon salt
¼ teaspoon cayenne pepper
1 cup chunky medium or hot salsa
1 (8-ounce) can tomato sauce
10–12 taco shells
2 cups grated Cheddar cheese
2 cups shredded lettuce
1 cup sour cream
1 cup chopped avocados
2 cups chopped tomatoes

1. In 5-quart slow cooker, combine onions, garlic, and jalapeño pepper. Sprinkle chicken with chili powder, cumin, salt, and cayenne pepper; place on top of onions.
2. Pour salsa and tomato sauce over all. Cover and cook on low for 6–7 hours or until chicken is thoroughly cooked.
3. Using two forks, shred chicken. Stir mixture in slow cooker.
4. Heat taco shells as directed on package. Serve chicken filling with the taco shells and remaining ingredients; let everyone make their own tacos.

*A new commandment I give to you,
that you love one another, even as I have loved you,
that you also love one another.*

—JOHN 13:34

Laura's Chicken Risotto

SERVES 8–10

Brown rice not only has more fiber and nutrients than white rice, but it cooks well in the slow cooker. Purists may look askance at this recipe, but it's delicious!

2 cups brown rice

2 onions, chopped

6 boneless, skinless chicken breasts, cubed

1 teaspoon salt

¼ teaspoon pepper

1 teaspoon dried thyme leaves

3 cups chicken broth

1 (10-ounce) can cream of chicken soup

3 cups frozen baby peas

3 tablespoons butter

1 cup grated Parmesan cheese

1. Combine brown rice and onions in 5-quart slow cooker. Top with chicken breasts. In large bowl, combine salt, pepper, thyme, chicken broth, and canned soup; mix with wire whisk until blended. Pour into slow cooker.
2. Cover and cook on low for 8–10 hours or until rice is tender and chicken is thoroughly cooked, stirring after 4 hours.
3. Stir in peas, butter, and cheese. Cover and cook on high for 20–30 minutes or until peas are hot and butter and cheese are melted. Stir gently and serve.

Chicken Dinner

SERVES 8–10

Now this is a meal in one dish! You could add any root vegetable you'd like to this easy recipe; turnips and rutabagas would be two good choices.

6 potatoes, cut into chunks

2 sweet potatoes, peeled and cut into chunks

6 carrots, cut into chunks

2 onions, chopped

¼ cup olive oil

2 tablespoons butter

4 cloves garlic, minced

1 teaspoon dried thyme

1 teaspoon dried basil

1½ teaspoons seasoned salt

¼ teaspoon pepper

2 (3-pound) cut-up chickens, skinned

1. In 6- to 7-quart slow cooker, combine potatoes, sweet potatoes, carrots, and onions. In small saucepan, heat olive oil and butter until butter melts; add garlic. Cook and stir for 2–3 minutes until garlic is tender.
2. Remove saucepan from heat and stir in thyme, basil, salt, and pepper. Brush some of this mixture over chicken. Pour remaining mixture into slow cooker over vegetables.
3. Place chicken in slow cooker. Cover and cook on low for 8–9 hours or until chicken is thoroughly cooked and vegetables are tender.

Turkey and Stuffing Casserole

SERVES 8–10

Classic turkey and stuffing cook beautifully in the slow cooker. The pattern the herbs make under the turkey skin is very beautiful too.

2 tablespoons butter, melted

2 onions, chopped

2 red bell peppers, chopped

1 (8-ounce) package sliced mushrooms

8 cups seasoned stuffing mix

2½ cups chicken broth

¼ teaspoon pepper

½ teaspoon dried sage leaves

1 teaspoon dried thyme leaves

1 (4–5 pound) boneless turkey breast

½ teaspoon salt

⅛ teaspoon pepper

¼ cup fresh sage leaves

2 tablespoons fresh rosemary leaves

3 tablespoons olive oil

1. In large bowl, combine melted butter, onions, bell peppers, and mushrooms; stir to coat. Add stuffing mix; toss to coat. Gradually add chicken broth, tossing to coat, until stuffing is just barely moist. Season with pepper, sage, and thyme.

2. Spray a 6- to 7-quart slow cooker with nonstick cooking spray. Place stuffing mixture in slow cooker.

3. Loosen skin from turkey breast and sprinkle flesh with salt and pepper. Arrange sage leaves and rosemary leaves in a pattern on the flesh. Carefully smooth skin back over the flesh, keeping the herbs in place.

4. Heat olive oil in large skillet. Add turkey, skin side down, and brown, moving turkey around as necessary, for 6–8 minutes.

5. Place turkey on top of stuffing, pressing down gently. Cover and cook on low for 8–10 hours or until turkey registers 165°F. Slice turkey and serve with stuffing.

*By this Jesus everyone who believes is
set free from all those sins from which you
could not be freed by the law of Moses.*

—ACTS 13:39

Chicken Dijon

SERVES 8

Dijon mustard adds a wonderful kick of spice and piquancy to this simple chicken dish. Serve it with mashed potatoes, noodles, or rice to soak up the flavorful sauce.

8 boneless, skinless chicken breasts

1 teaspoon salt

⅛ teaspoon white pepper

1 teaspoon dried tarragon leaves

1 onion, chopped

1 (16-ounce) bag baby carrots

1 (10-ounce) container refrigerated Alfredo sauce

¼ cup Dijon mustard

½ cup apple juice

½ cup chicken broth

2 tablespoons cornstarch

¼ cup water

1. In 5-quart slow cooker, combine all ingredients except cornstarch and water. Cover and cook on low for 6–7 hours or until chicken registers 165°F with a meat thermometer.

2. In small bowl, combine cornstarch and water; mix well. Add to slow cooker. Cover and cook on high for 20–30 minutes or until sauce is thickened. Serve over hot cooked noodles, rice, or mashed potatoes.

Turkey and Bean Cassoulet

SERVES 10–12

Cassoulet is French for "casserole." It's traditionally made with duck breasts and sausage, but this simplified version has just as much flavor, with less fat!

2 tablespoons olive oil

1 tablespoon butter

2 pounds turkey sausage links

2 onions, chopped

4 cloves garlic, minced

1 (16-ounce) bag baby carrots

2 (15-ounce) can navy beans, drained

2 (15-ounce) cans black beans, drained

1 (28-ounce) can tomato purée

½ cup red wine or chicken broth

1 teaspoon dried marjoram

¼ teaspoon pepper

1 bay leaf

1. Heat olive oil and butter in large saucepan over medium heat. Add turkey sausage; cook and stir until browned, but not cooked through. Remove sausage to plate and cut into 1" pieces.

2. Add onions and garlic to saucepan; cook and stir to loosen drippings. Place onions and garlic in 6- to 7-quart slow cooker along with sausage and remaining ingredients. Stir well to combine.

3. Cover and cook on low for 8–9 hours or until sausage is cooked and vegetables are tender. Remove bay leaf and serve.

Classic Chicken and Dumplings

SERVES 10–12

Pizza dough, when cut into small pieces, cooks into fluffy dumplings in this comforting and classic recipe. You may need the larger slow cooker depending on the size of the chicken breasts.

8 boneless, skinless chicken breasts
1 teaspoon salt
⅛ teaspoon pepper
1 teaspoon paprika
½ teaspoon poultry seasoning
4 stalks celery, sliced
½ cup chopped celery leaves
4 carrots, sliced
1 onion, chopped
6 cloves garlic, minced
1 (16-ounce) jar four-cheese Alfredo sauce
1 (16-ounce) jar Cheddar cheese pasta sauce
1 (10-ounce) can condensed cream of celery soup
1 cup heavy cream
1 (13.8-ounce) tube refrigerated pizza dough

1. Cut chicken breasts into cubes. Sprinkle with salt, pepper, paprika, and poultry seasoning; toss to coat.
2. Combine celery, celery leaves, carrots, onions, and garlic in 6- to 7-quart slow cooker; mix well. Add chicken breasts and stir.
3. In medium bowl, combine Alfredo sauce, pasta sauce, soup, and heavy cream; mix well. Pour into slow cooker. Cover and cook on low for 6–7 hours or until chicken and vegetables are tender.
4. On lightly floured surface, roll out the pizza dough to ½" thickness and cut into 1" pieces. Stir into slow cooker, making sure the dough is evenly distributed. Cover and cook on high for 1 to 1½ hours or until dumplings are cooked through. Serve immediately.

Woe to you, scribes and Pharisees, hypocrites! For you tithe mint, dill and cumin, and have neglected the weightier matters of the law: justice and mercy and faith. It is these you ought to have practiced without neglecting the others. You blind guides! You strain out a gnat but swallow a camel!

—MATTHEW 23:13–15

Chicken Lasagna

SERVES 10–12

Lasagna in the slow cooker is a great timesaver and is so easy. You don't have to boil the noodles separately!

5 boneless, skinless chicken breasts

1 teaspoon salt

⅛ teaspoon pepper

½ teaspoon paprika

2 tablespoons butter

2 tablespoons olive oil

1 onion, chopped

4 cloves garlic, minced

1 red bell pepper, chopped

1 (26-ounce) jar spaghetti sauce

½ cup water

1 teaspoon dried Italian seasoning

1 (8-ounce) package cream cheese, softened

2 eggs

1 (16-ounce) container ricotta cheese

2 cups frozen cut-leaf spinach, thawed and drained

½ cup grated Parmesan cheese

6–9 lasagna noodles

1 cup shredded mozzarella cheese

½ cup shredded Romano cheese

1. Cut chicken breasts into 1" cubes. Sprinkle with salt, pepper, and paprika; toss to coat.

2. Heat butter with olive oil in large saucepan over medium heat. Add chicken; cook and stir until chicken is thoroughly cooked, about 9 minutes. Remove chicken from pan with slotted spoon.

3. In drippings remaining in skillet, cook onion and garlic until tender. Stir in red bell peppers, spaghetti sauce, water, and Italian seasoning; bring to a simmer.

4. Meanwhile, in bowl combine cream cheese, eggs, and ricotta cheese; beat until smooth. Stir in drained spinach and Parmesan cheese.

5. Break lasagna noodles in half. Place about 1 cup of the chicken mixture in bottom of 6-quart casserole. Top with a layer of lasagna noodles, more chicken mixture, some cream cheese mixture, and mozzarella cheese. Repeat layers, ending with cheese.

6. Sprinkle with Romano cheese, cover, and cook on low for 6–7 hours or until noodles are tender. To serve, scoop down deeply into the slow cooker to get all the layers.

On that day there shall be inscribed on the bells of the horses, "Holy to the Lord." And the cooking pots in the house of the Lord shall be as holy as the bowls in front of the altar.

—ZECHARIAH 14:20

Spanish Chicken and Rice

SERVES 8–10

If you like it really spicy, add a minced jalapeño pepper or substitute cayenne pepper for the black pepper.

3 pounds boneless, skinless chicken breasts

1 teaspoon paprika

¼ teaspoon pepper

1 teaspoon salt

2 tablespoons olive oil

2 onions, chopped

4 cloves garlic, minced

1½ cups long grain brown rice

2 green bell peppers, chopped

1 cup barbecue sauce

2 (14-ounce) cans diced tomatoes, undrained

1 (8-ounce) can tomato sauce

1 cup chicken broth

1 teaspoon cumin

1 tablespoon honey

2 tablespoons apple cider vinegar

¼ cup chopped parsley

¼ cup chopped cilantro

1. Cut chicken breasts into 1" cubes. Sprinkle with paprika, pepper, and salt; mix well. Heat olive oil in large skillet over medium heat. Add chicken; cook and stir until chicken starts to brown, about 4–5 minutes.
2. Remove chicken from skillet and place in 6-quart slow cooker. Add onions and garlic to skillet; cook until onion is tender, stirring to remove pan drippings, about 5 minutes.
3. Add rice to skillet; cook and stir for 3–4 minutes until coated. Add rice mixture to slow cooker.
4. Stir in remaining ingredients except parsley and cilantro. Cover and cook on low for 6–7 hours or until chicken is thoroughly cooked and rice is tender. Stir in parsley and cilantro and serve.

Apple Chicken with Pecans

SERVES 8

Chicken, apples, and pecans are classic ingredients in chicken salad. When combined together in a hot casserole, the flavors and textures blend beautifully. Serve this dish over hot cooked rice.

8 boneless, skinless chicken breasts

1 teaspoon dried thyme leaves

¼ teaspoon pepper

1 teaspoon salt

2 onions, sliced

4 Granny Smith apples, cored, peeled and sliced

½ cup chicken broth

½ cup apple cider

½ cup brown sugar

3 tablespoons butter, melted

2 cups small whole pecans, toasted

1. Sprinkle chicken with thyme, pepper, and salt. Place onions in bottom of 5-quart slow cooker. Top with chicken and apples.
2. In small bowl, combine remaining ingredients except pecans and mix well. Pour into slow cooker.
3. Cover and cook on low for 6–7 hours or until chicken is thoroughly cooked and apples are tender. Stir in pecans and serve over hot cooked rice.

Pork and Ham Entrées

My maternal grandmother really loved pork, and so does my mother. We ate tender, juicy chops and roasts quite often when I was growing up. And my husband loves pork too, especially smoked pork, because he grew up in Germany, where it's practically the national meat.

Pork includes roasts, chops, ham, bacon, and ribs. These foods cook well in the slow cooker (except bacon) and can be transformed into hearty one-pot meals or elegant entrées. A pork loin roast is an inexpensive way to serve a crowd. And you can combine pork with everything from curry to chili powder!

Bacon is delicious used as a flavoring in many main dish recipes. Just cook it crisply in a skillet and use the drippings to sauté meat or vegetables. When using bacon with a slow cooker, it's best to refrigerate the cooked bacon and add it toward the end of cooking time so it retains its texture.

We don't have to cook pork to well-done any longer. Today's pork is bred to be leaner, and it's safe to cook pork until there's just a tinge of pink in the center. Using a food thermometer is always a good idea. Cook pork to 155°F. For roasts, let the pork stand, covered, for about 10 minutes after cooking before slicing to let the juices redistribute.

Deviled Spareribs

SERVES 12–15
A little bit of spice is the perfect finish for super-tender ribs. Serve these spareribs with lots of water or soft drinks and lots of napkins!

4–5 pounds spareribs
2 tablespoons butter
2 onions, chopped
3 cloves garlic, minced
1 (16-ounce) bottle barbecue sauce
¼ cup honey
¼ teaspoon cayenne pepper
1 cup chili sauce
½ teaspoon salt
⅛ teaspoon white pepper

1. Preheat broiler. Place spareribs on broiler rack and broil 6" from heat source for 4–5 minutes or until browned. Turn and broil for 4–5 minutes longer. Cut into serving-sized pieces, if necessary, and place in 7-quart slow cooker.
2. In large saucepan, melt butter over medium heat. Add onions and garlic; cook and stir until tender, about 5 minutes. Add remaining ingredients; cook and stir for 4 minutes.
3. Pour sauce over ribs in slow cooker. Cover and cook on low for 8–10 hours, until ribs are tender. Serve immediately.

Creamy Mustard Pork Chops

SERVES 8
Mustard was made for pork. The spicy, sweet-and-sour taste blends with the sweet and nutty flavor of pork chops. Serve this one with mashed potatoes.

8 boneless pork loin chops
½ teaspoon salt
⅛ teaspoon white pepper
2 tablespoons olive oil
2 onions, sliced
¼ cup Dijon mustard
1½ cups chicken broth
1 tablespoon prepared horseradish
2 tablespoons cornstarch
1 cup sour cream
2 tablespoons Dijon mustard

1. Sprinkle pork chops with salt and pepper. In large skillet, heat olive oil over medium heat. Add chops; brown, turning once, for about 4–6 minutes.
2. Place onions in the bottom of a 5- to 6-quart slow cooker. Add a layer of pork chops, then spread some of the mustard over. Repeat, using the rest of the pork chops and the mustard.
3. Add chicken broth to slow cooker. Cover and cook on low for 7–8 hours or until chops are tender and register 155°F.
4. Remove chops from slow cooker and cover to keep warm. In small bowl, combine horseradish, cornstarch, sour cream, and Dijon mustard; mix well. Pour into slow cooker and stir well.
5. Return chops to slow cooker, cover, and cook on high for 30 minutes until sauce is thickened. Serve immediately.

Hot German Potato Salad

SERVES 10–12

Hot potato salad is a classic German side dish. Adding sausages elevates it to a hearty main dish.

4 slices bacon	½ cup chicken broth
2 tablespoons butter	½ teaspoon celery seed
1 onion, chopped	⅛ teaspoon pepper
4 cloves garlic, minced	¼ cup flour
1½ pounds Polish sausage	½ cup apple cider vinegar
9 potatoes, cut into chunks	1 cup sour cream
½ cup sugar	

1. In large skillet, cook bacon until crisp. Drain bacon on paper towels, crumble, and set aside in refrigerator. Drain all but 1 tablespoon drippings from skillet. Add butter to skillet.
2. Add onion and garlic to skillet; cook and stir for 5 minutes. Remove from heat. Cut sausage into 1" chunks.
3. Combine potatoes and sausage in 5 to 6-quart slow cooker. Add sugar, chicken broth, celery seed, and pepper to skillet with onions and mix well. Pour into slow cooker.
4. Cover and cook on low for 8–10 hours or until potatoes are tender. In small bowl, combine flour, vinegar, and sour cream and mix well. Stir into slow cooker. Cover and cook on high for 20–30 minutes or until hot and blended. Sprinkle with reserved bacon before serving.

Ham and Cheese Potatoes

SERVES 8–10

Kids will love this recipe. It's hot, creamy, and comforting, made easy by starting with frozen potatoes.

1 (32-ounce) package frozen straight cut French fry potatoes

2 onions, chopped

4 cloves garlic, minced

3 cups cubed ham

2 cups shredded Havarti cheese

2 (10-ounce) cans cream of potato soup

1 cup ricotta cheese

⅛ teaspoon pepper

1 teaspoon dried marjoram

2 cups frozen baby peas, thawed

½ cup grated Romano cheese

1. In 5- to 6-quart slow cooker, combine potatoes, onions, garlic, ham, and Havarti cheese; mix well. In medium bowl, combine soup, cheese, pepper, and marjoram. Pour over potato mixture.
2. Cover and cook on low for 8–9 hours or until potatoes are tender. Stir in peas and Romano cheese. Cover and cook on high for 30–40 minutes or until peas are hot. Serve immediately.

Then he looked up at his disciples and said: "Blessed are you who are poor, for yours is the kingdom of God. Blessed are you who are hungry now, for you will be filled.

—LUKE 6:20–21

Aunt Peg's Pork Roast

SERVES 12

The combination of apricots and spicy onions is really delicious with tender and juicy pork loin. This will become a favorite!

2 onions, chopped
3 cloves garlic, minced
1 (4-pound) boneless pork loin roast
½ teaspoon salt
¼ teaspoon pepper
1 (12-ounce) jar apricot preserves
1 envelope dry onion soup mix
½ cup apricot nectar
½ cup chicken broth
2 tablespoons Dijon mustard
2 tablespoons cornstarch
¼ cup cold water

1. Place onion and garlic in bottom of 5- to 6-quart slow cooker. Sprinkle pork with salt and pepper and place in slow cooker.
2. In medium bowl, combine preserves, onion soup mix, nectar, chicken broth, and mustard; mix well. Pour over pork. Cover and cook on low for 7–9 hours until pork registers 155°F.
3. Remove pork from slow cooker and cover to keep it warm. In small bowl, combine cornstarch and water; blend well. Pour into slow cooker and stir with wire whisk. Return pork to slow cooker.
4. Cover and cook on high for 25 minutes or until sauce thickens. Slice pork and serve with sauce.

Sausage Sweet Potato Supper

SERVES 10

Sweet potatoes, apples, and pork really complement each other. Add curry powder and some onions and garlic, and you have a fabulous one-dish meal.

2 pounds sweet Italian sausage links
2 tablespoons butter
2 onions, chopped
4 cloves garlic, minced
¼ cup flour
1 teaspoon salt
⅛ teaspoon pepper
1 tablespoon curry powder
⅓ cup brown sugar
½ cup chicken broth
1 cup apple cider
6 sweet potatoes, peeled
3 apples, peeled and sliced
2 tablespoons brown sugar

1. In large skillet, cook sausage until almost done; remove from skillet. Add butter to drippings remaining in skillet. Add onions and garlic; cook and stir until tender, about 6 minutes.
2. Add flour, salt, pepper, and curry powder; cook and stir until bubbly. Add ⅓ cup brown sugar, then stir in chicken broth and cider. Cook and stir until thickened.
3. Slice sweet potatoes into ⅛" thick rounds. Slice the sausage into 1" chunks. Layer sweet potatoes, apples, sausage pieces, and onion mixture in 5- to 6-quart slow cooker. Top with 2 tablespoons brown sugar.
4. Cover and cook on low for 9–10 hours or until sweet potatoes are tender. Serve immediately.

Ham with Wild Rice

SERVES 12
Wild rice cooks perfectly in the slow cooker, unlike white rice.

2 onions, chopped
6 cloves garlic, minced
2 (4-ounce) jars sliced mushrooms
2 cups wild rice
1 (16-ounce) bag baby carrots
4 cups cubed cooked ham
1 (10-ounce) container refrigerated Alfredo sauce
1 (10-ounce) can condensed cream of mushroom soup
5 cups chicken stock
1 teaspoon dried tarragon leaves
⅛ teaspoon white pepper
½ cup grated Parmesan cheese

1. In 5-quart slow cooker, combine onions, garlic, mushrooms with their liquid, wild rice, carrots, and ham; stir gently.
2. In large bowl, combine Alfredo sauce, soup, chicken stock, tarragon, and pepper; mix well. Pour into slow cooker.
3. Cover and cook on high for 1 hour, then stir. Cover again and cook on low for 6 hours or until wild rice and carrots are tender. Stir in cheese and serve.

Blessed are those who hunger and thirst for righteousness, for they will be filled.

—MATTHEW 5:6

Tex-Mex Pork and Corn Bake

SERVES 8
Two kinds of corn add flavor and texture to this spicy dish. Serve it with some chopped fresh tomatoes and tortilla chips.

8 boneless pork loin chops
1 teaspoon salt
⅛ teaspoon pepper
1 tablespoon olive oil
1 tablespoon butter
2 onions, chopped
4 cloves garlic, minced
1 tablespoon chili powder
1 (4-ounce) can chopped green chiles
1 (16-ounce) can cream-style corn
2 cups frozen corn
2 green bell peppers, chopped
1 jalapeño pepper, chopped
2 cups grated Swiss or pepper jack cheese

1. Sprinkle chops with salt and pepper. In large skillet, heat olive oil and butter over medium heat. Add chops; brown on both sides, turning once, about 5 minutes total. Remove chops from pan.
2. Add onions and garlic to pan; cook and stir until tender, about 5 minutes. Add chili powder, green chiles with liquid, cream-style corn, and frozen corn. Cook and stir for 4 minutes.
3. In 5- to 6-quart slow cooker, layer corn mixture with pork chops and green bell peppers. Sprinkle top with jalapeño pepper. Cover and cook on low for 7–8 hours or until chops are tender.
4. Uncover and stir in cheese. Cover and cook on high for 20 minutes longer or until cheese melts. Serve immediately.

Spicy Fruited Pork Chops

SERVES 8

Dried fruit really complements the flavor of pork. You could use any combination you'd like; dried currants and peaches would be nice additions.

8 boneless pork loin chops	½ teaspoon allspice
1 teaspoon salt	2 cups chicken broth
⅛ teaspoon white pepper	10 dried apricots, chopped
2 tablespoons butter	1 cup golden raisins
1 tablespoon olive oil	10 dried prunes, chopped
⅓ cup brown sugar	2 tablespoons cornstarch
⅓ cup white wine vinegar	¼ cup water
1½ teaspoons cinnamon	

1. Sprinkle chops with salt and pepper. In skillet, heat butter and olive oil over medium heat. When butter melts, brown chops on both sides, about 5 minutes total. Place in 5-quart slow cooker.
2. Add brown sugar, vinegar, cinnamon, allspice, and chicken broth to skillet; bring to a simmer. Stir in apricots, raisins, and prunes. Pour over chops in slow cooker.
3. Cover and cook on low for 7 hours or until chops and fruit are tender. In bowl, combine cornstarch and water. Add to slow cooker; cover and cook on high for 20 minutes or until sauce thickens.

Keep falsehood and lies far from me; give me neither poverty nor riches, but give me only my daily bread.

—PROVERBS 30:8

Curried Pork

SERVES 8–10

Curry and chutney are Indian condiments that are sweet and spicy at the same time. Cooked with lots of fruit and pork and served over rice or mashed potatoes, this makes a delicious and easy dinner.

2 onions, chopped
4 cloves garlic, minced
3 tart apples, peeled, cored, and chopped
1 cup golden raisins
1 cup dark raisins
2½ pounds lean pork, cubed
1–2 tablespoons curry powder
1 teaspoon salt
¼ teaspoon white pepper
1 cup apple juice
1 cup chicken broth
2 tablespoons lemon juice
1 (16-ounce) jar mango chutney
2 tablespoons cornstarch
⅓ cup mango nectar

1. In 5- to 6-quart slow cooker, combine all ingredients except chutney, cornstarch, and mango nectar. Cover and cook on low for 8–9 hours or until pork is tender.
2. In medium bowl, combine chutney, cornstarch, and mango nectar. Stir into slow cooker. Cover and cook on high for 20–30 minutes or until sauce is thickened. Serve over hot cooked rice or mashed potatoes.

Ham and Potato Salad

SERVES 10–12

Cooking ham and potatoes together in the slow cooker makes a wonderful base for a ham salad. Add dressing and it's waiting for you in the fridge!

4 potatoes, peeled and cubed

4 sweet potatoes, peeled and cubed

2 onions, chopped

4 cloves garlic, minced

1 cup chicken broth

3 cups cubed ham

1½ cups mayonnaise

1½ cups plain yogurt

⅓ cup milk

½ cup yellow mustard

1 teaspoon salt

¼ teaspoon pepper

2 teaspoons dried basil leaves

2 green bell peppers, chopped

4 stalks celery, chopped

2 pints grape tomatoes

1. In 5- to 6-quart slow cooker, combine potatoes, sweet potatoes, onions, garlic, chicken broth, and cubed ham. Cover and cook on low for 8–9 hours or until potatoes are tender when pierced with fork. Drain if necessary.
2. In large bowl, combine mayonnaise, yogurt, milk, mustard, salt, pepper, and dried basil; mix well. Remove hot potato mixture from slow cooker with large slotted spoon or sieve. Stir into dressing in bowl, then add remaining ingredients and stir gently to coat.
3. Cover and refrigerate for 3–4 hours or until salad is cold. Stir gently before serving.

The Best Spareribs

SERVES 8–10

Spareribs are delicious for a summer picnic. Serve with Potato Salad (page 152) and a nice fruit salad.

4 pounds country-style pork spareribs

1 tablespoon olive oil

1 onion, chopped

3 cloves garlic, minced

1 cup chili sauce

½ cup barbecue sauce

¼ cup Dijon mustard

¼ cup honey

1 teaspoon salt

¼ teaspoon pepper

1. Cut spareribs into serving-sized pieces and place, meat side up, on broiler rack. Broil for 3–4 minutes or until spareribs brown; set aside.
2. In large saucepan, heat olive oil over medium heat. Add onion and garlic; cook and stir until tender, about 5 minutes. Add remaining ingredients and bring to a simmer.
3. Place ribs in 5- to 6-quart slow cooker and pour sauce over. Cover and cook on low for 7–8 hours or until ribs are cooked and tender. Uncover and cook on high for 30 minutes to help thicken sauce, if necessary.

Do not judge, so that you may not be judged. For with the judgment you make you will be judged, and the measure you give will be the measure you get.

—MATTHEW 7:1–5

Pulled Pork Burritos

SERVES 16

A dry rub helps season the meat in these excellent burritos. You also can use this pork filling for wrap sandwiches; spread corn tortillas with some refried beans, and then add the pork.

4-pound boneless pork loin roast

¼ cup brown sugar

1 teaspoon dry mustard powder

1 tablespoon chili powder

1 teaspoon salt

¼ teaspoon cayenne pepper

2 onions, chopped

6 cloves garlic, minced

1 cup vinegar

2 cups chicken stock

16 (10-inch) flour tortillas

2 (16-ounce) cans refried beans

2 cups shredded Muenster cheese

2 cups shredded sharp Cheddar cheese

1. Cut roast into 3 pieces. In small bowl, combine brown sugar, mustard powder, chili powder, salt, and cayenne pepper; mix well. Sprinkle over roast and rub into surface.
2. Cover and marinate pork in refrigerator overnight. In the morning, place onions and garlic in bottom of 5- or 6-quart slow cooker. Place pork on top. Pour vinegar and chicken stock over all. Cover and cook on low for 8–9 hours or until pork is very tender.
3. Remove pork from slow cooker along with onions. Shred pork, using two forks. Add vegetables and enough of the cooking liquid to moisten meat. At this point you can use the meat for wrap sandwiches or other purposes if you wish. If making burritos, continue with next steps.
4. Preheat oven to 375°F. Spread tortillas with refried beans. Top each with some of the shredded pork and the cheeses; then roll up. Place, seam side down, in two greased 13" × 9" casserole dishes.
5. Cover with foil and bake for 20–30 minutes or until cheese is melted and burritos are hot.

The hungry eat their harvest, and they take it even out of the thorns; and the thirsty pant after their wealth. For misery does not come from the earth, nor does trouble sprout from the ground, but human beings are born to trouble just as sparks fly upward.

—JOB 5:5–7

Pork Loin with Apple Chutney

SERVES 12

This is a delicious way to serve the Apple Chutney, which you can make in large quantities. The pork can be served on its own, too; the sauce can be thickened with cornstarch and water.

1 onion, chopped
3 cloves garlic, minced
1 (4-pound) boneless pork loin roast
½ teaspoon salt
¼ teaspoon pepper
1 teaspoon dried thyme leaves
1 cup chicken broth
½ cup apple cider
2 cups Apple Chutney (page 208)

1. Place onion and garlic in bottom of 5- to 6-quart slow cooker. Sprinkle pork with salt, pepper, and thyme. Place in slow cooker.
2. In medium bowl combine chicken broth and ½ cup apple cider; mix well. Pour over pork. Cover and cook on low for 8 hours until pork registers 155°F.
3. Slice pork and serve with chutney, either warm or cold.

"Did not your father eat and drink and do justice and righteousness? Then it was well with him. He judged the cause of the poor and needy; then it was well. Is not this to know me?" says the Lord.

—JEREMIAH 22:15–16

Spicy Ham and Corn Bake

SERVES 8

Corn muffin mix is the secret ingredient in this hearty casserole. You can substitute Canadian bacon for the ham.

2 tablespoons butter
1 onion, chopped
3 cloves garlic, minced
1–2 jalapeño peppers, minced
2 (8-ounce) boxes corn muffin mix
3 eggs
1 cup mascarpone cheese
3 cups chopped ham
2 cups frozen corn
1½ cups shredded Cheddar cheese
1 cup salsa
¼ cup chopped green onions, white and green parts
¼ cup sliced black olives

1. In large skillet, melt butter over medium heat. Add onion and garlic; cook and stir for 5 minutes. Add jalapeño peppers and remove from heat.
2. In large bowl, combine both boxes muffin mix with onion mixture, eggs, and mascarpone cheese; mix well.
3. Spray a 4-quart slow cooker with nonstick cooking spray. Place half of the muffin mixture in bottom of slow cooker. Top with half of the ham, corn, and cheese. Repeat layers, ending with cheese.
4. Cover and cook on high for 2½ to 3½ hours or until toothpick inserted in center comes out clean.
5. Meanwhile, in small bowl combine salsa, green onions, and olives; mix well. To serve, scoop casserole out of slow cooker onto serving plates. Offer salsa mixture as a topping.

Spicy Pork Tenderloin

SERVES 8–10

Mustard, honey, and tender pork combine beautifully in this simple recipe. Serve it with Herbed Brown Rice Pilaf (page 146) or mashed potatoes to soak up the sauce.

2 (2-pound) pork tenderloins

10 cloves garlic, peeled and sliced

1½ teaspoons salt

¼ teaspoon white pepper

1 teaspoon cumin

¼ cup Dijon mustard

⅓ cup honey

1½ cups chicken broth

2 tablespoons cornstarch

½ cup water

1. Poke 20 holes into each of the tenderloins with a knife. Cut each clove of garlic into four slices. Insert a slice of garlic into each hole. In small bowl, combine salt, pepper, cumin, mustard, and honey; mix well. Spread over tenderloins.
2. Place pork in 4- to 5-quart slow cooker. Pour chicken broth into slow cooker.
3. Cover and cook on low for 5–6 hours or until meat thermometer registers 155°F. Remove pork from slow cooker, cover, and let stand for 15 minutes.
4. Meanwhile, combine cornstarch and water in a small bowl. Stir into the liquid remaining in slow cooker. Cook on high for 15–20 minutes or until sauce thickens. Slice pork and serve with sauce.

Pork and Bean Tacos

SERVES 12

Make a pot of this filling, along with the other taco fillings in the book, and set up a taco bar. Ole!

2 tablespoons chili powder

1 teaspoon cumin

1 teaspoon salt

¼ teaspoon pepper

¼ cup flour

1 (4-pound) boneless pork loin roast

2 tablespoons butter

2 tablespoons oil

2 onions, chopped

6 cloves garlic, minced

1 (15-ounce) can refried beans

2 (15-ounce) cans kidney beans

1 (16-ounce) jar mild or medium salsa

12–14 taco shells

2 cups shredded lettuce

2 cups shredded Muenster cheese

2 cups chopped tomatoes

1. On shallow plate, combine chili powder, cumin, salt, pepper, and flour; mix well. Dredge pork in this mixture until completely coated.
2. In skillet, melt butter with oil over medium heat. Add pork; sear on all sides until browned, about 6 minutes. Place pork in 5- to 6-quart slow cooker.
3. Add onions and garlic to skillet; cook and stir until tender, stirring to scrape up drippings. Add refried beans and heat for 4 minutes, stirring well. Add kidney beans and salsa; pour over pork.
4. Cover and cook on low for 7–9 hours or until pork is very tender. Using two forks, shred pork. Stir to mix with rest of filling.
5. Heat taco shells as directed on package. Make tacos with filling, lettuce, cheese, and tomatoes.

Slow Cooker Tex-Mex Lasagna

Using corn tortillas instead of pasta works well in the slow cooker, which can overcook pasta. You can vary the spice level to suit your taste. Serve this spicy casserole with more sour cream, guacamole, and chopped chives.

2 pounds spicy bulk pork sausage

2 onions, chopped

4 cloves garlic, minced

1 (16-ounce) jar mild or medium salsa

1 (16-ounce) can refried beans

1 (6-ounce) can tomato paste

1 tablespoon chili powder

½ teaspoon salt

⅛ teaspoon cayenne pepper

1 (8-ounce) package cream cheese, softened

1 cup sour cream

2 tablespoons flour

2 cups frozen corn

1 (4-ounce) can chopped green chiles, drained

12 corn tortillas

2 cups shredded pepper jack cheese

1 cup shredded Cheddar cheese

1. In skillet, cook pork sausage with onions and garlic until sausage is cooked, stirring to break up meat. Drain well. Add salsa, refried beans, tomato paste, chili powder, salt, and cayenne pepper; stir until combined. Remove from heat.

2. In large bowl beat cream cheese until soft. Gradually add sour cream; beat well. Mix in flour. Add corn and drained chiles.

3. Place a layer of the pork mixture in the bottom of a 5- to 6-quart slow cooker. Top with some of four corn tortillas, overlapping slightly. Top with corn mixture, then some of the cheeses. Repeat layers, ending with cheese.

4. Cover and cook on low for 7–9 hours or until casserole is hot and bubbling. Serve with guacamole, more sour cream, and chopped chives if desired.

Owe no one anything, except to love one another; for the one who loves another has fulfilled the law. The commandments, "You shall not commit adultery; You shall not murder; You shall not steal; You shall not covet"; and any other commandment, are summed up in this word, "Love your neighbor as yourself." Love does no wrong to a neighbor; therefore, love is the fulfilling of the law.

—ROMANS 13:8–10

Sausage and Bean Casserole

SERVES 10–12

This sweet and spicy casserole is fun to make and serve. Just drain the beans; don't rinse them. The sweet sauce they are packed in adds flavor and texture to the dish.

2 pounds sweet bulk Italian sausage

2 onions, chopped

2 (15-ounce) cans lima beans, drained

1 (15-ounce) can chili beans, undrained

1 (15-ounce) can black beans, drained

4 carrots, sliced

1 (6-ounce) can tomato paste

½ cup chili sauce

½ cup honey

⅓ cup brown sugar

¼ cup Dijon mustard

1 teaspoon fennel seed

1. In large skillet, cook sausage with onions until sausage is browned, stirring to break up meat. Drain thoroughly.
2. Place sausage and onions in 5-quart slow cooker. Add carrots, all of the beans, and mix well.
3. In skillet combine remaining ingredients and stir over low heat until blended. Pour into slow cooker.
4. Cover and cook on low for 7–8 hours or until vegetables are tender and casserole is hot and bubbly. Serve immediately.

Amy's Root Beer Pork Roast

SERVES 8–10

Root beer helps tenderize the pork as it cooks. You can slice and serve this by itself, or shred the pork, return it to the sauce, and serve in tortillas or on toasted buns.

2 (2-pound) pork tenderloins

1 teaspoon garlic salt

⅛ teaspoon pepper

2 onions, sliced

1 (12-ounce) can root beer

½ cup ketchup

¼ cup chili sauce

1 tablespoon lemon juice

2 tablespoons Worcestershire sauce

2 tablespoons honey

1. Sprinkle tenderloins with garlic salt and pepper. Place onions in bottom of 5-quart slow cooker. Top with pork.
2. In medium bowl, combine remaining ingredients and stir with wire whisk until blended. Pour into slow cooker.
3. Cover and cook on low for 8–9 hours or until pork is tender. Shred pork and return to sauce. Turn slow cooker to high and cook uncovered for 30–40 minutes to thicken, or remove pork from sauce, slice, and serve with the sauce.

Honey-Glazed Ham

SERVES 16

You could have several slow cookers going with this ham for feeding a crowd at the holidays.

3 onions, sliced
4-pound fully cooked ham
½ cup brown sugar
¼ cup honey
¼ cup Dijon mustard
½ teaspoon dry mustard powder
2 tablespoons apple cider
⅛ teaspoon pepper

1. Place onions in bottom of 5- to 6-quart slow cooker. Place ham in slow cooker on top of onions.
2. In medium bowl, combine remaining ingredients and mix well. Spread over the ham.
3. Cover slow cooker and cook on high for 1 hour. Then turn heat to low and cook for 8–9 hours longer or until ham registers 140°F using a meat thermometer.

While they were eating, he took a loaf of bead, and after blessing it he broke it, gave it to them, and said, "Take, this is my body." Then he took a cup, and after giving thanks he gave it to them, and all of them drank from it. He said to them, "This is my blood of the covenant, which is poured out for many."

—MARK 14:22

Orange and Apricot Pork Chops

SERVES 10

This sweet and tangy sauce complements the tender pork beautifully. Serve with a wild rice pilaf and a fruit salad for the perfect Lenten meal.

10 boneless loin pork chops
1 teaspoon seasoned salt
¼ teaspoon white pepper
1 teaspoon paprika
¼ cup butter
2 onions, chopped
1 cup orange marmalade
1 cup apricot preserves
1 cup golden raisins
½ cup honey
¼ cup mustard
1 teaspoon grated orange peel

1. Sprinkle pork chops with seasoned salt, pepper, and paprika. In large skillet, melt butter over medium heat. Add pork chops; brown on both sides, about 4–5 minutes total.
2. Remove pork chops to a 6- to 7-quart slow cooker. Add onions to drippings remaining in pan; cook and stir for 4 minutes to loosen pan drippings, until onions are crisp-tender. Add to slow cooker.
3. In medium bowl, combine all remaining ingredients and mix well. Stir into slow cooker.
4. Cover and cook on low for 7–9 hours or until pork registers 155°F and is tender. Serve with hot cooked rice or mashed potatoes.

Vegetarian Entrées

I've tried to become a vegetarian, I really have, but I just can't do it. I really admire those who are vegetarian. Not only are they eating lower on the food chain, but they usually eat more fruits and vegetables than do non-vegetarians.

At any rate, it's important to offer vegetarian foods in any large gathering. In fact, more people than you think will choose the vegetarian entrée, because it is automatically lower in fat and usually contains more vegetables and fiber.

Vegetarian food doesn't have to be beans and tofu, although that can be delicious too! Inventive recipes that use vegetables, potatoes, and cheese in new ways will satisfy any appetite, and no one will miss the meat.

Vegetarians and vegans must be concerned about protein intake. Legumes (beans) and grains do not provide complete proteins by themselves, so they must be combined in a recipe or a meal. The combination of beans and grains, or beans and corn, will supply you with all the needed amino acids. Soy, buckwheat, quinoa, and amaranth do contain complete proteins. Ovo-lacto vegetarians who eat dairy products don't need to worry about this.

There are quite a few vegetarian substitutes and fake-outs on the market. Meatless soy crumbles look and taste just like ground beef, and there's a version that mimics pork sausage. You can even find "fake" chicken and chicken chunks! If you do use these products, be sure to label the finished dish so vegetarians won't think they're accidentally eating meat!

Mexican Torte

SERVES 8–10

Frozen meatless soy crumbles taste almost like ground beef, and have the exact same texture. They're delicious in this hearty casserole.

2 tablespoons olive oil

2 onions, chopped

4 cloves garlic, minced

2 (16-ounce) packages frozen meatless soy crumbles

2 (4-ounce) cans chopped green chiles, undrained

1 tablespoon chili powder

2 teaspoons dried oregano leaves

1 teaspoon salt

¼ teaspoon cayenne pepper

1 (14-ounce) can diced tomatoes, undrained

2 cups salsa

1 (16-ounce) can refried beans

12 (6-inch) corn tortillas

2 cups shredded Colby cheese

2 cups shredded pepper jack cheese

1 cup sour cream

1 cup chopped tomatoes

½ cup chopped green onions

1. In large skillet, heat olive oil over medium heat. Add onions and garlic; cook and stir until tender, about 6 minutes. Add crumbles, green chiles, chili powder, oregano, salt, pepper, and tomatoes; bring to a simmer.

2. In large bowl, combine salsa and refried beans and mix well. In 6-quart slow cooker, layer ¼ of the crumbles mixture, ¼ of the tortillas, ¼ of the salsa mixture, and ¼ of each of the cheeses.

3. Cover and cook on low for 6–7 hours or until hot and bubbly. Serve with sour cream, chopped tomatoes, and green onions.

He who supplies seed to the sower and bread for food will supply and multiply your seed for sowing and increase the harvest of your righteousness. You will be enriched in every way for your great generosity, which will produce thanksgiving to God through us.

—2 CORINTHIANS 9:10–11

Potato Gratin

SERVES 12–14

This fabulously rich and creamy vegetarian main dish will be a hit with all ages. You could also serve it as a side dish, but if you do, scoop out small portions.

2 tablespoons butter
1 tablespoon olive oil
2 onions, chopped
6 cloves garlic, minced
2 tablespoons flour
1 teaspoon salt
¼ teaspoon pepper
⅛ teaspoon nutmeg
1 cup milk
1 cup heavy cream

1 (8-ounce) package cream cheese, cubed
1 cup mascarpone cheese
3 pounds russet potatoes, peeled, sliced ⅛" thick
2 (8-ounce) jars mushrooms, drained
2 cups diced Swiss or Havarti cheese
½ cup grated Romano cheese

1. In large saucepan, melt butter with olive oil over medium heat. Add onions and garlic; cook and stir until tender, about 6 minutes.
2. Add flour, salt, pepper, and nutmeg to onion mixture; cook and stir until bubbly. Add milk and cream all at once, stirring with wire whisk; then stir in cream cheese and mascarpone cheese. Cook and stir until cheese melts and mixture is smooth.
3. Spray a 6-quart slow cooker with nonstick cooking spray. Layer ⅓ of potatoes, mushrooms, and Swiss cheese in slow cooker. Pour ⅓ of onion mixture over. Repeat layers, ending with onion mixture.
4. Sprinkle with Romano cheese. Cover and cook on low for 8–9 hours or until potatoes are tender.

Potato Omelet

SERVES 10

Topping a moist and hearty potato omelet with an herb-and-tomato mixture really perks up the flavor and wakes up your taste buds.

1 (32-ounce) package frozen hash brown potatoes
2 onions, diced
4 cloves garlic, minced
1 cup shredded Cheddar cheese
1 cup shredded Muenster cheese
12 eggs
½ cup heavy cream
½ cup sour cream
1 teaspoon salt
¼ teaspoon pepper
2 cups chopped tomatoes
¼ cup chopped green onions, white and green parts
1 tablespoon fresh thyme leaves

1. Spray a 5-quart slow cooker with nonstick cooking spray. Layer potatoes, onions, garlic, and cheeses in slow cooker.
2. In large bowl, combine eggs with cream and sour cream and beat until blended. Stir in salt and pepper and mix well. Pour into slow cooker.
3. Cover and cook on high for 4–5 hours or until eggs are set. In medium bowl, combine tomatoes, green onion, and thyme; mix gently. Serve tomato topping with omelet.

Vegetarian Chili

SERVES 8–10

Serve this hearty and filling dish with sour cream, shredded cheese, chopped jalapeños, guacamole, and tortilla chips for a satisfying meal in a bowl.

2 onions, chopped
5 cloves garlic, minced
2 jalapeño peppers, minced
2 (10-ounce) packages frozen meatless soy crumbles
2 green bell peppers, chopped
2 red bell peppers, chopped
3 (14-ounce) cans diced tomatoes, undrained
2 cups frozen corn
2 tablespoons chili powder
1 teaspoon cumin
1 teaspoon salt
1 teaspoon dried oregano
¼ teaspoon cayenne pepper
2 (15-ounce) cans kidney beans, drained
2 (15-ounce) cans black beans, drained
3 tablespoons cornstarch
⅓ cup water

1. In 6-quart slow cooker, combine all ingredients except cornstarch and water; mix gently. Cover and cook on low for 8–9 hours or until chili is blended.
2. In small bowl, combine cornstarch and water and mix well. Stir into slow cooker, cover, and cook on high for 20–30 minutes until thickened.

Vegetarian Gumbo

SERVES 10–12

Increase the chipotle chiles and adobo sauce to add a spicy, smoky richness to this thick meatless stew.

2 tablespoons butter
¼ cup olive oil
6 tablespoons flour
1 teaspoon seasoned salt
¼ teaspoon pepper
2 onions, chopped
4 stalks celery, chopped
8 cloves garlic, minced
4 chipotle peppers in adobo sauce, chopped
3 tablespoons adobo sauce from chipotle chilies
2 (15-ounce) cans black beans, drained
1 (14-ounce) can diced tomatoes, undrained
2 cups vegetable broth
6 plum tomatoes, chopped
4 cups frozen corn
2 tablespoons Cajun seasoning
1 teaspoon dried thyme leaves
5 cups hot cooked rice

1. In heavy saucepan over low heat, combine butter and olive oil. When butter melts, add flour. Cook and stir over low heat until the flour turns brown. Watch it carefully so it doesn't burn.
2. Place in 6-quart slow cooker. Add salt, pepper, and remaining ingredients except for rice.
3. Cover and cook on low for 7–8 hours or until vegetables are tender. If the stew needs thickening, remove cover and cook on high for about 1 hour until thickened. Serve over hot cooked rice.

Tex-Mex Egg Casserole

SERVES 8

Three kinds of cheese make this spicy casserole rich and creamy. Top each hot serving with cold salsa to create a delicious contrast.

1 tablespoon butter

1 tablespoon olive oil

2 onions, chopped

4 cloves garlic, minced

1 red bell pepper, chopped

1 jalapeño pepper, minced

¼ cup flour

1 cup heavy cream

12 eggs, beaten

1 cup cottage cheese

½ teaspoon hot pepper sauce

1 teaspoon dried oregano

1 teaspoon salt

¼ teaspoon pepper

⅛ teaspoon cayenne pepper

2 cups shredded pepper jack cheese

1 cup shredded Cheddar cheese

2 cups salsa

1. Spray a 4-quart slow cooker with nonstick cooking spray and set aside. In large skillet, melt butter and olive oil over medium heat. Add onions and garlic; cook and stir until tender, about 6 minutes. Add red bell pepper and jalapeño pepper; cook and stir for 3 minutes longer.

2. Sprinkle flour into skillet; cook and stir until bubbly, about 3–4 minutes. Stir in heavy cream and cook until thickened. Remove from heat; let stand for 20 minutes.

3. In large bowl, beat eggs with cottage cheese, hot pepper sauce, oregano, salt, pepper, and cayenne pepper. Stir in pepper jack and Cheddar cheeses; then stir in vegetable mixture. Pour into prepared slow cooker.

4. Cover and cook on low for 7–8 hours or until set. Serve with cold salsa.

Let them gather all the food of these good years that are coming, and lay up grain under the authority of Pharaoh for food in the cities, and let them keep it.

—GENESIS 41:33

Vegetarian Curry

SERVES 12

Chickpeas and wild rice, a legume and a grain, combine to make a complete protein in this wonderful and delicious one-dish meal.

2 tablespoons olive oil

2 onions, chopped

5 cloves garlic, minced

2 tablespoons minced gingerroot

2 tablespoons curry powder

2 cups wild rice

2 pears, peeled, cored, and chopped

2 apples, peeled, cored, and chopped

1 cup golden raisins

½ cup dark raisins

½ cup dried currants

1 teaspoon salt

¼ teaspoon white pepper

3 (15-ounce) cans chickpeas, drained

2 (14-ounce) cans vegetable broth

2 cups water

1 (10-ounce) jar mango chutney

1. In large skillet, heat olive oil over medium heat. Add onions, garlic, gingerroot, and curry powder; cook and stir for 5 minutes.
2. Place wild rice in bottom of 6-quart slow cooker. Layer pears, apples, raisins, and currants on top.
3. Add salt, pepper, chickpeas, broth, water, and chutney to vegetables in skillet; bring to a simmer. Pour mixture into slow cooker.
4. Cover and cook on low for 8–9 hours or until wild rice is tender. Stir gently to mix.

Beans and "Sausage"

SERVES 16–18

Meatless soy vegetarian crumbles flavored to taste like sausage really do—taste like sausage, that is. This hearty casserole is tasty and filling.

2 tablespoons butter

2 onions, chopped

2 (12-ounce) packages sausage-style meatless soy vegetarian crumbles

2 (15-ounce) cans black beans, drained

2 (15-ounce) cans kidney beans, drained

1 (15-ounce) can navy beans, drained

1 (16-ounce) bag frozen lima beans, thawed

1 cup chili sauce

½ cup barbecue sauce

½ cup brown sugar

⅓ cup yellow mustard

1. In large skillet, melt butter over medium heat. Add onions; cook and stir until tender.
2. Combine onions with all remaining ingredients in a 6-quart slow cooker. Cover and cook on low for 7–8 hours or until everything is blended and crumbles are tender. Stir and serve immediately.

He raises up the poor from the dust; he lifts the needy from the ash heap, to make them sit with princes and inherit a seat of honor.

—1 SAMUEL 2:8

Shepherd's Pie

SERVES 8

Eggplant and mushrooms add a meaty flavor to this hearty and filling meatless main dish. You could flavor the potatoes that top it with everything from Cheddar cheese to green onions.

2 tablespoons olive oil

2 tablespoons butter

2 eggplants, peeled and cubed

2 onions, chopped

2 (8-ounce) packages sliced fresh mushrooms

5 cloves garlic, minced

1 teaspoon salt

¼ teaspoon pepper

1 teaspoon dried thyme leaves

4 carrots, sliced

1 (14-ounce) can diced tomatoes, undrained

1 (6-ounce) can tomato paste

¾ cup chili sauce

2 tablespoons Worcestershire sauce

1 (24-ounce) package refrigerated mashed potatoes

½ cup sour cream

½ cup grated Parmesan cheese

1. In large skillet, heat olive oil and butter over medium heat. When butter melts, add eggplant; cook and stir until almost tender. Remove with slotted spoon; set aside.

2. Add onions, mushrooms, and garlic to skillet; cook and stir for 5–6 minutes until crisp-tender. Stir in salt, pepper, thyme, carrots, tomatoes, tomato paste, chili sauce, and Worcestershire sauce, along with the eggplant; bring to a simmer.

3. Prepare mashed potatoes as directed on package. Stir in sour cream and Parmesan cheese.

4. Pour vegetable mixture into 6-quart slow cooker. Top with potato mixture. Cover and cook on low for 7–8 hours or until mixture is hot and bubbling.

Then she gave the king one hundred twenty talents of gold, a very great quantity of spices, and precious stones. There were no spices such as those that the queen of Sheba gave to King Solomon.

—2 CHRONICLES 9:9

Black Bean Tortilla Torte

SERVES 10–12

Black beans are delicious; hearty and meaty-tasting. In this well-seasoned casserole, they blend beautifully with salsa, cheese, and tortillas.

2 tablespoons olive oil

3 onions, chopped

6 cloves garlic, minced

3 (15-ounce) cans black beans, drained

2 (16-ounce) jars mild or medium salsa

2 envelopes taco seasoning mix

1 (6-ounce) can tomato paste

1½ cups sour cream

2 cups shredded CoJack cheese

1 cup shredded pepper jack cheese

2 green bell peppers, chopped

12 (6-inch) corn tortillas

⅓ cup grated Cotija cheese

2 cups chopped tomatoes

1 (4-ounce) can green chiles, drained

½ cup chopped fresh cilantro leaves

1. In large skillet, heat olive oil over medium heat. Add onions and garlic; cook and stir until crisp-tender, about 5 minutes. Stir in black beans, salsa, taco seasoning mix, and tomato paste. Bring to a simmer; simmer uncovered for 5 minutes.

2. In medium bowl, combine sour cream, CoJack cheese, pepper jack cheese, and green peppers. Mix well.

3. Spray a 6-quart slow cooker with nonstick cooking spray. Place a spoonful of the black bean mixture in bottom. Layer some tortillas on top and add a layer of the sour cream mixture. Repeat layers, ending with sour cream mixture.

4. Sprinkle top with Cotija cheese. Cover and cook on low for 7–8 hours until casserole is bubbly. In small bowl, combine tomatoes, green chiles, and cilantro. Serve casserole with tomato mixture.

And she came to Jerusalem with a very great train, with camels that bore spices, and very much gold, and precious stones, and when she came to Solomon, she told him all that was in her heart.

—1 KINGS 10:2

Gourmet Mac and Cheese

SERVES 12–14

Five kinds of cheese make this dish rich and creamy. Use an oval slow cooker, and fill it just over half full.

2 tablespoons butter

2 onions, chopped

2 (13-ounce) cans evaporated milk

½ cup whole milk

¾ cup sour cream

⅓ cup Dijon mustard

½ teaspoon salt

¼ teaspoon white pepper

2 cups shredded sharp Cheddar cheese

3 cups shredded American cheese

2 cups shredded provolone cheese

1 (8-ounce) package cream cheese, cubed

1 (16-ounce) package elbow macaroni

½ cup grated Parmesan cheese

1 teaspoon paprika

1. In large skillet, melt butter over medium heat. Add onions; cook and stir until tender, about 6 minutes.
2. Add evaporated milk, whole milk, sour cream, mustard, salt, and pepper; heat until steaming. Remove from heat and stir in Cheddar, American, provolone, and cream cheeses.
3. Stir in macaroni and pour into 6-quart slow cooker. Sprinkle top with Parmesan cheese and paprika. Cover and cook on high for 2–3 hours or until macaroni is tender. Stir well and serve.

Greek Stew over Couscous

SERVES 14–16

The flavors of Greece mingle in this delicious stew. You can find feta in several flavors: plain; with garlic and herbs; or with tomatoes and herbs.

1 acorn squash, peeled and cubed

1 butternut squash, peeled and cubed

2 onions, chopped

6 cloves garlic, minced

4 carrots, sliced

4 cups vegetable broth

4 cups water

1 teaspoon salt

1 teaspoon dried oregano

1 teaspoon dried thyme

¼ teaspoon white pepper

2 (15-ounce) cans chickpeas, drained

1 cup golden raisins

4 cups couscous

6 cups vegetable broth

1 cup crumbled feta cheese

1. Combine all ingredients except couscous, broth, and feta in a 6-quart slow cooker. Cover and cook on low for 9–10 hours or until vegetables are very tender.
2. Place broth in saucepan and bring to a boil over high heat. Stir in couscous, cover, and remove from heat. Let stand for 5 minutes, then fluff with fork. Place couscous in large serving bowl.
3. Stir mixture in slow cooker and spoon over couscous. Sprinkle with feta cheese and serve.

A ruler who oppresses the poor is
a beating rain that leaves no food.

—PROVERBS 28:3

Meatless Lasagna

SERVES 12–14

The squash and mushrooms add great texture and meaty flavor to this filling dish. If you vary the cheese (use Gruyère or Colby), you can create a new recipe.

3 tablespoons butter

2 tablespoons olive oil

1 zucchini, peeled and cubed

1 eggplant, peeled and cubed

1 yellow summer squash, peeled and cubed

1 (8-ounce) package sliced mushrooms

2 cups sliced portobello mushrooms

1 onion, chopped

4 cloves garlic, minced

3 (14-ounce) cans diced tomatoes, undrained

2 cups vegetable broth

1 (6-ounce) can tomato paste

1 teaspoon dried basil leaves

1 teaspoon dried oregano leaves

1½ teaspoons salt

¼ teaspoon white pepper

1 (15-ounce) container part-skim ricotta cheese

2 eggs

1 (12-ounce) tub soft cream cheese

2 cups shredded mozzarella cheese

½ cup grated Parmesan cheese, divided

12 lasagna noodles

1. In skillet, heat butter and olive oil over medium heat. Add zucchini and eggplant; cook and stir until crisp-tender, about 5 minutes. Remove vegetables to a large bowl with slotted spoon.

2. Add squash and both kinds of mushrooms to skillet; cook and stir until crisp-tender, about 5 minutes. Remove to same bowl with slotted spoon.

3. Add onions and garlic to skillet; cook and stir until crisp-tender, about 5 minutes. Stir in tomatoes, vegetable broth, tomato paste, basil, oregano, salt, and pepper; bring to a simmer.

4. In another large bowl combine ricotta cheese, eggs, and cream cheese; beat until blended. Stir in mozzarella cheese and ¼ cup Parmesan cheese.

5. Spray a 6- to 7-quart oval slow cooker with non-stick cooking spray. Add a spoonful of the tomato sauce to the bottom. Top with 4 lasagna noodles, then a layer of the squash mixture. Top with ricotta mixture. Repeat layers, ending with ricotta mixture.

6. Sprinkle top with remaining ¼ cup Parmesan cheese. Cover and cook on high for 4–5 hours or until lasagna noodles are tender. Turn off heat, remove cover, and let stand for 15 minutes before serving.

And all the people went their way to eat and drink and to send portions and to make great rejoicing, because they had understood the words that were declared for them.

—NEHEMIAH 8:12

Cheesy Polenta Casserole

SERVES 12–14

You use two slow cookers to make this casserole—one for the topping and one for the polenta—but the time saving is huge!

2½ cups yellow cornmeal

6½ cups vegetable broth

2 cups water

3 tablespoons butter

1½ teaspoons salt

¼ teaspoon white pepper

2 cups shredded extra-sharp Cheddar cheese

1 (8-ounce) package cream cheese, cubed

2 tablespoons butter

1 onion, chopped

2 green bell peppers, chopped

1 (14-ounce) can diced tomatoes, drained

1 (8-ounce) can tomato sauce

2 (15-ounce) cans chickpeas, drained

1 teaspoon dried oregano

⅛ teaspoon pepper

½ cup grated Parmesan cheese

1. Place cornmeal in a 4-quart slow cooker. In large saucepan, combine broth, water, 3 tablespoons butter, salt, and pepper; bring to a boil. Stir into cornmeal.

2. Cover and cook on high for 2 hours, or until liquid is absorbed. Stir polenta thoroughly, add Cheddar and cream cheese, stir gently, and turn off heat.

3. In large skillet, melt 2 tablespoons butter over medium heat. Add onion; cook and stir until tender, about 6 minutes. Add bell peppers, tomatoes, tomato sauce, chickpeas, oregano, and pepper; bring to a simmer. Remove from heat.

4. Place polenta in bottom of 7-quart slow cooker. Top with chickpea mixture, then sprinkle with Parmesan cheese. Cover and cook on low for 5–6 hours or until casserole is thoroughly heated.

Just then a lawyer stood up to test Jesus. "Teacher," he said, "what must I do to inherit eternal life?" He said to him, "What is written in the law? What do you read there?" He answered, "You shall love the Lord your God with all your heart, and with all your soul, and with all your strength, and with all your mind, and your neighbor as yourself." And He said to him, "You have given the right answer: do this, and you will live."

—LUKE 10:25–28

Black-Eyed Pea and Rice Salad

SERVES 18–20

The peas and rice combine to provide complete protein in this excellent and colorful main dish salad.

1 (16-ounce) bag dried
    black-eyed peas

1 cup wild rice

2 onions, chopped

4 jalapeño peppers,
    minced

1 (16-ounce) bag baby
    carrots

2 (32-ounce) boxes
    vegetable broth

2 cups water

2 tablespoons olive oil

1 teaspoon salt

1 cup mayonnaise

½ cup olive oil

⅓ cup Dijon mustard

¼ cup apple cider vinegar

1 teaspoon salt

1 teaspoon dried thyme
    leaves

¼ teaspoon pepper

2 red bell peppers,
    chopped

1. Sort and rinse peas. Place in large saucepan and cover with water. Bring to a boil; boil hard for two minutes. Remove saucepan from heat, cover, and let stand for 2 hours.
2. Drain peas and place in 6-quart slow cooker with wild rice, onions, jalapeño peppers, baby carrots, vegetable broth, water, 2 tablespoons olive oil, and 1 teaspoon salt. Cover and cook on low for 8 hours or until peas and rice are tender. Drain.
3. In large bowl, combine mayonnaise, ½ cup olive oil, mustard, vinegar, salt, thyme, and pepper; mix well. Stir in drained peas and rice mixture along with red bell peppers.
4. Cover and chill for 4–5 hours. Stir gently before serving.

Vegetarian Spaghetti

SERVES 10–12

Carrots help keep the sauce from becoming watery, and add nutrition and flavor. The sauce can be served over any pasta; linguine or penne would be good.

3 onions, chopped

6 cloves garlic, minced

2 cups shredded carrots

2 (8-ounce) packages sliced fresh mushrooms

2 tablespoons olive oil

1 (6-ounce) can tomato paste

1 (15-ounce) can tomato sauce

2 (14-ounce) cans diced tomatoes, undrained

2 cups water

2 teaspoons dried Italian seasoning

1 bay leaf

1 teaspoon salt

¼ teaspoon pepper

2 (16-ounce) packages pasta

1 cup grated Parmesan cheese

1. Combine all ingredients except pasta and cheese in a 5-quart slow cooker. Cover and cook on low for 8–9 hours, stirring once during cooking time, until sauce is blended and thickened.
2. When sauce is ready, bring two pots of salted water to a boil. Add one package pasta to each pot; cook according to package directions until al dente. Drain pasta and place on two warmed serving dishes. Remove and discard bay leaf. Stir sauce and spoon over pasta. Sprinkle with cheese and serve.

Curried Barley and Potato Salad

SERVES 10–12
Barley adds a great chewy texture and nutty flavor to potato salad. You can find vegan mayonnaise, mustard, and milk if you're serving strict vegans.

1 cup pearl barley
4 pounds russet potatoes
2 onions, chopped
6 cloves garlic, minced
1½ teaspoons salt
¼ teaspoon white pepper
1 teaspoon dried tarragon
3 cups water
1½ cups mayonnaise
1 cup sour cream

½ cup plain yogurt
⅓ cup mustard
3 tablespoons Dijon mustard
⅓ cup whole milk
1 red bell pepper, chopped
1 green bell pepper, chopped
1 yellow bell pepper, chopped
2 pints grape tomatoes

1. Place barley in the bottom of 6-quart slow cooker. Peel potatoes and cut into cubes. Place on top of barley along with onions and garlic. Sprinkle with salt, pepper, and tarragon, then pour the water over all.
2. Make sure barley is covered with liquid. Cover and cook on low for 8–9 hours or until potatoes and barley are tender.
3. In bowl, combine mayonnaise, sour cream, yogurt, mustard, Dijon mustard, and milk; mix with wire whisk. Stir in remaining ingredients and mix well.
4. Remove hot potato mixture from slow cooker with large slotted spoon or sieve. Add to bowl and stir gently to coat. Cover and chill for 4–5 hours until cold. Stir gently before serving.

Grandma's Tomatoes and Pierogies

SERVES 10–12
Pierogies are large ravioli-like pasta, stuffed with a mixture of potatoes and cheese or onions. They are found in the frozen entrées section of the supermarket.

2 onions, chopped
6 cloves garlic, minced
6 tomatoes, chopped
6 plum tomatoes, chopped
2 (15-ounce) cans tomato paste
2 cups vegetable broth
1 teaspoon salt
1 teaspoon dried marjoram leaves
3 (12-count) packages frozen pierogies, thawed
2 cups shredded pizza blend cheese

1. Combine all ingredients except pierogies and cheese in a 6-quart slow cooker. Cover and cook on low for 6–7 hours or until sauce is blended.
2. Separate the pierogies and add them to the slow cooker, distributing them evenly. Make sure all of the pierogies are covered with sauce.
3. Cover and cook on high for 1–2 hours longer, or until pierogies are hot in the center. Sprinkle with cheese and serve.

And whoever gives even a cup of water to one of these little ones—none of these will lose their reward.

—MATTHEW 10:42

Ratatouille

SERVES 10

The vegetables will cook down quite a bit in this recipe, so don't be alarmed if the slow cooker is really full right at the beginning.

1½ teaspoons salt

¼ teaspoon pepper

¼ teaspoon white pepper

1 teaspoon dried oregano leaves

1 teaspoon dried basil leaves

1 teaspoon dried Italian seasoning

1 tablespoon sugar

3 tablespoons olive oil

1 eggplant, sliced ½" thick

3 onions, chopped

6 cloves garlic, minced

3 yellow summer squash, sliced

2 zucchini, sliced

3 tomatoes, sliced

2 (8-ounce) packages sliced mushrooms

1 red bell pepper, sliced

2 green bell peppers, sliced

1 yellow bell pepper, sliced

¼ cup extra-virgin olive oil

1 (26-ounce) jar spaghetti sauce

1 (6-ounce) can tomato paste

3 tablespoons balsamic vinegar

1 cup diced feta cheese, if desired

1. In bowl combine salt, pepper, white pepper, oregano, basil, Italian seasoning, and sugar. Mix well and set aside. In large skillet, heat 3 tablespoons olive oil over medium heat. Add eggplant; sauté for 2–3 minutes on each side and then remove eggplant to a separate bowl. Add onions and garlic to skillet; cook and stir for 5 minutes.
2. Spray a 7-quart slow cooker with nonstick cooking spray. Layer all of the vegetables in the slow cooker, sprinkling each layer with some of the salt mixture and drizzling with some of the extra-virgin olive oil.
3. In food processor, combine half of the spaghetti sauce with the tomato paste; blend until smooth. Stir in remaining spaghetti sauce along with the vinegar. Pour into slow cooker.
4. Cover and cook on low for 7–9 hours or until vegetables are very tender. Sprinkle with cheese, if desired, and serve.

If you offer your food to the hungry and satisfy the needs of the afflicted, then your light shall rise in the darkness and your bloom be like the noonday. The Lord will guide you continually, and satisfy your needs in parched places, and make your bones strong; and you shall be like a watered garden, like a spring of water, whose waters never fail.

—ISAIAH 58:10–11

Spicy Risotto

SERVES 10–12

To seed tomatoes, cut in half and gently squeeze out the seeds and jelly. Then chop the tomatoes coarsely and set aside in a dish until it's time to add them to the recipe.

¼ cup olive oil

2 onions, chopped

4 cloves garlic, minced

1 or 2 jalapeño peppers, minced

2½ cups Arborio rice

1 (8-ounce) package sliced fresh mushrooms

1 teaspoon salt

¼ teaspoon white pepper

1 teaspoon cumin seeds

½ teaspoon crushed red pepper flakes

7 cups vegetable broth

1 cup tomato juice

6 tomatoes, seeded and chopped

1 cup heavy cream

1 cup grated Parmesan cheese

1. Heat oil in large skillet. Add onions, garlic, and jalapeño pepper; cook and stir for 4–5 minutes. Then stir in rice; cook and stir for 3–4 minutes longer.

2. Place onion mixture in 5-quart slow cooker. Add mushrooms, salt, pepper, cumin seeds, red pepper flakes, broth, and tomato juice.

3. Cover and cook on high for 2 hours, stirring twice during cooking time. Stir in chopped tomatoes, then continue cooking on high for another 1–2 hours, stirring every half hour, until rice is al dente (slightly firm in the center).

4. Stir in cream and cheese. Uncover and cook for 15–25 minutes longer or until risotto is creamy and hot. Serve immediately.

The Lord has comforted his people, and will have compassion on his suffering ones. But Zion said, "The Lord has forsaken me, my Lord has forgotten me." Can a woman forget her nursing child, or show no compassion for the child of her womb? Even these may forget, yet I will not forget you.

—ISAIAH 49:14–15

Side Dishes

I still remember lunches at the parochial grade school I attended. At almost every meal, the lunch ladies served the most marvelous mashed potatoes (made from scratch, of course), topped with melted butter. A lady would scoop mashed potatoes onto your plate, then make an indentation with the back of a tiny ladle, and pour some butter in. The combination was, and is, sublime.

A church can't function without its supporting cast: volunteers, secretaries, and deacons. So, too, no meal is complete without a side dish. And no matter what you choose for a main dish, side dishes cook perfectly in the slow cooker. Using a slow cooker for your side dishes means you can free up the stovetop and oven to make the entrée, desserts, and breads.

For a Thanksgiving service, or a Christmas buffet when you want to serve turkey and dressing, make extra dressing and let it slowly cook in the slow cooker. No turkey has enough stuffing to satisfy a large gathering, so you'll be able to easily feed a crowd using this technique.

When cooking side dishes in the slow cooker, be aware that many root vegetables and dried beans need to cook for a longer time than meats. These foods should be placed on the bottom of the slow cooker, where they can be surrounded by heat. Salt and acidic ingredients, including tomatoes and citrus juices, can prevent these foods from tenderizing, so add them toward the end of cooking time.

Gingered Baked Beans

SERVES 10–12

Adding ginger to baked beans wakes them up a bit. The onion and ginger become tender and mild during the long cooking time, forming the perfect complement to the beans.

2 tablespoons butter

1 onion, chopped

2 tablespoons minced fresh gingerroot

1/3 cup maple syrup

1/3 cup brown sugar

1/3 cup ketchup

2 tablespoons yellow mustard

2 (16-ounce) cans baked beans, undrained

1 (15-ounce) can black beans, drained

1 (15-ounce) can navy beans, drained

1. In medium skillet, melt butter over medium heat. Add onion; cook and stir until tender, about 6 minutes. Place in 4-quart slow cooker along with gingerroot, maple syrup, brown sugar, ketchup, and mustard; mix well.
2. Add undrained baked beans, drained black beans, and drained navy beans; mix well. Cover and cook on low for 7–9 hours.

He has brought down the powerful from their thrones, and lifted up the lowly; he has filled the hungry with good things, and sent the rich away empty.

—LUKE 1:52

Anne's Cheesy Carrots

SERVES 10–12

Even picky eaters will love this recipe. A creamy, cheesy sauce surrounds tender baby carrots. It's the perfect side dish for any entrée.

3 (16-ounce) packages baby carrots

2 cups water

2 tablespoons butter

1 (8-ounce) package processed American cheese, cubed

1 (8-ounce) package cream cheese, cubed

1 teaspoon dried thyme leaves

1/3 cup milk

1. In 4-quart slow cooker, combine carrots, water, and butter. Cover and cook on low for 5–6 hours or until carrots are tender.
2. Drain carrots and return to slow cooker. Stir in American cheese, cream cheese, thyme, and milk; mix gently. Cover and cook on low for 2 hours, stirring once during cooking time, until smooth sauce forms. Serve immediately.

But he said to them, "You give them something to eat."

—LUKE 9:13

Creamy Potatoes

SERVES 10–12

This creamy, cheesy recipe will be a hit at any gathering. Kids, especially, love this concoction, so it's perfect for a church potluck.

2 (32-ounce) packages frozen hash brown potatoes
2 onions, chopped
4 cloves garlic, minced
2 (10-ounce) cans condensed cream of potato soup
1 (8-ounce) package cream cheese, cubed
1 cup sour cream
2 cups grated Havarti or Swiss cheese

1. In 4- to 5-quart slow cooker, combine potatoes, onions, and garlic. In medium bowl, combine remaining ingredients; mix. Pour into slow cooker.
2. Cover and cook on low for 4 hours; then stir to mix. Cover and continue cooking on low for 3–4 hours longer, until potatoes and onions are tender.

Why do you pass judgment on your brother or sister? Or you, why do you despise your brother or sister? For we will all stand before the judgment seat of God.

—ROMANS 14:10

Spicy Corn Spoon Bread

SERVES 8–10

Baking bread in the slow cooker makes a moist and tender loaf, more like a spoon bread, which is a cross between a soufflé and bread. Make this a mild casserole by omitting the chili powder and green chiles.

2 (8-ounce) packages corn muffin mix
1 tablespoon chili powder, divided
2 eggs, beaten
⅓ cup milk
⅓ cup sour cream
1½ cups frozen corn
1 red bell pepper, chopped
1 (4-ounce) can chopped green chiles, drained
1 cup shredded Colby cheese
⅓ cup mild or medium salsa

1. In large bowl, combine both packages muffin mix and 2 teaspoons chili powder; mix to combine. In medium bowl, combine eggs, milk, and sour cream; mix well. Add to muffin mix and stir just until combined. Stir in corn and bell pepper.
2. In small bowl, combine drained chiles, cheese, and salsa. Spray a 3½- quart slow cooker with nonstick baking spray containing flour. Spoon half of the muffin mix batter into the slow cooker. Top with the green chile mixture, then add remaining batter. Smooth top and sprinkle with remaining 1 teaspoon chili powder.
3. Cover slow cooker and cook on high for 2–3 hours, or until top springs back when lightly touched. Uncover, then top with foil, leaving a corner vented, and cool for 20 minutes. Serve by scooping out hot bread with a large spoon.

Curried Rice

SERVES 6–8

Curried Rice is gently seasoned, and the perfect complement to everything from roasted chicken to Curried Pork (page 117).

3 cups vegetable stock
2 cloves garlic, minced
1½ cups long grain white rice
2 teaspoons curry powder
1 tablespoon butter
2 teaspoons dried parsley flakes
⅛ teaspoon pepper
½ teaspoon salt
½ cup sliced almonds, toasted

1. In small saucepan, bring stock and garlic to a simmer. Pour into 2-quart slow cooker. Add remaining ingredients except almonds. Stir and cover. Cook on low for 4 hours.
2. Turn off slow cooker and add almonds. Let stand for 5 minutes, then fluff to incorporate almonds and mix the rice.

Take wheat and barley, beans and lentils, millet and spelt; put them in a storage jar and use them to make bread for yourself.

—EZEKIEL 4:9

Garlicky Green Beans

SERVES 10–12

When cooked for a long time at low temperatures, garlic becomes tender, mild, and nutty. It adds a wonderful spark of flavor to green beans.

3 (16-ounce) packages frozen whole green beans
1 onion, chopped
6 cloves garlic, minced
½ teaspoon salt
⅛ teaspoon pepper
1 cup water
2 tablespoons butter

1. Combine all ingredients except butter in 4-quart slow cooker. Cover and cook on low for 4–5 hours or until beans and onions are tender.
2. Drain off water and return ingredients to slow cooker. Add butter, cover, and cook for 30 minutes longer. Stir and serve.

What good is it, my brothers and sisters, if you say you have faith but do not have works? Can faith save you? If a brother or sister is naked and lacks daily food, and one of you says to them, "Go in peace, keep warm and eat your fill," and yet you do not supply their bodily needs, what is the good of that?

—JAMES 2:14–17

Herbed Brown Rice Pilaf

SERVES 6

Rice pilaf goes with everything: chicken, beef, pork, and fish. And brown rice, besides being good for you, cooks to perfection in the slow cooker.

1 tablespoon olive oil
1 tablespoon butter
1 onion, chopped
2 cloves garlic, minced
2 cups long grain brown rice
2 cups water
2 cups vegetable broth
1 teaspoon dried thyme leaves
½ teaspoon dried marjoram leaves
½ teaspoon salt
⅛ teaspoon pepper

1. In medium skillet, heat olive oil and butter over medium heat until butter melts. Add onion and garlic; cook and stir for 3 minutes. Add rice; cook and stir until rice is slightly toasted, about 5–6 minutes longer.
2. Transfer rice mixture to 2-quart slow cooker. To the skillet, add water, broth, and remaining ingredients; bring to a simmer. Pour into slow cooker.
3. Cover and cook on low for 6–7 hours or until rice is tender. Stir well and serve.

Risi Bisi

SERVES 8

Risi bisi, or rice with peas, is a classic Italian side dish. A little sour cream and cheese make it decadent and delicious.

2 tablespoons butter
1 onion, chopped
2 shallots, finely chopped
2 cups long grain rice
4 cups water
1 vegetable soup bouillon cube
1 teaspoon dried Italian seasoning
⅛ teaspoon pepper
1½ cups frozen baby peas, thawed
½ cup sour cream
¼ cup grated Parmesan cheese

1. In small saucepan, melt butter over medium heat. Add onion and shallots; cook and stir for 4 minutes. Add rice; cook and stir for 3 minutes longer. Place into 2-quart slow cooker.
2. Add water, bouillon cube, Italian seasoning, and pepper. Cover and cook on low for 5–6 hours or until rice is almost tender.
3. Stir in peas; cover and cook for 30 minutes. Then add sour cream and cheese; cover and cook for 30 minutes longer. Stir and serve immediately.

Clara's Creamed Corn

SERVES 12

Corn combined with two kinds of cheese makes one delicious side dish. Try this one alongside a baked ham.

2 (16-ounce) packages frozen corn
2 (15-ounce) cans creamed corn
1 cup mascarpone cheese
2 (3-ounce) packages cream cheese, cubed
⅓ cup butter
2 tablespoons honey
1 cup whole milk
¼ teaspoon white pepper
1 teaspoon dried thyme leaves

1. In 4-quart slow cooker, combine all ingredients and mix well. Cover and cook on low heat for 3 hours.
2. Stir gently to combine. Serve or hold on low heat for 2 hours, stirring occasionally.

Every third year you shall bring out the full tithe of your produce for that year, and store it within your towns; the Levites, because they have no allotment or inheritance with you, as well as the resident aliens, the orphans, and the widows in your towns, may come and eat their fill so that the Lord your God may bless you.

—DEUTERONOMY 14:28–29

Potato Apple Gratin

SERVES 10–12

In French, apples are *pommes*, while potatoes are *pommes de terre*, or apples of the earth. These two foods combine beautifully in a rich casserole.

1 cup whole milk
1 cup heavy cream
1 (10-ounce) can condensed cream of potato soup
4 egg yolks
⅛ teaspoon white pepper
⅛ teaspoon nutmeg
3 cloves garlic, minced
1 onion, finely chopped
2 pounds small red potatoes, unpeeled, thinly sliced
3 Winesap apples, peeled, cored, and thinly sliced
1 cup shredded Havarti cheese
¼ cup grated Parmesan cheese
½ teaspoon paprika

1. In medium bowl, combine milk, cream, soup, egg yolks, pepper, nutmeg, and garlic; mix well. In 4- to 5-quart slow cooker, layer ⅓ of the onion, potatoes, and apples, sprinkling some Havarti cheese over each layer. Repeat layers.
2. Pour milk mixture over all. Sprinkle with Parmesan cheese and paprika. Cover and cook on low for 7–8 hours or until potatoes and apples are tender and gratin is bubbling. Serve immediately.

Wild Rice Salad

SERVES 12

Wild rice and brown rice cook well in the slow cooker. This salad can be made into a main dish salad with the addition of 3–4 cups chopped cooked chicken, made according to the instructions in Chapter 7.

2 cups wild rice

2 cups brown rice

2 onions, chopped

2 cups water

4 cups vegetable broth

2 cups apple juice

1 teaspoon salt

⅛ teaspoon pepper

1 teaspoon dried thyme leaves

1 cup mayonnaise

1 cup plain yogurt

½ cup sour cream

¼ cup tarragon vinegar

2 tablespoons sugar

2 red bell peppers, chopped

2 green bell peppers, chopped

2 pints grape tomatoes

1. In 4-quart slow cooker, combine wild rice, brown rice, onions, water, broth, and apple juice. Add salt, pepper, and thyme; stir.
2. Cover and cook on high for 3–4 hours or until liquid is absorbed and the rice is tender.
3. In large bowl, combine mayonnaise, yogurt, sour cream, tarragon vinegar, and sugar; mix well. Add bell peppers and tomatoes.
4. Drain rice mixture if any liquid remains, and stir into mayonnaise mixture. Cover and chill for 3–4 hours. Stir gently before serving.

Garlic and Herb Mashed Potatoes

SERVES 12–14

First cook the potatoes to tender perfection in the slow cooker, then mash them with delicious ingredients to make some of the best mashed potatoes anywhere!

6 pounds red potatoes, peeled

6 cloves garlic, minced

2 (5-inch) sprigs fresh thyme

1 cup vegetable broth

1 cup butter, cut into cubes

1 teaspoon dried thyme leaves

1 (8-ounce) package cream cheese, cubed

1 cup mascarpone cheese

1 cup whole milk

1 teaspoon salt

¼ teaspoon white pepper

1. In a 7-quart slow cooker, combine potatoes with garlic, thyme, and vegetable broth. Cover and cook on low for 7–8 hours or until potatoes are tender.
2. Drain potatoes and return to hot slow cooker. Remove thyme stems, leaving leaves with the potatoes. Add butter and dried thyme leaves; mash until smooth.
3. Beat in remaining ingredients until potatoes are fluffy. Cover and cook on low for 2 hours longer, stirring once during cooking time. You can hold the potatoes on low for another hour before serving.

Matha's Best Crunchy Sweet Potatoes

SERVES 8–10

Since the granola is added at the end of cooking time, it stays crunchy. This recipe has a wonderful combination of flavors and textures.

6 sweet potatoes, peeled and cubed
½ cup brown sugar
½ cup pineapple juice
1 teaspoon cinnamon
2 tablespoons honey
1 teaspoon salt
⅛ teaspoon pepper
2 tablespoons butter
½ cup coconut
1 cup granola

1. In 4- to 5-quart slow cooker, combine cubed sweet potatoes, brown sugar, pineapple juice, cinnamon, honey, salt, pepper, and butter. Cover and cook on low for 7–9 hours or until potatoes are tender.
2. Using a potato masher, partially mash the potatoes; stir well. In small saucepan over medium heat, toast coconut, stirring frequently, until browned, about 5–7 minutes. Sprinkle over potatoes, then top with granola.
3. Cover and cook on high for 20–30 minutes longer until hot, then serve.

Creamed Peas and Onions

SERVES 10–12

Creamed peas are a classic side dish. Add two kinds of cheese, onions, and garlic, and you have a side dish fit for company.

2 (16-ounce) packages frozen green peas
2 onions, finely chopped
4 cloves garlic, minced
1 (16-ounce) jar four-cheese Alfredo sauce
1 (10-ounce) container refrigerated Alfredo sauce
½ cup light cream
1 (8-ounce) package cream cheese, cubed
2 cups shredded Muenster cheese

1. Combine all ingredients except cheeses in a 4-quart slow cooker and stir gently to blend. Cover and cook on low for 4 hours.
2. Uncover, add cheeses, and stir to blend. Cover and cook on high for 30–40 minutes longer, or until peas are hot and sauce is blended. Serve immediately.

Then he lay down under the broom tree and fell asleep. Suddenly an angel touched him and said to him, "Get up and eat." He looked, and there at his head was a cake baked on hot stones, and a jar of water. He ate and drank, and lay down again.

—1 KINGS 19:5–6

Mom's Green Bean Casserole

SERVES 12–14

Red peppers and mushrooms add great flavor to this updated casserole. And the topping, toasted in butter on the stovetop, is just superb.

2 (16-ounce) packages frozen cut green beans

2 onions, chopped

6 cloves garlic, minced

2 red bell peppers, chopped

1 (8-ounce) package fresh mushrooms, chopped

1 (16-ounce) jar Alfredo sauce

2 (10-ounce) cans golden cream of mushroom soup

¼ cup butter, melted

1 cup heavy cream

1 teaspoon dried thyme leaves

¼ teaspoon white pepper

¼ cup butter

2 cups soft bread crumbs

1 cup crumbled canned French-fried onions

1. In 5-quart slow cooker, combine green beans, onions, garlic, bell peppers, and mushrooms; mix well.
2. In large bowl, combine Alfredo sauce, soup, melted butter, heavy cream, thyme, and pepper; mix well. Pour into slow cooker.
3. Cover and cook on high for 4–5 hours or until mixture is bubbling.
4. In large saucepan, melt ¼ cup butter. Add bread crumbs and crumbled onions; cook and stir until toasted and golden brown.
5. Uncover slow cooker and turn heat to high. Sprinkle with bread crumb mixture and cook for 30 minutes longer.

Wild Rice Pilaf

SERVES 8–10

Wild rice cooks to perfection in the slow cooker. You could add another container of Alfredo sauce if you think the dish needs it. Pilafs should be rather firm, not soupy.

2½ cups wild rice

1 onion, finely chopped

1 cup orange juice

4 cups vegetable broth

1 teaspoon salt

¼ teaspoon white pepper

1 (10-ounce) container refrigerated Alfredo sauce

⅓ cup chopped parsley

1 teaspoon grated orange rind

1 cup chopped pecans

1. Combine all ingredients except Alfredo sauce, parsley, orange rind, and pecans in 3-quart slow cooker. Cover and cook on low for 5–7 hours or until rice is almost tender.
2. Stir in Alfredo sauce, parsley, and orange rind. Cover and cook on high for 1 hour, then stir and add pecans. Cover, turn off heat, and let stand for 10 minutes. Stir again and serve.

For why should my liberty be subject to the judgment of someone else's conscience?

—1 CORINTHIANS 10:29

Carol Sue's Broccoli and Carrots

SERVES 10–12

Broccoli and carrots are cooked to perfection in a cheese sauce, and topped with butter-toasted bread crumbs.

1 (16-ounce) package frozen chopped broccoli

1 (13-ounce) package frozen broccoli florets

1 (16-ounce) package frozen sliced carrots

1 tablespoon olive oil

1 tablespoon butter

1 onion, chopped

4 cloves garlic, minced

2 (16-ounce) jars four-cheese Alfredo sauce

½ cup heavy cream

2 cups shredded Swiss cheese

2 tablespoons cornstarch

⅓ cup butter, melted

2 cups soft bread crumbs

½ cup grated Parmesan cheese

1. Spray a 4- to 5-quart slow cooker with nonstick cooking spray. Combine broccoli, broccoli florets, and carrots in slow cooker.
2. In large skillet, heat olive oil and 2 tablespoons butter over medium heat. Add onion and garlic; cook and stir until tender, about 6 minutes. Stir in Alfredo sauce and heavy cream and stir well.
3. Pour onion mixture into slow cooker. Cover and cook on high for 3–4 hours or until vegetables are hot and tender.
4. Toss cheese with cornstarch and stir into slow cooker. Cover and cook on high for 20 minutes.
5. In large skillet, melt ⅓ cup butter over medium heat. Add bread crumbs; cook and stir until toasted, about 6–8 minutes. Stir in Parmesan cheese and sprinkle over mixture in slow cooker. Serve.

Orange Cauliflower

SERVES 10–12

Orange adds a nice spark to cauliflower, especially when it is used in three forms! This is a good side dish to serve with a ham or pork chop dinner.

4 heads cauliflower

½ cup orange juice

1 cup orange marmalade

1 tablespoon chopped fresh tarragon leaves

1 teaspoon salt

⅛ teaspoon white pepper

1 tablespoon grated orange zest

1. Remove florets from cauliflower, trimming ends. Discard stems and center of cauliflower.
2. Place cauliflower in 5- to 6-quart slow cooker. In small bowl, combine remaining ingredients. Pour over cauliflower in slow cooker.
3. Cover and cook on low for 5–6 hours, or until cauliflower is tender when pierced with a knife, stirring once during cooking time.

He brought me to the banqueting house, and his intention toward me was love.

—SONG OF SOLOMON 2:4

Creamy Spicy Carrots

SERVES 10–12

This simple dish can be kept in the slow cooker on low or warm for 2 hours after it's finished. This is perfect for a buffet lunch before Christmas caroling.

3 (16-ounce) bags baby carrots
2 onions, chopped
2 cups vegetable broth
1 teaspoon salt
¼ teaspoon pepper
1 tablespoon curry powder
½ cup heavy cream
3 tablespoons butter

1. In 4-quart slow cooker, combine carrots, onions, broth, salt, pepper, and curry powder. Cover and cook on low for 5–7 hours or until carrots are tender.
2. Uncover and add cream and butter. Turn off slow cooker; using a potato masher or immersion blender, mash the carrots until smooth. Cover and cook on low for 1 hour longer until hot. Serve immediately.

May God give you the dew of heaven, and of the fatness of the earth, and plenty of grain and wine.

—GENESIS 27:28

Potato Salad

SERVES 10–12

Cook your potatoes so easily in the slow cooker. They turn out tender and moist, with practically no effort on your part, perfect for potato salad.

5 pounds russet potatoes
2 onions, chopped
6 cloves garlic, minced
1½ teaspoons salt
¼ teaspoon white pepper
1 cup water
1½ cups mayonnaise
1 cup whipped salad dressing
½ cup plain yogurt
⅓ cup yellow mustard
2 tablespoons Dijon mustard
⅓ cup whole milk
1 cup chopped green onions, green and white parts
1 cup thinly sliced radishes

1. Peel potatoes and cut into cubes. Combine in 5- to 6-quart slow cooker with onions and garlic. Sprinkle with salt and pepper, then pour water over.
2. Cover and cook on low for 8–9 hours or until potatoes are tender. Drain potato mixture.
3. In large bowl, combine remaining ingredients and mix well. Add hot potato mixture and stir gently to coat. Cover and chill for 4–5 hours until cold. Stir gently before serving.

Tater Tot Casserole

SERVES 12–14

This delicious recipe uses Tater Tots to make a rich and creamy side dish. Serve this with fried chicken, some cooked carrots, and a gelatin salad.

2 (16-ounce) bags frozen Tater Tots, thawed
2 (16-ounce) jars four-cheese Alfredo sauce
1 (12-ounce) can evaporated milk
⅓ cup chopped fresh chives
¼ teaspoon white pepper
3 cups shredded Cheddar cheese
½ cup grated Romano cheese
1 teaspoon paprika

1. In 5-quart slow cooker, combine all ingredients except Romano cheese and paprika; mix well. Sprinkle with Romano cheese and paprika.
2. Cover and cook on low for 5–7 hours, stirring twice during cooking time, until mixture is hot and potatoes are tender. Serve immediately.

For by grace are you saved through faith, and that not of yourselves; it is the gift of God, not of works, lest anyone should boast.

—EPHESIANS 2:8

Grandma's Peas and Carrots

SERVES 12

Carrots take a long time to cook in the slow cooker, while peas just a brief period, mainly to heat through. They both turn out perfectly in this simple recipe.

10 carrots, sliced
2 onions, chopped
4 cloves garlic, minced
1 cup vegetable broth
⅓ cup butter
2 tablespoons honey
1 teaspoon salt
¼ teaspoon white pepper
1 teaspoon dried marjoram leaves
4 cups frozen baby peas

1. In 4- to 5-quart slow cooker, combine all ingredients except peas and mix well. Cover and cook on low heat for 7–8 hours or until carrots are tender.
2. Stir gently and turn heat to high. Add frozen peas and stir again. Cover and cook on high for 15–25 minutes or until peas are hot and tender. Serve immediately.

Squash and Apple Bake

SERVES 10–12

This delicious side dish is perfect for the holidays, or anytime you want to serve a ham or turkey. Peel the squash using a sharp knife, then scrape out the seeds with a spoon. Save the seeds to roast for snacks, if you'd like.

1 (3-pound) butternut squash
1 (2-pound) acorn squash
4 Granny Smith apples, peeled, cored, and cubed
2 onions, chopped
6 cloves garlic, minced
¼ cup butter
½ cup brown sugar
2 teaspoons salt
¼ teaspoon white pepper
1 teaspoon dried tarragon leaves
⅓ cup apple cider vinegar
½ cup water

1. Peel, seed, and cube both types of squash. Combine with apples, onions, and garlic in 5-quart slow cooker.
2. In small saucepan, melt butter over medium heat. Add sugar, salt, pepper, and tarragon; remove from heat. Stir in vinegar and water until blended.

3. Pour this mixture into slow cooker. Cover and cook on low for 7–9 hours or until squash is tender when pierced with a fork. Using a potato masher, partially mash the ingredients, then stir to combine.

Then Levi gave a great banquet for him in his house; and there was a large crowd of tax collectors and others sitting at the table with them. The Pharisees and their scribes were complaining to his disciples, saying "Why do you eat and drink with tax collectors and sinners?" Jesus answered, "Those who are well have no need of a physician, but those who are sick do; I have come to call not the righteous, but sinners to repentance."

—LUKE 5:29

Sandwiches

*Y*es, you can make sandwiches in the slow cooker. It's the perfect place to cook tender fillings that you can use with everything from tortillas to hoagie buns to popovers. You can also transform classic sandwich recipes into stratas and casseroles that are perfectly suited to this appliance.

Sandwiches are ideal for youth gatherings and for casual potlucks. You'll create an air of community when you involve the congregation in meal preparation. And having parishioners make their own sandwiches makes the whole event easier on you!

It's easy to prepare a few different fillings in several slow cookers, then just put out different types of rolls and buns, along with toppings such as shredded cheese, sliced tomatoes, lettuces, mustard, mayonnaise, ketchup, pickle relish, and various vegetables, and let everybody make their own sandwiches.

By using the broiler in the oven, you can easily toast or brown bread slices, English muffins, or cut sandwich buns to use with these fillings. Toasting the bread will help give the sandwich more texture and character.

Also think about using leftover meats from any of the previous chapters to make your own favorite sandwiches or sandwich fillings. Even a rice pilaf or leftover vegetables can be combined with some cheeses and condiments to make a delicious wrap with lettuce leaves or colored flour tortillas.

Alice's Crunchy Apricot Ham Wraps

SERVES 10–12

This recipe is ideal for a Ladies' Guild luncheon. Place a pretty slow cooker on the table, along with a selection of homemade rolls and some lettuce leaves for those on a low-carb diet.

3 pounds fully cooked ham, cubed
1 (10-ounce) jar apricot preserves
2 onions, chopped
3 cloves garlic, minced
1 cup chopped dried apricots
2 tablespoons prepared mustard
2 green bell peppers, chopped
1 cup sour cream
2 tablespoons cornstarch
1 cup chopped pistachios

1. In 5-quart slow cooker, combine ham, preserves, onions, garlic, apricots, and mustard; mix well. Cover and cook on low for 8 hours.
2. Add bell peppers to slow cooker. Cover and cook on low for 1 hour. In small bowl, combine sour cream and cornstarch. Stir into ham mixture. Cover and cook on low for 30 minutes.
3. Stir mixture and add pistachios. Serve in homemade buns, tortillas, and lettuce wraps.

In response to his people the Lord said: I am sending you grain, wine, and oil, and you will be satisfied.

—JOEL 2:19

Christine's Best BBQ Sandwiches

SERVES 12

Combining beef and pork makes a rich and savory sandwich filling. Use tortillas to make wrap sandwiches.

1 (3-pound) boneless beef chuck roast
1 (1½-pound) boneless pork loin roast
2 onions, chopped
6 stalks celery with leaves, chopped
½ cup barbecue sauce
½ cup chili sauce
½ cup ketchup
¼ cup brown sugar
2 tablespoons apple cider vinegar
12–16 onion buns, split and toasted

1. Cut beef and pork into 2" cubes. Place onions and celery in bottom of 5- to 6-quart slow cooker and top with meat. In bowl combine remaining ingredients except onion buns; stir well. Pour into slow cooker. Cover and cook on low for 8–9 hours or until meat is very tender. Stir well, using a fork if necessary, to help break up meat.
2. To serve, spoon some barbecue on the onion buns, making sandwiches.

So faith by itself, if it has no works, is dead. But someone will say, "You have faith and I have works." Show me your faith apart from your works, and I by my works will show you my faith.

—JAMES 2:18

Sloppy Joe in the Round

SERVES 16

You do have to bake the bread for this fun sandwich, but that only takes a few minutes. The filling is rich and flavorful, just right for a picnic. You can serve this filling in plain hamburger buns too.

4 pounds 90% lean ground beef

4 onions, chopped

6 cloves garlic, minced

3 carrots, chopped

1 (8-ounce) can tomato sauce

1 (6-ounce) can tomato paste

¼ cup tomato juice

1 tablespoon chili powder

¼ cup Worcestershire sauce

2 tablespoons cornmeal

4 (11-ounce) cans refrigerated French bread dough

2 tablespoons olive oil

1 teaspoon dried thyme leaves

1. In large skillet, cook ground beef until browned, stirring to break up meat. Drain thoroughly, but do not wipe out skillet. In a 6-quart slow cooker, combine cooked beef with onions, garlic, and carrots; mix well.

2. In skillet that you used for the beef, combine tomato sauce, paste, juice, chili powder, and Worcestershire sauce. Bring to a simmer over medium heat, stirring until a sauce forms. Pour into slow cooker.

3. Cover and cook on low for 8–9 hours. Meanwhile, preheat oven to 350°F. Grease two large cookie sheets and sprinkle with cornmeal. Open dough; do not unroll. Place the four rolls on work surface, seam side down.

4. Form two large rings with the dough by attaching the ends of two rolls together; pinch the ends thoroughly to seal. Place on prepared cookie sheets. Cut ¼" slashes diagonally across the top of the dough rings. Drizzle with oil and sprinkle with thyme. Bake for 25–35 minutes, rearranging cookie sheets in oven once, until loaves are golden brown.

5. Remove loaves from cookie sheet and cool on wire rack. Then store, covered, at room temperature. When ready to eat, cut each loaf in half crosswise to make two rings. Spoon the ground beef mixture onto bottom half of loaf and top with the other half. Cut into wedges to serve.

May God give you the dew of heaven, and of the fatness of the earth, and plenty of grain and wine.

—GENESIS 27:28

Pulled Pork Sandwiches

SERVES 12
Pulled Pork from Pulled Pork Burritos (page 119) combines with flavorful coleslaw in these fabulous sandwiches.

6 cups Pulled Pork (page 119)
2 cups shredded cabbage
1 cup shredded carrots
½ cup chopped green onions, green and white part
½ cup mayonnaise
2 tablespoons yellow mustard
1 teaspoon celery seed
12 onion rolls, cut in half
¼ cup butter

1. Shred and moisten the Pulled Pork with cooking liquid according to recipe directions.
2. In large bowl, combine cabbage, carrots, green onions, mayonnaise, mustard, and celery seed; mix well.
3. Spread cut sides of rolls with butter and place, cut side up, on broiler pan. Broil until golden brown.
4. Make sandwiches with the Pulled Pork and the cabbage mixture. Serve immediately.

BBQ Chicken Sandwiches

SERVES 12–14
Chicken thighs cook perfectly in the slow cooker while staying moist and tender. These flavorful sandwiches are delicious served with potato salad and apple wedges.

4 pounds boneless, skinless chicken thighs
1 teaspoon celery salt
1 teaspoon seasoned salt
½ teaspoon pepper
2 onions, chopped
6 cloves garlic, minced
1 (18-ounce) bottle barbecue sauce
1 (6-ounce) can tomato paste
¼ cup honey
1 teaspoon dried Italian seasoning
12–14 sandwich rolls

1. Sprinkle chicken with celery salt, seasoned salt, and pepper. Place onions in bottom of 5- to 6-quart slow cooker and top with chicken and garlic.
2. In medium bowl, combine barbecue sauce, tomato paste, honey, and Italian seasoning; mix well. Pour over chicken.
3. Cover and cook on low for 8–9 hours or until chicken is cooked. Using two large forks, shred chicken in the sauce. Serve on split and toasted sandwich rolls.

Beef and Bean Wraps

SERVES 10–12

These are burritos made in the slow cooker. The refried beans add a rich flavor and smooth texture to this hearty filling. If the filling isn't thick enough at the end of cooking time, thicken with cornstarch as directed.

2 pounds ground beef

2 onions, chopped

5 cloves garlic, minced

1 (15-ounce) can refried beans

1 (15-ounce) can kidney beans, drained

2 (10-ounce) cans enchilada sauce

1 (4-ounce) can chopped green chiles, drained

1 tablespoon chili powder

1 teaspoon cumin

1 teaspoon salt

⅛ teaspoon pepper

12–14 (6-inch) corn tortillas

2 cups shredded Cheddar cheese

1 cup sour cream

2 cups chopped tomatoes

2 cups shredded lettuce

1. In large skillet, cook ground beef with onions and garlic over medium heat, stirring to break up beef, until beef is thoroughly cooked.
2. Combine beef mixture with refried beans, kidney beans, enchilada sauce, green chiles, chili powder, cumin, salt, and pepper in 4-quart slow cooker; mix well.
3. Cover and cook on low for 8–9 hours until mixture is hot and blended. If necessary, thicken with a mixture of 2 tablespoons cornstarch and ¼ cup water.
4. Serve mixture with tortillas, cheese, sour cream, tomatoes, and lettuce, and let people make their own wraps.

Veggie Submarine Sandwich

SERVES 14–16

Vegetables cook to tender perfection in the slow cooker to save you time and energy. Then make a buffet and let everybody create their own masterpiece!

2 onions, chopped

3 red bell peppers, sliced

2 zucchini, sliced

3 yellow summer squash, sliced

1 pound fresh green beans, trimmed

2 (8-ounce) packages sliced mushrooms

5 cloves garlic, minced

1½ teaspoons salt

¼ teaspoon white pepper

1 cup water

½ cup mustard

⅓ cup honey

1 cup mayonnaise

14–16 hoagie buns, split

2–3 cups shredded Cheddar cheese

1. Combine all vegetables in 5- to 6-quart slow cooker. Sprinkle with salt and pepper; toss. Pour water into slow cooker. Cover and cook on low for 5–7 hours or until vegetables are tender.
2. Drain vegetables and place in large bowl. In medium bowl, combine mustard, honey, and mayonnaise; mix well.
3. Lay out the split buns, cheese, mayonnaise mixture, and vegetables. Let people make their own sandwiches.

Flaky Tex-Mex Braid

SERVES 18–20

If you have a couple of events on the weekend, or around the holidays, plan on serving Tender Pot Roast one day, and make these sandwiches the next!

3 cups shredded leftover Tender Pot Roast (page 64)

3 (4-ounce) cans chopped green chiles, drained

3 red bell peppers, chopped

4 (8-ounce) cans refrigerated crescent rolls

1 (15-ounce) can refried beans

3 cups shredded pepper jack cheese

1. In large bowl, combine Pot Roast with drained chiles and red bell peppers; mix well.
2. On work surface, unroll crescent roll dough. Divide into eight 14" × 9" rectangles. Spread a 12" × 3" rectangle of refried beans on each dough rectangle. Divide beef mixture on top of beans and sprinkle with cheese.
3. Using a sharp knife, make cuts 1" apart on the 14" sides of the dough almost to the filling. Cross the strips alternately over the filling, pressing gently to seal, to create a braided appearance.
4. You can refrigerate the sandwiches, unbaked, for up to 2 hours at this point. To bake, preheat oven to 350°F. Bake the sandwiches for 30–35 minutes or until crust is deep golden brown. Cut into slices to serve.

Turkey Enchilada Sandwiches

SERVES 16–18

You can use this filling to make enchiladas, too. Just roll up flour or corn tortillas with the filling and some cheese, place in a greased baking dish, top with more cheese, and bake until hot.

2 onions, chopped

6 cloves garlic, minced

3 jalapeño peppers, minced

2 (10-ounce) cans enchilada sauce

3 (15-ounce) cans black beans, drained

1 (16-ounce) jar salsa

1 teaspoon cumin

¼ teaspoon cayenne pepper

2 (2-pound) turkey tenderloins

1 (8-ounce) package cream cheese, cubed

16–18 (8-inch) flour tortillas

3 cups shredded CoJack cheese

4 cups shredded lettuce

2 cups chopped tomatoes

1. In 5-quart slow cooker, combine the onions, garlic, jalapeño peppers, enchilada sauce, black beans, salsa, cumin, and cayenne pepper. Mix well and place the turkey on top.
2. Cover and cook on low for 8–9 hours or until turkey is thoroughly cooked. Remove turkey from slow cooker and, using two forks, shred it. Stir back into slow cooker along with cream cheese.
3. Uncover and cook on high for 20–30 minutes or until mixture is thickened. Serve with tortillas and remaining ingredients to make wrap sandwiches.

Grandmother's Best Chicken Salad Sandwiches

SERVES 16–20

You could serve this salad on split and toasted English muffins, in pita breads, or with lettuce to make low-carb wraps.

8 Poached Chicken Breasts (page 208), cubed
3 cups seedless red grapes, cut in half
6 stalks celery, chopped
1 cup golden raisins
1 cup dark raisins
1 cup broken pecans
1 cup mayonnaise
1 cup vanilla yogurt
1 teaspoon salt
¼ teaspoon white pepper
1 teaspoon paprika
½ cup heavy whipping cream
32 slices raisin bread, toasted, or other breads

1. In large bowl, combine cubed poached chicken breasts, grapes, celery, golden and dark raisins, and pecans; toss gently.
2. In bowl, combine mayonnaise, yogurt, salt, pepper, and paprika. In small bowl, beat cream until stiff peaks form. Fold into mayonnaise mixture.
3. Fold mayonnaise mixture into chicken mixture. Cover and chill for 1–2 hours. Use to make sandwiches with toasted raisin bread, other breads, or sandwich buns.

Thai Chicken Wraps

SERVES 18

Use the preshredded carrots you can find in the produce aisle of your supermarket to make these flavorful wrap sandwiches.

3 pounds ground chicken
2 onions, chopped
6 cloves garlic, minced
2 tablespoons minced fresh gingerroot
1 cup chicken broth
2 tablespoons Worcestershire sauce
2 tablespoons soy sauce
⅔ cup peanut butter
1 tablespoon sugar
¼ teaspoon pepper
3 tablespoons cornstarch
⅓ cup lime juice
3 cups shredded carrots
1½ cups chopped cashews
24–30 large lettuce leaves

1. In large skillet, cook chicken in two batches until almost done, stirring to break up meat. Drain chicken and place in 4-quart slow cooker.
2. Add onions, garlic, gingerroot, chicken broth, Worcestershire sauce, soy sauce, peanut butter, sugar, and pepper; stir.
3. Cover and cook on low for 4–5 hours or until chicken is thoroughly cooked and mixture is hot and blended. In small bowl, combine cornstarch and lime juice and mix well. Stir into slow cooker.
4. Cover and cook on high for 20–25 minutes or until mixture thickens. To serve, set out filling, shredded carrots, chopped cashews, and lettuce leaves to use for wraps.

Mu Shu Turkey Wraps

SERVES 14

Mu Shu Pork is traditionally served in pancakes with hoisin sauce. This updated version substitutes turkey and flour tortillas, and is delicious.

2 (2-pound) turkey tenderloins, cubed
2 onions, chopped
2 red bell peppers, chopped
2 (8-ounce) packages sliced fresh mushrooms
2 (4-ounce) cans bamboo shoots, drained
½ cup hoisin sauce
¼ cup soy sauce
¼ teaspoon pepper
1 cup chopped green onions
4 cups hot cooked rice
2 teaspoons sesame oil
14 flour tortillas or lettuce leaves

1. In 5-quart slow cooker, combine all ingredients except green onions, rice, sesame oil, and tortillas or lettuce leaves. Cover and cook on low for 8–9 hours or until turkey is thoroughly cooked and vegetables are tender.
2. Stir in green onions and turn slow cooker to high. Cover and cook on low for 20–30 minutes until hot; drain and return to slow cooker.
3. Stir in sesame oil, then set out tortillas and/or lettuce leaves and offer the filling to add and roll up.

Roast Beef Wraps

SERVES 12–14

You can combine lots of leftover slow cooker recipes to make wrap sandwiches. Just use your imagination and what you have on hand!

1 (12-ounce) tub soft cream cheese
1 cup sour cream
6 cups shredded leftover Roast Beef (page 66)
½ cup thinly sliced green onions
2 cups leftover Wild Rice Pilaf (page 206)
12 (10-inch) flour tortillas
2 cups shredded Swiss cheese

1. In large bowl, beat cream cheese with sour cream. Stir in beef, green onions, and pilaf.
2. Place tortillas on work surface. Spread with the beef mixture and sprinkle with cheese. Roll up tortilla, fold in ends, and roll to enclose filling. Cut in half diagonally and serve.

And God is able to provide you with every blessing in abundance, so that by always having enough of everything, you may share abundantly in every good work. As it is written, "He scatters abroad, he gives to the poor; his righteousness endures forever."

—2 CORINTHIANS 9:8–9

Monte Cristo Sandwich Strata

SERVES 12–14

Monte Cristo sandwiches are layered chicken and ham sandwiches that traditionally are deep-fried. This method, using two slow cookers, makes a bunch and is much easier.

1 (1-pound) loaf sourdough bread, cubed

3 cups chopped cooked chicken

2 cups shredded Havarti cheese

2 cups shredded Swiss cheese

2 cups chopped cooked ham

12 eggs

2 cups whole milk

1 cup heavy cream

1 teaspoon salt

¼ teaspoon pepper

1 teaspoon dried oregano leaves

⅓ cup cider vinegar

⅔ cup currant jelly

⅓ cup water

2 tablespoons honey

½ teaspoon paprika

2 tablespoons butter

½ cup powdered sugar

1 cup crisp rice cereal crumbs

1. Spray a 6-quart slow cooker with nonstick cooking spray. Layer cubed bread, chicken, cheeses, and ham in slow cooker.

2. In large bowl, combine eggs, milk, cream, salt, pepper, and oregano; beat well. Pour into slow cooker. Let mixture stand for 20 minutes, pushing bread back down into the egg mixture as necessary. Cover and cook on low for 4–5 hours or until egg mixture is set.

3. In 2-cup slow cooker, combine vinegar, jelly, water, honey, paprika, and butter. Cover and cook on low for 2–3 hours, stirring twice during cooking time, until sauce is blended and slightly thickened.

4. To serve strata, scoop out of slow cooker and drizzle with currant jelly sauce. Sprinkle with powdered sugar and cereal crumbs, and serve immediately.

The one who sows sparingly will also reap sparingly, and the one who sows bountifully will reap bountifully. Each of you must give as you have made up your mind, not reluctantly or under compulsion, for God loves a cheerful giver.

—2 CORINTHIANS 8:6–7

Ham and Veggie Wraps

SERVES 18–20

You can add just about any vegetable to this hearty wrap sandwich. Think about using different colors and flavors of tortillas to add interest to the spread.

2 onions, chopped
5 carrots, sliced
4 potatoes, peeled and cubed
1 teaspoon dried basil leaves
2 cups chicken broth
2 green bell peppers, chopped
4 cups cubed cooked ham
1½ cups mayonnaise
3 cups shredded Cheddar cheese
18–20 flour tortillas

1. Place onions, carrots, potatoes, basil, and chicken broth in 5-quart slow cooker. Cover and cook on low for 6 hours or until vegetables are almost tender.
2. Add bell peppers and ham to slow cooker. Cover and cook on low for 2–3 hours longer or until ham is hot and bell peppers are crisp-tender.
3. Drain mixture and place in large bowl. Add mayonnaise and cheese, and mix well. Make wraps with flour tortillas; serve immediately.

I do not judge anyone who hears my words and does not keep them, for I came not to judge the world, but to save the world.

—JOHN 12:47

Meatloaf Sandwiches

SERVES 16–18

You could substitute two pounds of frozen precooked meatballs for the meatloaf if you'd like. But this is an excellent way to use up any kind of leftover meatloaf.

1 recipe Mom's Meatloaf (page 68), cubed
1 (26-ounce) jar spaghetti sauce
1 (6-ounce) can tomato paste
1 (15-ounce) can tomato sauce
1 teaspoon dried oregano leaves
1 teaspoon dried Italian seasoning
3 cups cubed mozzarella cheese
16–18 hoagie buns, split and toasted
16–18 slices American cheese

1. In 4-quart slow cooker, combine cubed meatloaf and remaining ingredients except for mozzarella cheese, hoagie buns, and American cheese.
2. Cover and cook on high for 2–3 hours or until mixture is hot, stirring once during cooking time. Stir in mozzarella cheese.
3. Place American cheese on bottom half of each toasted hoagie bun. Top with some of the meatloaf mixture, then the bun tops. Serve immediately.

The Lord sits enthroned over the flood, the Lord is enthroned as King forever. The Lord gives strength to his people; the Lord blesses his people with peace.

—PSALMS 29:10–11

Cranberry Turkey Sandwiches

SERVES 10–12

All of the flavors of Thanksgiving are contained in this easy-to-make sandwich. And the cream cheese spread is the perfect finishing touch.

2 onions, chopped
6 cloves garlic, minced
1 envelope onion soup mix
2 (2-pound) turkey tenderloins, cubed
1 teaspoon salt
1/8 teaspoon pepper
1 teaspoon dried sage leaves
1 (16-ounce) can whole berry cranberry sauce
1/2 cup chicken broth
1/3 cup butter, softened
10–12 hoagie buns, split
1 (12-ounce) container soft cream cheese

1. Place onions, garlic, and onion soup mix in bottom of 4- to 5-quart slow cooker. Sprinkle turkey with salt, pepper, and sage, and place in slow cooker. In medium bowl combine cranberry sauce with chicken broth; mix well. Pour into slow cooker.
2. Cover and cook on low for 6–8 hours or until turkey is thoroughly cooked.
3. Spread butter on split hoagie buns and toast in the oven under the broiler. Spread cut sides with cream cheese, and make sandwiches with the turkey mixture. Serve immediately.

Shredded Beef Tacos

SERVES 20–24

Use a mild salsa for children, and a spicy hot one for adults. This can be part of a taco buffet. For toppings, set out shredded lettuce, guacamole, fresh chopped tomatoes, salsa, cilantro, and shredded cheese.

4 pounds beef sirloin tip, cubed
3 onions, chopped
8 cloves garlic, minced
1 (10-ounce) can condensed tomato soup
1 (16-ounce) jar salsa
1/3 cup apple cider vinegar
1 (16-ounce) can tomato paste
2 (4-ounce) cans chopped green chiles, drained
24 taco shells

1. Combine beef, onions, and garlic in 6- to 7-quart slow cooker. In large bowl, combine soup, salsa, vinegar, tomato paste, and chiles; mix well. Pour into slow cooker.
2. Cover and cook on low for 7–8 hours or until beef is tender. Stir vigorously to break up meat.
3. Heat taco shells as directed on package. Serve beef mixture in taco shells and offer the lettuce, guacamole, etc. as toppings.

I have no silver or gold, but what I have I give to you.

—ACTS 3:6

Greek Pita Turkey Sandwiches

SERVES 24–30

Greek flavors include lemon, feta, yogurt, oregano, and olives. This easy sandwich is simple to make and fun, too.

1 pound spicy bulk turkey sausage

2 onions, chopped

6 cloves garlic, minced

¼ cup flour

2 cups chicken or turkey broth

3 pounds turkey tenderloins, cubed

1½ teaspoons salt

½ teaspoon lemon pepper

1 teaspoon dried oregano leaves

2 cups plain yogurt

1 cup grated Parmesan cheese

3 cucumbers, peeled, seeded, and chopped

1 teaspoon dried oregano leaves

2 tablespoons lemon juice

1 cup sliced black olives

1 cup crumbled feta cheese

24 whole wheat pita breads

1. In large skillet, brown sausage with onions and garlic over medium heat, stirring to break up meat. When done, sprinkle with flour; cook and stir for 1 minute.

2. Add chicken or turkey broth; cook and stir to loosen pan drippings. Bring to a boil.

3. Pour into 4- or 5-quart slow cooker. Sprinkle turkey with salt, lemon pepper, and 1 teaspoon oregano; add to slow cooker. Cover and cook on low for 6–7 hours or until turkey is thoroughly cooked.

4. Meanwhile, combine remaining ingredients except pita breads in large bowl; cover and refrigerate.

5. When turkey is done, use a slotted spoon to remove the mixture from the slow cooker. Make sandwiches with the pita breads and the yogurt filling; serve immediately.

For when the time comes to eat, each of you goes ahead with your own supper, and one goes hungry and another becomes drunk. What! Do you not have homes to eat and drink in? Or do you show contempt for the church of God and humiliate those who have nothing? What should I say to you? Should I commend you? In this matter I do not commend you!

—1 CORINTHIANS 11:21–22

Canadian Bacon Pitas

SERVES 18–20

Pineapple and green bell peppers combine with Canadian bacon to make a hearty and flavorful sandwich that's a bit like Hawaiian pizza.

3 onions, chopped
1 (20-ounce) can pineapple tidbits in juice, undrained
1 (16-ounce) can crushed pineapple in juice, undrained
6 carrots, sliced
2 green bell peppers, chopped
4 (4-ounce) packages sliced Canadian bacon, chopped
¼ cup cornstarch
½ cup chicken broth
20–24 pita breads
1 head butter lettuce
1 head green lettuce

1. Combine onions, both kinds of pineapple, and carrots in 5-quart slow cooker. Cover and cook on low for 6–7 hours or until carrots are tender. Stir in green bell peppers and Canadian bacon.
2. In small bowl, combine cornstarch with chicken broth; mix well. Stir into slow cooker. Cover and cook on high for 20–25 minutes or until sauce thickens.
3. Cut pita breads in half and gently open. Line with lettuce leaves and spoon Canadian bacon mixture into each bread. Serve immediately.

Sloppy Janes

SERVES 12

What do you call a Sloppy Joe filling made from turkey? Sloppy Janes, of course! Serve a choice of beef or turkey fillings for your next youth gathering.

3 pounds ground turkey
3 onions, chopped
4 cloves garlic, minced
3 stalks celery
3 carrots, chopped
1 (8-ounce) can tomato sauce
1 (6-ounce) can tomato paste
½ cup tomato juice
1 teaspoon dried basil leaves
1 teaspoon poultry seasoning
¼ cup white wine Worcestershire sauce
12 slices American cheese
12 hamburger buns, split

1. In skillet, cook turkey until browned, stirring to break up meat. Drain thoroughly, but do not wipe skillet. In a 5-quart slow cooker, combine cooked turkey with onions, garlic, celery, and carrots; mix.
2. In skillet that you used for the turkey, combine tomato sauce, paste, juice, basil, poultry seasoning, and Worcestershire sauce. Bring to a simmer over medium heat, stirring until a sauce forms. Pour into slow cooker.
3. Cover and cook on low for 8 hours. Place one slice American cheese on each split hamburger bun, and make sandwiches with the turkey filling.

Desserts

Ah, dessert. Many people feel that no meal is complete without it. I myself have a great sweet tooth, and have fond memories of many bake sales at church in which I both prepared offerings and was a consumer.

At any church gathering, dessert is mandatory, whether as simple cookies or candy or an elaborate cake or pudding. And yes, you can make dessert in the slow cooker. Cakes turn out moist and tender, pudding is creamy and sweet, and the gentle heat is perfect for melting chocolate for candies.

You may need to use an insert or cake or bread pan for some of these recipes. There are special molds and pans you can buy that are made for the slow cooker, but many recipes will work just fine in ordinary pans and molds. Just be sure to fill the pan about half full, and be sure that there is a small space between the pan and the slow cooker sides so heat can circulate.

Fondue is a natural for the slow cooker. The appliance should be used as the serving container as well; it will keep the mixture at the correct temperature. As with appetizers, think about crisp, cool, and crunchy accompaniments to these recipes. For fondue, crisp cookies, cool fruit, and tender cake make great dippers. Serve warm cakes with ice cream, warm puddings with whipped topping, and poached fruits with cakes and crushed nuts.

Black and White and Red Fondue

SERVES 12–14

Fondue is such a wonderful communal dessert. Strawberries are the best choice for dipping into this creamy and sweet mixture.

2 (14-ounce) cans sweetened condensed milk

3 (12-ounce) packages semisweet chocolate chips

4 (1-ounce) squares unsweetened baking chocolate, chopped

⅓ cup unsweetened cocoa powder

¼ cup honey

2 teaspoons vanilla

2 (12-ounce) packages white chocolate chips

2 (8-ounce) bars white chocolate with almonds, chopped

60 strawberries

Long wooden skewers

Mini marshmallows

1. In 4-quart slow cooker, combine condensed milk, semisweet chocolate, baking chocolate, cocoa, and honey; mix well. Cover and cook on low for 1–2 hours or until chocolate is melted and mixture is smooth. Stir well and add vanilla.
2. Add white chocolate chips and the chopped candy bars. Stir just to combine, then cook on low for 10 minutes. Do not stir; serve immediately with skewered strawberries.
3. To serve a crowd, choose large strawberries. Wash and hull berries; then place one strawberry on each long wooden skewer and hold in place with a mini marshmallow. Everyone can dip to their heart's content, but only use each skewer once!

Chocolate-Caramel Fondue

SERVES 8

Serve this dip with cookies, pieces of pound and angel food cake, and fresh fruits such as strawberries, pineapple, and apple slices.

1 (12-ounce) package semisweet chocolate chips

1 (12-ounce) package milk chocolate chips

1 (8-ounce) bittersweet chocolate bar, chopped

1 (14-ounce) can sweetened condensed milk

1 (13-ounce) can dulce de leche sweetened condensed milk

14 caramels, unwrapped and chopped

1. In 3-quart slow cooker, combine semisweet chocolate chips with milk chocolate chips, chopped chocolate bar, and both kinds of sweetened condensed milk. Stir to combine.
2. Cover and cook on low for 1 to 1½ hours or until chocolate is melted and mixture is smooth. Stir in caramels; cover and cook on low for another 30 minutes to melt caramels. Serve immediately.

For the mountains may depart and the hills be removed, but my steadfast love shall not depart from you, and my covenant of peace shall not be removed, says the Lord, who has compassion on you.

—ISAIAH 54:10

Caramel Chocolate Cake

SERVES 10

A cake baked in the slow cooker! This one has the best combination of textures and flavors. Serve warm with some ice cream on top.

1 (3-ounce) package cream cheese, cubed

½ cup milk

1 cup sour cream

¼ cup unsweetened cocoa powder

1 egg

2 (8.2-ounce) packages chocolate chip muffin mix

2 tablespoons butter

½ cup brown sugar

½ cup caramel ice cream topping

½ cup water

1. In small microwave-safe bowl, combine cream cheese and milk. Microwave on 50% power for 1 minute; remove and stir. Continue microwaving for 30-second intervals until cream cheese melts; stir with wire whisk to blend.
2. Place in large bowl; stir in sour cream, cocoa powder, and egg. Mix well. Add both packages muffin mix and stir just until combined.
3. Spray a 3½-quart slow cooker with nonstick baking spray containing flour. Spread batter evenly in slow cooker.
4. In small saucepan, combine butter, brown sugar, ice cream topping, and water; heat to boiling, stirring until blended. Carefully pour over batter in slow cooker.
5. Cook on high for 2½ to 3 hours or until cake springs back when lightly touched. Uncover, turn off slow cooker, top loosely with foil, and let stand for 30 minutes.
6. Gently run a sharp knife around the edges of the cake and invert over serving plate until cake drops out. If any sauce remains in slow cooker, spoon over cake. Cool for 30–45 minutes before serving.

You prepare a table before me in the presence of my enemies; you anoint my head with oil; my cup overflows.

—PSALMS 23:5

Lisa's Pineapple Upside-Down Cake

SERVES 9

A pineapple upside-down cake is always a treat. This special recipe has a moist, fine-textured cake resting on pineapple rings coated with a sweet brown sugar syrup.

9 canned pineapple rings in juice

¼ cup reserved pineapple juice

2 tablespoons butter, melted

½ cup brown sugar

2 tablespoons corn syrup

½ cup butter

¾ cup brown sugar

1 egg

1½ cups flour

¼ teaspoon salt

½ teaspoon cinnamon

¼ teaspoon ginger

1 teaspoon baking powder

1 teaspoon baking soda

½ cup mascarpone cheese

½ cup reserved pineapple juice

1. Line a 3½ quart slow cooker with a double layer of foil, making sure the foil extends over the top. Spray foil with nonstick baking spray containing flour and set aside. Drain pineapple, reserving juice.

2. In small saucepan, combine ¼ cup reserved juice, 2 tablespoons butter, ½ cup brown sugar, and corn syrup. Cook and stir over low heat until butter melts and mixture is smooth. Pour into the slow cooker and spread evenly. Top with pineapple rings.

3. In large bowl, beat ½ cup butter with ¾ cup brown sugar until fluffy. Add egg, beating well. Sift together flour with salt, cinnamon, ginger, baking powder, and baking soda. Add flour mixture to butter and brown sugar mixture alternately with cheese and ½ cup reserved juice, beginning and ending with dry ingredients.

4. Carefully spoon batter over the pineapple in the slow cooker. Cover and cook on low for 2½ to 3½ hours until cake is brown around edges and springs back lightly when touched.

5. Remove cover and turn off slow cooker; let cake stand for 15 minutes. Using foil, carefully lift out cake. Peel foil away from edges and invert onto serving plate. Peel away foil, let stand for 30 minutes more, and serve.

My child, eat honey, for it is good, and the drippings of the honeycomb are sweet to your taste.

—PROVERBS 24:13

Butterscotch Pears

SERVES 16

This delicious combination can be served alone, with sweetened whipped cream, or as a topping for ice cream or angel food cake.

8 large, firm pears
2 tablespoons lemon juice
½ cup dark brown sugar
⅓ cup butter, softened
¼ cup flour
½ teaspoon cinnamon
¼ teaspoon salt
1 cup chopped pecans
1 cup pear nectar
¼ cup honey

1. Cut pears in half and remove core; do not peel. Brush pears with lemon juice. In medium bowl, combine brown sugar, butter, flour, cinnamon, and salt; mix well. Stir in pecans.
2. Fill the pear halves with the brown sugar mixture, mounding the filling. Place, filling side up, in 3½ to 4-quart slow cooker; layer the pears. In small bowl, combine nectar and honey; stir to blend. Pour around pears.
3. Cover and cook on high for 2–3 hours or until pears are tender. Serve immediately.

Cranberry Pudding Cake

SERVES 12

Cranberries and white chocolate complement each other beautifully in this easy and delicious slow cooker cake.

1 (16-ounce) package pound cake mix
1 (4-ounce) package French vanilla pudding mix
1¾ cups sour cream
3 eggs, beaten
¾ cup vegetable oil
½ cup water
¼ cup cranberry juice
1 cup fresh cranberries, chopped
½ cup dried cranberries, chopped
1 cup white chocolate chips

1. Spray a 4-quart slow cooker with nonstick baking spray containing flour. In large bowl, combine cake mix, pudding mix, sour cream, eggs, oil, water, and cranberry juice. Beat with electric mixer until combined, then scrape sides and beat for 2 minutes longer.
2. Fold in the cranberries, dried cranberries, and white chocolate chips. Pour batter into prepared slow cooker, cover, and cook on low for 6–7 hours or until the cake begins to pull away from sides of pan.
3. To serve, scoop cake out of slow cooker and top with ice cream or whipped cream.

Melba Fudge Pudding Cake

SERVES 8

Melba is a combination of peaches and raspberries. Add a moist fudge pudding cake and you have a spectacular dessert.

2 cups peeled, chopped fresh peaches
1 tablespoon lemon juice
½ cup sugar
½ cup brown sugar
1¼ cups flour
¼ cup unsweetened cocoa
1½ teaspoons baking powder
½ teaspoon baking soda
¼ teaspoon salt
½ cup peach nectar
3 tablespoons butter, melted
½ cup semisweet chocolate chips
¾ cup brown sugar
3 tablespoons unsweetened cocoa
1 cup water
½ cup peach nectar
1 cup fresh raspberries

1. Spray a 3½ quart slow cooker with nonstick baking spray containing flour. Place peaches in bottom of slow cooker; sprinkle with lemon juice.
2. In medium bowl, combine ½ cup sugar, ½ cup brown sugar, flour, ¼ cup cocoa, baking powder, baking soda, and salt; mix with wire whisk to combine.
3. In small bowl, combine ½ cup peach nectar and melted butter; stir to combine. Add to flour mixture and stir just until blended. Stir in chocolate chips and spoon batter over peaches in slow cooker.
4. Sprinkle batter with ¾ cup brown sugar. In microwave-safe glass measuring cup, combine 3 tablespoons cocoa, water, and ½ cup peach nectar; microwave on high for 2–3 minutes until boiling. Pour over batter.
5. Cover and cook on high for 2–3 hours or until toothpick inserted in center of cake comes out clean. Scoop out of slow cooker and turn over each scoop to serve. Top each serving with raspberries.

"Let me bring a little bread, that you may refresh yourselves, and after that you may pass on—since you have come to your servant." So they said, "Do as you have said." And Abraham hastened into the tent to Sarah, and said, "Make ready quickly three measures of choice flour, knead it, and make cakes."

—GENESIS 18:5–6

Caramel Apple Crisp

SERVES 8

Caramels melt together with apples in this delicious recipe, and the topping melts into a candy-like mixture. Serve with sweetened whipped cream or vanilla ice cream. Yum!

¼ cup butter
½ cup chopped pecans
1 cup rolled oats
½ cup brown sugar
1 teaspoon cinnamon
⅛ teaspoon cardamom
½ teaspoon salt
2 cups granola cereal
4 cups cored, peeled apple slices
14 unwrapped caramels, chopped
3 tablespoons flour
¼ cup apple juice

1. Spray a 3-quart slow cooker with nonstick cooking spray and set aside. In large skillet, melt butter. Add pecans and rolled oats; cook and stir until toasted and fragrant. Stir in brown sugar, cinnamon, cardamom, and salt.
2. Add granola cereal; stir and remove from heat. Place apple slices and chopped caramels in prepared slow cooker. Sprinkle with flour and top with apple juice. Top with granola mixture.
3. Cover and cook on low for 6–7 hours or until apples are tender and topping is set. Serve with ice cream or whipped cream.

White Chocolate Cherry Cobbler

SERVES 12

White chocolate is a fabulous contrast to sour pie cherries in this excellent cobbler. It adds sweetness and a great melting texture. This is also delicious with vanilla ice cream or sweetened whipped cream.

2 (15-ounce) cans sour pie cherries
1½ cups sugar
⅓ cup flour
1½ cups reserved cherry juice
¾ cup butter
1½ cups rolled oats
1½ cups brown sugar
½ teaspoon salt
1 teaspoon cinnamon
2¼ cups flour
1 teaspoon baking soda
1 (11.5-ounce) package white chocolate chips

1. Drain cherries, reserving juice. In large saucepan, combine sugar and flour; mix with wire whisk. Add 1½ cups reserved cherry juice and stir. Cook over medium heat until mixture thickens and boils. Stir in cherries and remove from heat.
2. Spray a 4-quart slow cooker with nonstick cooking spray. Place cherry mixture in bottom of slow cooker.
3. In skillet, melt butter over medium heat. Add oats; cook and stir until fragrant and lightly toasted. Remove from heat and add brown sugar, salt, and cinnamon; mix well. Stir in flour and baking soda until crumbly. Stir in white chocolate chips.
4. Sprinkle skillet mixture over cherry mixture in slow cooker. Cover and cook on low for 5–6 hours. Serve immediately with ice cream or whipped cream.

Dried Cherry Bread Pudding

SERVES 10–12

Dried cherries are tart and delicious. It's best to chop them and examine them carefully before stirring into the topping, because they can still contain pits.

9 cups French bread cubes

3 cups dried cherries, chopped

1½ cups chopped pecans

4 eggs, beaten

2 cups heavy cream

2 cups whole milk

1¼ cups sugar

⅓ cup butter, melted

1 tablespoon vanilla

½ teaspoon salt

1 cup caramel ice cream topping

1. Turn oven to 300°F. Place bread cubes on cookie sheet. Toast in the oven for 30 minutes or until dry to the touch. Place in 4-quart slow cooker along with cherries and pecans; mix gently.
2. In large bowl, combine eggs, cream, milk, sugar, butter, vanilla, and salt; beat until combined. Pour into slow cooker. Let stand for 15 minutes, pushing down on bread mixture occasionally so it absorbs the sauce.
3. Cover and cook on high for 1 hour, then reduce heat to low and cook for 5–6 hours longer until pudding is fluffy and set. Spoon into dessert bowls and top with a drizzle of caramel ice cream topping.

Peanut Butter Fondue

SERVES 8–10

If the fondue is too thick, you can stir in more evaporated milk. This can also be served as a sauce over ice cream or pudding.

2 cups peanut butter

1 (14-ounce) can sweetened condensed milk

1 (13-ounce) can evaporated milk

1 (11-ounce) package peanut butter flavored chips

⅓ cup butter

Sliced bananas

Sliced cored apples

Marshmallows

1 cup chopped peanuts

1. In 3-quart slow cooker, combine peanut butter, both kinds of milk, chips, and butter; mix well. Cover and cook on low for 3–4 hours or until mixture is smooth, stirring once during cooking time.
2. Arrange dippers on a platter around the fondue, and provide forks, skewers, or toothpicks. Dip fruits into the fondue and roll into peanuts. Remind people to use each fork or skewer only once.

Every generous act of giving, with every perfect gift, is from above, coming down from the Father of lights, with whom there is no variation or shadow due to change.

—JAMES 1:17

Carol's Chocolate Marshmallow Dip

SERVES 12–14

Sweetened condensed milk is the creamy basis for this velvety dip. Use your imagination when choosing dippers. This is a great way to use up leftover angel food cake or plain cookies.

2 (14-ounce) cans sweetened condensed milk

1 (12-ounce) package semisweet chocolate chips

1 (11-ounce) package milk chocolate chips

2 (1-ounce) squares unsweetened baking chocolate, chopped

1 (7-ounce) jar marshmallow crème

2 cups miniature marshmallows

Sugar cookies, graham crackers, gingersnaps, angel food cake

1. In 3-quart slow cooker, combine milk, both kinds of chocolate chips, and baking chocolate. Cover and cook on low for 2 hours, then stir.
2. Cover and cook on low for another 1–2 hours, as necessary, until chocolate melts and mixture is smooth.
3. Stir in marshmallow crème and miniature marshmallows to blend. Serve immediately with sugar cookies, graham crackers, gingersnaps, or angel food cake for dipping.

Toffee Peach Crisp

SERVES 8–10

Peaches and toffee are a wonderful combination. The toffee melts in the topping, adding a sweet burst of flavor, while the peaches become soft and tender. Serve with ice cream or whipped cream.

8 peaches, peeled and sliced

3 tablespoons lemon juice

1 teaspoon cinnamon

½ cup caramel ice cream topping

2 cups rolled oats

1 cup brown sugar

1 cup flour

½ teaspoon salt

1 teaspoon cinnamon

½ cup butter, melted

1 cup granola

1 cup crushed toffee

1. Spray 4-quart slow cooker with nonstick cooking spray. Place peaches, lemon juice, and cinnamon in slow cooker and mix. Drizzle with caramel ice cream topping.
2. In large bowl, combine oatmeal, brown sugar, flour, salt, and cinnamon; mix well. Add melted butter; stir until crumbly. Stir in granola and toffee.
3. Sprinkle over peach mixture in slow cooker. Cover and cook on low for 4–5 hours or until peaches are tender and topping is hot. Serve with ice cream or sweetened whipped cream.

Slow Cooker Chocolate Cheesecake

SERVES 8–10

Many cheesecakes crack in the dry heat of the oven. The slow cooker is the perfect environment for making moist and tender cheesecake.

1 cup chocolate sandwich cookie crumbs
¼ cup butter, melted
¼ cup chopped walnuts
1 (8-ounce) package cream cheese, softened
1 cup mascarpone cheese
½ cup ricotta cheese
½ cup sugar
½ cup brown sugar
⅓ cup unsweetened cocoa
¼ cup heavy cream
¼ teaspoon salt
2 tablespoons cornstarch
1 tablespoon flour
2 teaspoons vanilla
½ cup sour cream
⅓ cup powdered sugar
½ teaspoon vanilla

1. Spray a 7-inch springform pan with nonstick baking spray containing flour. In small bowl, combine cookie crumbs, melted butter, and nuts; mix well. Press onto bottom of prepared pan.

2. In large bowl, beat cream cheese until fluffy. Add mascarpone cheese and beat until smooth, then beat in ricotta cheese. Add sugar, brown sugar, cocoa, cream, and salt; beat until combined. Stir in cornstarch, flour, and vanilla. Pour mixture into pan over crust.

3. Place a rack, or a ring of crumpled aluminum foil, in the bottom of a 4-quart slow cooker. Place the pan on top of the rack. Make sure that there is at least 1" around the sides of the springform pan so heat can circulate.

4. Cover and cook on high for 2–3 hours or until cheesecake is barely set in the center. Turn slow cooker off, remove lid, and let cheesecake stand for 30 minutes, then remove from slow cooker and refrigerate for 1 hour.

5. In small bowl, combine sour cream, powdered sugar, and ½ teaspoon vanilla; mix well. Spread over cheesecake, return to refrigerator, and let chill until set, about 4–5 hours.

Further, he distributed to all the people, to all the multitude of Israel, both to men and women, a cake of bread and one of dates and one of raisins to each one. Then all the people departed each to his house.

—2 SAMUEL 6:19

Chocolate Steamed Pudding with Sauce

SERVES 8–10

This decadent recipe is comforting and delicious. The Hard Sauce melts into the warm pudding as you eat it. Yum.

½ cup butter, softened
½ cup sugar
½ cup brown sugar
⅓ cup unsweetened cocoa
2 eggs
1 teaspoon vanilla
1½ cups flour
½ teaspoon salt
1 teaspoon baking powder
1 teaspoon baking soda
½ cup mascarpone cheese
¼ cup heavy cream
1 cup semisweet chocolate chips
⅓ cup butter, softened
½ cup powdered sugar
Pinch salt
1 teaspoon vanilla

1. Spray a 6-cup mold or 2-pound coffee can with nonstick baking spray containing flour. In large bowl, combine butter, sugar, and brown sugar; beat well.

2. Add cocoa, eggs, and vanilla; beat until fluffy. Sift together flour, salt, baking powder, and baking soda. Add alternately to the butter mixture with mascarpone cheese and heavy cream, beginning and ending with dry ingredients. Stir in chocolate chips.

3. Pour mixture into prepared mold or can. Place a rack or crumpled foil in bottom of 4-quart slow cooker. Place the mold on top of the rack. Cover and cook on high for 4–5 hours or until pudding is set. Remove the mold from slow cooker, then cool for 30 minutes.

4. For Hard Sauce, in medium bowl combine ⅓ cup butter, powdered sugar, pinch salt, and 1 teaspoon vanilla. Beat until fluffy.

5. Unmold pudding and serve warm with Hard Sauce.

Then the king will say to those at his right hand, "Come, you that are blessed by my Father, inherit the kingdom prepared for you from the foundation of the world; for I was hungry and you gave me food, I was thirsty and you gave me drink, I was a stranger and you welcomed me, I was naked and you gave me clothing, I was sick and you took care of me, I was in prison and you visited me."

—MATTHEW 25:34–36

Marlene's Apricot Rice Pudding

SERVES 8–10

Rice pudding is wonderful comfort food. When flavored with apricot nectar, cardamom, and nutmeg, it becomes a gourmet dessert.

1 cup medium grain white rice

1 cup sugar

¼ cup butter

¼ teaspoon salt

⅛ teaspoon cardamom

⅛ teaspoon nutmeg

2 cups apricot nectar

2 cups whole milk

2 teaspoons vanilla

½ cup finely chopped dried apricots

1 cup chopped canned apricots in juice, drained

1. Combine all ingredients except canned apricots in 3½ quart slow cooker. Cover and cook on low for 2 hours, then remove lid and stir.
2. Cover and continue cooking on low for 2–3 hours longer, until rice is tender and pudding is desired thickness. Stir in canned apricots, cover, and cook for another 30 minutes. Serve warm or cold.

Whoever is generous to the poor lends to the Lord, and he will repay him for his deed.

—PROVERBS 19:17

Apple Pecan Pudding Cake

SERVES 8

Apples and pecans, baked in a cake surrounded by an apple-brown sugar sauce; this dessert is spectacular.

2 tart apples, peeled, cored, and chopped

2 tablespoons lemon juice

1 cup brown sugar

1 cup apple cider

¼ cup butter, softened

½ cup brown sugar

½ cup sugar

1 egg

2 cups flour

1½ teaspoons baking powder

½ teaspoon baking soda

1 teaspoon cinnamon

⅛ teaspoon cardamom

¼ teaspoon salt

1 cup whole milk

1 cup chopped pecans

1. Spray a 3 quart slow cooker with nonstick baking spray containing flour. Place apples in bottom of slow cooker; sprinkle with lemon juice.
2. In medium saucepan, combine 1 cup brown sugar with apple cider and bring to a boil. Remove from heat and set aside.
3. In large bowl, combine butter with ½ cup brown sugar and ½ cup sugar; beat well. Add egg and beat until combined. Stir in flour, baking powder, baking soda, cinnamon, cardamom, and salt; beat to combine. Stir in milk and pecans.
4. Spoon batter over apples in slow cooker. Pour brown sugar syrup over batter.
5. Cover and cook on high for 2–3 hours or until toothpick inserted in center of cake comes out clean. Scoop out of slow cooker and turn over each scoop to serve.

Carrot Cake Pudding

SERVES 6

Serve this excellent pudding, which tastes like carrot cake, with Hard Sauce (page 180), or butter pecan ice cream.

1 (14.5-ounce) can sliced carrots, drained
1 (8-ounce) can crushed pineapple in juice, undrained
½ cup heavy cream
¾ cup brown sugar
⅓ cup flour
¼ teaspoon salt
½ teaspoon baking soda
½ teaspoon cinnamon
⅛ teaspoon cardamom
2 beaten eggs
2 tablespoons butter, melted
2 teaspoons vanilla
½ cup coconut
½ cup chopped pecans
¼ cup brown sugar
3 tablespoons butter, melted

1. Spray 3½-quart slow cooker with nonstick baking spray containing flour and set aside. Place carrots in large bowl and mash with potato masher until smooth. Stir in the undrained pineapple and cream; mix well.
2. Add brown sugar, flour, salt, baking soda, cinnamon, and cardamom; mix. Stir in eggs, 2 tablespoons melted butter, and vanilla. Mix well.
3. Pour batter into prepared slow cooker. Cover and cook on low for 6–7 hours or until pudding is set when lightly touched.
4. About half an hour before pudding is done, place coconut and pecans in a small dry skillet. Toast over low heat, stirring frequently, until light brown and fragrant. Stir in ¼ cup brown sugar and 3 tablespoons butter. Cook and stir until sugar melts and coats coconut and pecans.
5. Sprinkle coconut mixture over pudding and serve warm.

For I am convinced that neither death, nor life, nor angles, nor rulers, nor things present, nor things to come, now powers, nor height, nor depth, nor anything else in all creation, will be able to separate us from the love of God in Christ Jesus our Lord.

—ROMANS 8:38–39

Brownie Fudge Cake

SERVES 8
Peanut butter, caramel, and chocolate—yum!

1⅔ cups flour

¾ cup brown sugar

¼ cup unsweetened cocoa powder

½ teaspoon baking soda

¼ teaspoon salt

1 egg

¼ cup water

3 tablespoons peanut butter

2 tablespoons butter, melted

1 teaspoon vanilla

1 cup milk chocolate chips

½ cup chopped pecans

¼ cup caramel ice cream topping

¼ cup brown sugar

¾ cup water

1 (1-ounce) square unsweetened baking chocolate, chopped

½ teaspoon vanilla

1. In large bowl, combine flour, ¾ cup brown sugar, cocoa, baking soda, and salt; mix well. In small bowl, combine egg with ¼ cup water, peanut butter, 2 tablespoons melted butter, and vanilla; mix well.
2. Stir peanut butter mixture into flour mixture until combined. Add milk chocolate chips and pecans. Spray a 3-quart slow cooker with nonstick baking spray containing flour. Add batter to slow cooker.
3. In small saucepan, combine ice cream topping, brown sugar, ¾ cup water, and baking chocolate; cook and stir over medium heat until chocolate melts and mixture is smooth. Stir in ½ teaspoon vanilla and pour over batter.
4. Cover and cook on high for 2 to 2½ hours. Turn off slow cooker, place lid ajar, and let stand for 40 minutes. Serve with ice cream or sweetened whipped cream.

Raspberry-Pineapple Strata

SERVES 12–14
There are lots of fruity flavors in this pudding-like strata. You could use dark chocolate chips instead of the white. Serve with chocolate ice cream topping.

14 cups cubed white bread

½ cup butter, melted

½ cup sugar

2 cups fresh raspberries

2 cups white chocolate chips

1 (13-ounce) can evaporated milk

1 (8-ounce) can crushed pineapple in juice, undrained

3 eggs

1 cup heavy cream

1 (6-ounce) container frozen lemonade concentrate

1. Preheat oven to 400°F. Place cubed bread on two cookie sheets. Drizzle with butter and sprinkle with sugar; toss. Bake for 10–15 minutes or until bread is lightly toasted. Remove from oven and let cool.
2. Layer cooled toasted bread, raspberries, and chocolate chips in 5- to 6-quart slow cooker.
3. In food processor or blender, combine evaporated milk and crushed pineapple. Add eggs and process or blend until smooth. Pour into large bowl and add remaining ingredients. Stir until blended.
4. Pour into slow cooker. Let stand for 15 minutes, pushing bread back into liquid as necessary. Cover and cook on low for 6 hours or until pudding is set. Serve with chocolate sauce and fresh raspberries.

No-Bake Cookies

YIELDS 48 COOKIES

Yes, you can make cookies in the slow cooker! This excellent recipe could be varied several ways. Use white or dark chocolate chips, or dried blueberries or currants instead of the dried cranberries.

4 eggs

⅔ cup sugar

1 cup brown sugar

¼ cup butter, melted

⅛ teaspoon salt

1½ cups finely chopped dates

1 teaspoon vanilla

3½ cups crisp rice cereal

1 cup chopped dried cranberries

1 cup powdered sugar

1. Spray a 1½ quart slow cooker with nonstick cooking spray. In medium bowl, beat eggs with sugar, brown sugar, butter, and salt. Stir in dates. Pour into prepared slow cooker.
2. Cover and cook on high for 3–4 hours, stirring twice during cooking time, being sure to scrape the sides of the slow cooker. You may need to turn the slow cooker to low if the edges get too dark.
3. When the temperature reaches 160°F, empty the mixture into a large bowl. Stir in vanilla, then add cereal and cranberries.
4. Let the mixture cool for 10 minutes, then drop by teaspoons into powdered sugar. Shape into balls, then place on waxed paper. Store, covered, in refrigerator.

Curried Fruit

SERVES 12

This fragrant sauce can be served over pound cake or angel food cake, or spooned on top of ice cream for a summertime treat.

½ cup butter

1 cup brown sugar

1 tablespoon curry powder

1 (16-ounce) can sliced pears

1 (24-ounce) jar mango slices

2 (15-ounce) cans mandarin oranges

2 (15-ounce) cans apricot halves

1. Combine butter, brown sugar, and curry powder in a 4-quart slow cooker. Cover and cook on high for 1 hour or until butter melts.
2. Drain all of the fruits. Add all of the fruits to the slow cooker and stir very gently.
3. Cover and cook on high for 1–2 hours longer, or until fruits are hot but not falling apart. Serve as a compote or as a topping for cakes or ice cream.

For the whole law is summed up in a single commandment, "You shall love your neighbor as yourself."

—GALATIANS 5:14

Just for Kids

I remember being a picky eater. I didn't even like sandwiches as a child because there were too many flavors all bunched together. And I sat for a long time at the kitchen counter as my Brussels sprouts and cauliflower got very, very cold.

Getting kids to eat can be one of the biggest challenges of parenthood. Here are a few tips. Kids usually like mild foods, and foods they are used to. It takes as many as 20 introductions of a new food before a child will try it! So keep adding new foods to your child's diet; he or she will eventually try it, and may even like it!

One of the tricks to getting children to enjoy new foods is to introduce them slowly. Don't add too many foods to their diet at once. And make sure they see you eating fruits, vegetables, and other healthy foods with relish and enjoyment.

When you're feeding a crowd of kids, the simpler the better. Children generally do not like complicated recipes, with lots of different flavors. Every parent has the experience of a sweet little toddler refusing to touch her peas because they are touching the mashed potatoes.

And you have to be extra careful with food safety when you're cooking for kids. Never serve them undercooked eggs or meat, and strictly follow the 2-hour rule; refrigerate foods that have been left out at room temperature for 2 hours.

Mini Meatloaves

SERVES 12–14 KIDS

Kids love this recipe. The mini meatloaves are like large meatballs, but shaped differently. They are easy to serve at a buffet.

1½ cups soda cracker crumbs

2 eggs, beaten

½ cup ketchup

2 tablespoons brown sugar

2 tablespoons yellow mustard

⅛ teaspoon pepper

3 pounds 90% lean ground beef

3 tablespoons vegetable oil

1 (26-ounce) jar pasta sauce

½ cup ketchup

¼ cup honey

2 tablespoons apple cider vinegar

1. In large bowl, combine crumbs, eggs, ½ cup ketchup, brown sugar, mustard, and pepper; mix well. Add ground beef and mix gently but thoroughly with hands.
2. Scoop out individual balls, using a ¼-cup measure. Form into an oblong shape. When all the meatloaves are formed, heat oil in a large skillet over medium heat. Brown the meatloaves on both sides, turning once, about 4–6 minutes total. As they are cooked, place in 5- to 6-quart slow cooker.
3. In medium bowl, combine pasta sauce, ½ cup ketchup, honey, and vinegar; mix well. Pour over meatloaves. Cover and cook on low for 8–9 hours until meatloaves are tender and internal temperature reaches 165°F. Stir gently and serve.

Cheeseburgers

SERVES 10–12 KIDS

If you don't want to add onions to this recipe, add another half-pound of ground beef. But for authentic cheeseburger flavor, you need to use the processed cheese spread.

2 pounds ground beef

2 onions, chopped, if desired

2 (10-ounce) cans condensed tomato soup

1 (6-ounce) can tomato paste

1 cup water

2 tablespoons yellow mustard

1 teaspoon dried basil leaves

⅛ teaspoon pepper

10–12 English muffins, split and toasted

1 (8-ounce) jar processed cheese spread

10–12 tomato slices

1. In large skillet, cook ground beef until done, stirring to break up meat. In 4- or 5-quart slow cooker, combine beef, onions, tomato soup, tomato paste, water, mustard, basil, and pepper; stir well.
2. Cover and cook on low for 6–8 hours until blended. To serve, spread processed cheese spread thinly on both cut halves of each English muffin. Top half with a tomato, then the beef mixture. Cover with second half of English muffin and serve.

Slow Cooker Lasagna

SERVES 12 KIDS

Lasagna is everyone's favorite. You can omit the onions and garlic if you're serving very young kids, but add another ¾ pound of ground beef to keep the volume the same.

2 pounds lean ground beef

3 onions, chopped, if desired

4 cloves garlic, minced, if desired

1 (28-ounce) jar pasta sauce

1 (6-ounce) can tomato paste

1 cup tomato juice

1 teaspoon dried Italian seasoning

1 (8-ounce) package cream cheese, softened

¾ cup milk

1 tablespoon cornstarch

1 (15-ounce) package ricotta cheese

2 eggs

1 (16-ounce) package regular lasagna noodles

4 cups grated mozzarella cheese

⅓ cup grated Parmesan cheese

1. Spray a 6- or 7-quart slow cooker with nonstick cooking spray and set aside. In large skillet, cook ground beef until partially cooked, stirring to break up meat. Add onions and garlic, if using; cook and stir until beef is browned. Drain thoroughly.

2. Add pasta sauce, tomato paste, tomato juice, and Italian seasoning to beef mixture, and bring to a simmer. Simmer, stirring frequently, for 10 minutes.

3. In medium microwave-safe bowl, combine cream cheese and milk. Microwave on 50% power for 1 minute, then stir. Microwave on 50% power for 2 minutes longer; then remove and stir until smooth sauce forms. Stir in cornstarch, ricotta cheese and eggs.

4. Break lasagna noodles into irregular pieces. In prepared slow cooker, layer noodles, beef mixture, cream cheese mixture, and mozzarella cheese. Continue layering until slow cooker is ¾ full. Top with Parmesan cheese.

5. Cover slow cooker and cook on low for 4–5 hours or until noodles are tender and lasagna is bubbling around the edges. Let cool for 15 minutes, then serve.

May the Lord give you the dew of heaven, and of the fatness of the earth, and plenty of grain and wine.

—GENESIS 27:28

Penne Pasta Pizza

SERVES 8–10 KIDS

Pasta and pizza combine in a fun layered casserole. Serve with a gelatin fruit salad and small dinner rolls.

1½ pounds pork bulk sausage

1 onion, chopped

1 (8-ounce) package mushrooms, sliced

1 (26-ounce) jar pasta sauce

1 (10-ounce) can con-densed tomato soup

1 (16-ounce) package penne pasta

1 (10-ounce) can golden cream of mushroom soup

1 cup ricotta cheese

1 cup shredded mozzarella cheese

1 cup shredded Cheddar cheese

1 (4-ounce) package sliced pepperoni

1. Spray a 6-quart slow cooker with nonstick cooking spray and set aside. Bring a large pot of salted water to a boil. In skillet, cook pork sausage until partially cooked, stirring to break up meat. Add onion and mushrooms; cook and stir until sausage is cooked. Drain thoroughly, then add pasta sauce and tomato sauce and bring to a simmer.
3. Cook penne pasta for half of the time directed on package; drain. Combine in bowl with cream of mushroom soup and ricotta cheese; stir to blend.
4. In prepared slow cooker, place half of pork mixture, half of pasta mixture, half of mozzarella and Cheddar cheeses, and half of the pepperoni. Repeat layers. Cover and cook on low for 4 hours or until pasta is tender and casserole is bubbling. Let cool for 15 minutes, then serve.

Hot Pizza Dip

SERVES 10–12 KIDS

Heat some bakery focaccia in the oven until hot and crisp, then cut into small wedges to serve with this dip for the ultimate pizza experience!

1½ pounds ground beef

1 onion, chopped

4 cloves garlic, minced

2 red bell peppers, chopped

1 (16-ounce) jar pizza sauce

1 teaspoon dried oregano

1 teaspoon dried basil

½ teaspoon dried thyme leaves

¼ teaspoon pepper

1 (8-ounce) package cream cheese, cubed

1 cup diced mozzarella cheese

1½ cups diced Cheddar cheese

2 cups sliced pepperoni

¼ cup grated Parmesan cheese

20 breadsticks

4 cups pita chips

1. In large skillet, cook beef with onion and garlic until beef is browned, stirring to break up meat. Drain well. Add bell peppers to mixture along with pizza sauce, oregano, basil, thyme, and pepper; stir and remove from heat.
2. In 4-quart slow cooker, layer beef mixture with cream cheese, mozzarella cheese, and Cheddar cheese. Top with pepperoni and Parmesan cheese.
3. Cover and cook on low for 3–4 hours or until cheese is melted and dip is bubbling. Serve with breadsticks, hot pizza crust, and pita chips.

Chicken Tenders with Mustard Dip

SERVES 8–10 KIDS

Children love chicken tenders; they're so easy to eat. And because they are mild, they can be seasoned any way you'd like.

3–4 pounds chicken tenders
½ cup honey
⅓ cup yellow mustard
1 teaspoon salt
⅛ teaspoon pepper
1 cup sour cream
1 cup mayonnaise
⅓ cup honey
¼ cup yellow mustard
1 teaspoon onion salt

1. In 3- to 4-quart slow cooker, combine chicken tenders with honey, ⅓ cup mustard, salt, and pepper; mix well. Cover and cook on low for 6–7 hours or until chicken is thoroughly cooked.
2. While chicken is cooking, in medium bowl combine sour cream, mayonnaise, ⅓ cup honey, ¼ cup mustard, and onion salt; mix well.
3. Drain chicken and let cool on wire racks for 5–7 minutes. Serve the tenders with sour cream dip.

This is the day that the Lord has made.
I will rejoice and be glad in it.

—PSALMS 118:24

Tater Tot Hot Dish

SERVES 8–10 KIDS

Kids of all ages adore Tater Tots. These crunchy little cubes of potato combine easily with other ingredients in the slow cooker. They won't be crunchy, but they'll be delicious!

2 tablespoons butter
2 (12-ounce) packages brown and serve breakfast sausage
3 cups sliced carrots
1 cup sour cream
1 cup ricotta cheese
1 (16-ounce) jar four-cheese Alfredo sauce
2-pound package frozen Tater Tots, thawed
2 cups shredded Colby cheese
¼ cup grated Parmesan cheese

1. Melt butter in heavy skillet over medium heat. Add sausages; cook until brown and hot. Drain sausages on paper towels.
2. Add carrots to skillet; cook and stir for 3–4 minutes or until carrots are glazed. Add sour cream, ricotta cheese, and Alfredo sauce to skillet; heat through.
3. Cut sausages in half. Layer the sausages, Tater Tots, and Colby cheese in 5-quart slow cooker. Pour carrot mixture over all and stir gently to mix. Top with Parmesan cheese.
4. Cover and cook on low for 5–7 hours or until casserole is hot and blended. Serve immediately.

Cheesy Mini Sloppy Joes

SERVES 24 KIDS

Kids love anything that's small. These tiny sandwiches are fun to make and easy for small children to eat.

3 pounds ground beef
2 cups finely grated carrots
1 (10-ounce) can condensed tomato soup
1 (10-ounce) can condensed Cheddar cheese soup
1 cup ketchup
½ cup grated Parmesan cheese
24 mini sandwich buns, split
12 slices American cheese, quartered

1. In large skillet, cook ground beef until done, stirring to break up meat. Drain well.
2. Combine all ingredients except Parmesan cheese, buns, and American cheese in 4-quart slow cooker. Cover and cook on low for 5–6 hours or until mixture is hot. Stir in Parmesan cheese until blended.
3. Split the sandwich buns in half and place one-quarter of a slice of cheese on each half. Using the meat mixture, make sandwiches and serve immediately.

But grow in the grace and knowledge of our Lord and Savior Jesus Christ.

—2 PETER 3:18

Easy Spaghetti

SERVES 12–14 KIDS

Carrots not only sneak in some nutrition, but they help keep the sauce thick. The pasta will be very soft, kind of like canned pasta, but that's what kids like!

1 pound ground beef
1 cup shredded carrots
1 (16-ounce) package mini frozen meatballs
2 (10-ounce) cans condensed tomato soup
2 (8-ounce) cans tomato sauce
1 cup tomato juice
1 (16-ounce) package spaghetti pasta
1 cup grated Parmesan cheese, divided

1. In medium skillet, cook ground beef until done, stirring to break up meat. Drain well. Combine in 4- to 5-quart slow cooker with all remaining ingredients except ½ cup of the Parmesan cheese.
2. Cover and cook on low for 6–7 hours or until pasta is tender and meatballs are hot. Sprinkle with remaining ½ cup cheese and serve.

Do unto others as you would have them do unto you.

—LUKE 6:31

Chicken Potato Casserole

SERVES 12–14 KIDS

Tater Tots make another appearance in this chicken casserole. You could add or subtract vegetables that you think the kids would/would not like.

6 boneless, skinless
   chicken breasts, cubed
½ teaspoon salt
⅛ teaspoon pepper
2 tablespoons butter
1 (16-ounce) package
   baby carrots
2 cups frozen corn
2-pound package frozen
   Tater Tots, thawed
1 cup sour cream

1 cup whole milk
2 (16-ounce) jars four-
   cheese Alfredo sauce
1 cup shredded Muenster
   cheese
1 cup shredded Cheddar
   cheese
¼ cup grated Parmesan
   cheese

1. Sprinkle chicken cubes with salt and pepper. Melt butter in heavy skillet over medium heat. Add chicken; cook and stir until almost cooked through.
2. Place chicken in 6- to 7-quart slow cooker. Add carrots, corn, and Tater Tots; mix gently.
3. Add sour cream, milk, and both jars of sauce to skillet and bring to a simmer. Add Muenster and Cheddar cheeses, stir, and remove from heat. Pour into slow cooker. Sprinkle top with Parmesan cheese.
4. Cover and cook on low for 6–7 hours or until chicken is thoroughly cooked and casserole is hot and blended. Serve immediately.

Pretzel Snack Mix

YIELDS 16 CUPS; SERVES 32 KIDS

Sweet and salty is a wonderful flavor combination. This mix has lots of fun ingredients and textures; the kids will love it.

1 (16-ounce) package pretzel sticks
4 cups pecan halves
4 cups crisp square corn cereal
4 cups salted cashew halves
1 cup butter, melted
1 cup powdered sugar
½ cup brown sugar
2 teaspoons cinnamon

1. Combine pretzels, pecans, cereal, and cashews in 6-quart slow cooker. Melt butter in medium saucepan over low heat. Stir in both kinds of sugar and cinnamon; stir until blended.
2. Drizzle over mixture in slow cooker. Cook, uncovered, for 2–3 hours on high, until mixture is glazed. Cool on paper towels. Store, covered, in airtight container.

Simple Cheesy Tomato Soup

SERVES 14–16 KIDS
American cheese melts beautifully into a mild tomato soup in this delicious and healthy recipe.

2 (28-ounce) cans stewed tomatoes
3 shallots, minced
4 stalks celery, including leaves, chopped
1 teaspoon salt
⅛ teaspoon white pepper
2 tablespoons sugar
2 (16-ounce) jars four-cheese Alfredo sauce
1 cup heavy cream
3 cups cubed processed American cheese

1. In small batches, in blender or food processor, purée the tomatoes with shallots and celery. Place in 5-quart slow cooker along with salt, pepper, sugar, and Alfredo sauce.
2. Cover and cook on low for 6–7 hours or until soup is hot and blended. Stir in heavy cream.
3. Place some cheese in the bottom of each bowl, and ladle hot soup over the top. Serve immediately.

But the fruit of the Spirit is love, joy, peace, patience, kindness, goodness, faithfulness, gentleness and self-control. Against such things there is no law.

—GALATIANS 5:22

Mom's Mac and Cheese

SERVES 12–14 KIDS
This macaroni and cheese is pure, simple, cheesy, and rich. Make sure to check it at the minimum cooking time so the pasta doesn't overcook.

1 (16-ounce) container cottage cheese
2 (12-ounce) cans evaporated milk
1 cup heavy cream
3 cups cubed processed American cheese
2 cups shredded Colby cheese
1 (16-ounce) box elbow macaroni
¼ cup butter

1. Spray a 6-quart slow cooker with nonstick cooking spray. In food processor, process cottage cheese until smooth. Pour into prepared slow cooker and stir in milk and cream; mix well.
2. Add remaining ingredients and stir. Cover and cook on low for 5–7 hours or until macaroni is tender. Stir gently and serve.

Train up a child in the way he should go, and when he is old he will not depart from it.

—PROVERBS 22:6

Chicken Noodle Soup

SERVES 14–16 KIDS
The shredded carrots will melt into the soup, adding a sweet flavor. This hearty soup is healthy and delicious.

6 boneless, skinless chicken breasts
2 (10-ounce) cans condensed cream of chicken soup
1 cup shredded carrots
2 cups baby carrots
2 (32-ounce) boxes chicken broth
2 cups water
3 cups baby frozen peas
1 (12-ounce) package egg noodles

1. In 7-quart slow cooker, combine chicken, condensed soup, both types of carrots, chicken broth, and water. Cover and cook on low for 5–6 hours.
2. Remove chicken from slow cooker and chop. Return to slow cooker along with frozen peas and noodles. Cover and cook on high for 30 minutes or until noodles are tender.

Like a roaring lion or a charging bear is a wicked
ruler over a poor people. A ruler who lacks under-
standing is a cruel oppressor, but one who hates unjust
gain will enjoy a long life.

—PROVERBS 28:15–16

Taco Soup

SERVES 12 KIDS
Use the smaller amount of taco seasoning mix if the kids are picky. If they like it spicy, add more spices!

2 pounds ground beef
2 (15-ounce) cans tomato sauce
1 or 2 envelopes taco seasoning mix
3 (15-ounce) cans kidney beans, drained
3 cups tomato juice
3 cups water
4 cups frozen corn
6 cups corn chips
3 cups shredded Colby cheese

1. In large skillet, brown ground beef, stirring to break up meat. Drain thoroughly.
2. In 7-quart slow cooker, mix beef with remaining ingredients except corn chips and cheese. Cover and cook on low for 4–5 hours or until soup is hot and blended.
3. Serve with corn chips and cheese.

The Lord enters into judgment with the elders and
princes of his people; it is you who have devoured
the vineyard; the spoil of the poor is in your houses.
"What do you mean by crushing my people, by grind-
ing the face of the poor?" says the Lord God of hosts.

—ISAIAH 3:14–15

Pizza Fondue

SERVES 18–20 KIDS

Sausage and pepperoni combine in a cheesy tomato sauce for a wonderful dip. You can also serve this with breadsticks.

1½ pounds pork bulk sausage

2 (16-ounce) jars Cheddar cheese pasta sauce

3 (10-ounce) cans pizza sauce

1 (4-ounce) package thinly sliced pepperoni

1 cup heavy cream

2 cups diced processed American cheese

2 cups shredded mozzarella cheese

3 (12-ounce) rolls refrigerated pizza dough

1. In large skillet, cook sausage until browned, stirring to break up meat. Drain well and place in 5-quart slow cooker. Stir in remaining ingredients except for pizza dough.
2. Cover and cook on low for 3–4 hours or until cheese is melted, stirring once during cooking time.
3. Preheat oven to 400°F. Roll out pizza dough onto cookie sheets as directed on package. Bake for 15–20 minutes or until crust is golden brown. Immediately cut into small rectangles and serve with fondue.

Burger Ravioli Casserole

SERVES 12–16 KIDS

You can leave out the onion if you think the kids won't like it, but it does get soft and sweet when cooked this way.

2 pounds ground beef

1 onion, chopped

1 cup shredded carrots

2 (26-ounce) jars pasta sauce

1 (15-ounce) can tomato sauce

1 cup tomato juice

1 cup beef broth

1 (25-ounce) package frozen cheese ravioli

2 cups shredded mozzarella cheese

⅓ cup grated Parmesan cheese

1. In large skillet, cook ground beef with onion and shredded carrots, stirring to break up beef. When beef is done, drain thoroughly.
2. Combine beef mixture in 7-quart slow cooker with pasta sauce, tomato sauce, tomato juice, and beef broth. Cover and cook on low for 7–8 hours.
3. Uncover and stir in ravioli, making sure ravioli is well distributed in the slow cooker. Cover and cook on low for 20–30 minutes longer or until ravioli is hot and tender. Sprinkle with cheeses, cover, and let stand for 5 minutes, then serve.

Oatmeal Fruit Cookie Crisp

SERVES 18 KIDS

Apples and cherries combine in this simple crisp, which gets extra texture from crumbled oatmeal cookies.

4 apples, peeled, cored, and chopped
2 tablespoons lemon juice
½ cup sugar
2 (21-ounce) cans cherry pie filling
2 cups brown sugar
2 cups rolled oats
1 cup flour
2 teaspoons cinnamon
1 cup butter, melted
12 oatmeal cookies, crumbled

1. Sprinkle apples with lemon juice. Place in 5-quart slow cooker and stir in ½ cup sugar and both cans cherry pie filling.
2. In large bowl, combine brown sugar, oatmeal, flour, and cinnamon. Add butter and stir until mixture is crumbly. Stir in crumbled oatmeal cookies.
3. Sprinkle oatmeal mixture over fruit mixture in slow cooker. Cover and cook on low for 5–6 hours or until apples are tender and topping is hot.

Mini Chicken Cheese Sandwiches

SERVES 18 KIDS

If the kids will eat them, add other vegetables to this simple recipe. Chopped green bell peppers, chopped celery, or mushrooms will add more nutrition.

6 boneless, skinless chicken breasts
1 teaspoon salt
⅛ teaspoon white pepper
2 cups chicken broth
2 cups shredded carrots
1 cup mayonnaise
½ cup plain yogurt
2 cups diced processed American cheese
18–20 mini sandwich buns

1. Cut chicken breasts in half and sprinkle with salt and pepper. Place in 4- to 5-quart slow cooker and add chicken broth.
2. Cover and cook on low for 6–7 hours or until chicken registers 165°F on a meat thermometer.
3. Remove chicken from slow cooker and shred; place in large bowl. Add enough broth from the slow cooker to moisten. Stir in carrots, mayonnaise, yogurt, and cheese; mix well.
4. Cover and refrigerate for 2–3 hours before serving. Make sandwiches with split mini buns.

They feast on the abundance of your house, and you give them drink from the river of your delights.

—PSALMS 36:8

Large Quantity

In the elementary parochial school I attended, those wonderful ladies would make a hot lunch for us every day. The food was simply delicious—tender meatloaf, fried chicken, mashed potatoes, cooked vegetables, fruit salad, pies, and cakes—yum. I have nothing but admiration for those who cook every day for schoolchildren.

Church ladies have to be ready to tackle quantity cooking. When you're cooking a lot of food in several slow cookers, it's important to remember the ½ to ¾ rule, as explained in the Introduction. Use enough slow cookers so the food fills them to the proper amount. It may help to place a timer next to each slow cooker so you can keep track of when each one started cooking, or use timers with multiple functions.

It's also important to follow food safety regulations when you're cooking in quantity. Check with your local extension service that's part of the University near you for the latest laws and rules. Use a food thermometer to make sure that meat is thoroughly cooked, and that casseroles reach a temperature of 165°F.

These recipes may also inspire you to use your slow cookers in different ways. I love the idea of making a large quantity of each ingredient for, say, a salad, in different slow cookers, then combining them with a dressing in several very large bowls. You can cook rice, meats, vegetables, and even fruits this way in the slow cooker.

Enjoy these recipes, and let them help you cook for your church family.

Apple Pies

YIELDS 4 PIES; SERVES 32
Use apples that are best for cooking in this recipe: Granny Smith, Jonathan, McIntosh, and Winesap are good choices. This recipe assumes that the pie crust holds 3 cups.

16 medium tart apples, peeled, cored, and sliced
3 tablespoons lemon juice
1 cup brown sugar
1½ cups sugar
2 cinnamon sticks
2 teaspoons cinnamon
1 teaspoon nutmeg
¼ teaspoon cardamom
1½ teaspoons salt
2 cups applesauce
2 cups apple juice
¾ cup cornstarch
1 cup apple cider
4 premade vanilla wafer pie crusts
2 cups heavy cream
½ cup powdered sugar
2 teaspoons vanilla

1. In 6- to 7-quart slow cooker, combine apples with lemon juice and toss to coat. Add cinnamon sticks.

2. In large bowl, combine remaining ingredients except cornstarch, apple cider, pie crusts, cream, powdered sugar, and vanilla; mix well. Pour into slow cooker.

3. Cover and cook on low for 5–6 hours or until apples are tender when pierced with a fork, stirring once during cooking time. In small bowl, combine cornstarch with apple cider and mix well. Pour into slow cooker.

4. Cover and cook on high for 20–30 minutes or until mixture thickens. Remove and discard cinnamon sticks. Pour filling into the pie crusts and refrigerate immediately.

5. When filling is set and pies are cold, whip cream with powdered sugar and vanilla in medium bowl. Spoon cream on top of apples and serve.

The righteous know the rights of the poor; the wicked have no such understanding.

—PROVERBS 29:7

Southwest Potato Salad

SERVES 24–26

Cook the potatoes for this spicy salad in the slow cooker. If you don't like spicy food, leave out the jalapeño peppers.

10 pounds russet potatoes
4 onions, chopped
1 head garlic, peeled and minced
5 jalapeño peppers, minced
3 tablespoons chili powder
2 teaspoons cumin
3 teaspoons salt
1 teaspoon white pepper
6 cups frozen corn
2 cups water
3 cups mayonnaise
1 cup plain yogurt
1 (15-ounce) can creamed corn
3 (4-ounce) cans diced green chiles, undrained
2 tablespoons chili powder
2 teaspoons salt
¼ teaspoon cayenne pepper
4 cups cubed pepper jack cheese
1 cup grated Cotija cheese

1. Peel potatoes and cut into cubes. Combine in two 5- to 6-quart slow cookers with onions, garlic, and jalapeños. Sprinkle with chili powder, cumin, salt, and pepper; then pour 1 cup water into each slow cooker.

2. Cover and cook on low for 8–9 hours or until potatoes are tender. Drain potato mixture.

3. In two or three large bowls, combine remaining ingredients and mix well. Add hot potato mixture and stir gently to coat. Cover and chill for 5–6 hours until cold. Stir gently before serving.

So speak and so act as those who are to be judged by the law of liberty. For judgment will be without mercy to anyone who has shown no mercy; mercy triumphs over judgment.

—JAMES 2:12–13

Smoked Turkey Strata

SERVES 24

This is a great recipe for using leftover turkey after Thanksgiving or Christmas. Or you could use ham or cooked chicken instead.

3 (16-ounce) packages frozen Tater Tots, thawed

4 onions, chopped

5 cloves garlic, minced

2 pounds plain cooked or smoked turkey breast, chopped

6 carrots, sliced

2 cups shredded Swiss cheese

2 cups shredded provolone cheese

2 (13-ounce) cans evaporated milk

18 eggs

⅓ cup yellow mustard

2 teaspoons dried basil leaves

2 teaspoons salt

½ teaspoon pepper

1. Spray two 6- to 7-quart slow cookers with non-stick cooking spray. Layer Tater Tots, onions, garlic, turkey, carrots, and cheeses in both slow cookers, making three layers of each.
2. In large bowl, combine remaining ingredients and beat until blended. Pour into slow cookers.
3. Cover and cook on low for 8–10 hours or until casseroles are set. Serve immediately.

Cranberry Cherry Pies

YIELDS 4 PIES; SERVES 32

These tart pies aren't too sweet. For a nice finish, add some cocoa powder and powdered sugar to the whipped cream you dollop on top.

2 (15-ounce) cans whole berry cranberry sauce

3 (21-ounce) cans cherry pie filling

1 (16-ounce) bag fresh cranberries, chopped

1 cup brown sugar

½ cup sugar

¼ cup lemon juice

1 teaspoon salt

2 teaspoons cinnamon

¼ cup butter

3 (1-ounce) envelopes unflavored gelatin

1 cup cranberry juice

4 baked and cooled 9" pie crusts

2–3 cups frozen whipped topping, thawed

1. In 5-quart slow cooker, combine cranberry sauce, pie filling, cranberries, brown sugar, sugar, lemon juice, salt, cinnamon, and butter. Cover and cook on low for 7–8 hours or until cranberries are soft.
2. In small bowl, combine gelatin and cranberry juice and let stand for 5 minutes. Stir into slow cooker until gelatin dissolves.
3. Turn off slow cooker and let mixture stand for 30 minutes. Spoon into pie crusts and refrigerate immediately. When pies are set and cold, top with thawed frozen whipped topping or sweetened whipped cream and slice to serve.

Roasted Corn Stew

SERVES 32–36

This thick and rich chowder starts with roasted corn for wonderful caramelized sweetness and chewy texture.

18 cups frozen corn
½ cup olive oil
1½ teaspoons salt
½ teaspoon white pepper
½ cup butter
6 onions, sliced
1 head garlic, peeled and sliced
6 tablespoons flour
1 (32-ounce) box chicken broth
4 cups water
3 (15-ounce) cans cream-style corn
4 (16-ounce) jars four-cheese Alfredo sauce
2 cups heavy cream
3 cups shredded Muenster cheese

1. Preheat oven to 400°F. Place frozen corn on three cookie sheets. Drizzle with olive oil and sprinkle with salt and pepper. Roast for 20–30 minutes until corn begins to turn brown around the edges.
2. Divide corn between two 6- or 7-quart slow cookers. In each of two large skillets, melt ¼ cup butter over medium heat. Add onions and garlic, and cook and stir for 5–6 minutes.
3. Divide flour between the skillets and cook and stir until bubbly. Add half of chicken broth to each skillet and bring to a simmer. Pour into both slow cookers. Add half of water, canned corn and Alfredo sauce to each slow cooker; stir gently.
4. Cover and cook on low for 6–7 hours or until soup is blended and thick. Stir 1 cup of heavy cream and 1½ cups cheese into each slow cooker. Uncover and cook on high for 15–20 minutes or until cheese melts. Serve immediately.

Whoever has a bountiful eye will be blessed, for he shares his bread with the poor.

—PROVERBS 22:9

Mom's Goulash

SERVES 30–32

Wow—this goulash has a fabulous blend of flavors and textures. The combination of sausage with ground beef makes it rich and delicious. It will satisfy any hearty appetite.

1 (16-ounce) package bacon

3 tablespoons butter

3 onions, chopped

1 head garlic, peeled and minced

2 pounds pork bulk sausage

2 pounds ground beef

½ cup flour

2 teaspoons salt

½ teaspoon pepper

3 tablespoons sweet paprika

2 (32-ounce) boxes beef stock

⅔ cup red wine vinegar

4 carrots, sliced

2 (8-ounce) packages fresh sliced mushrooms

6 potatoes, peeled and cubed

30 cups hot cooked noodles

1. In large skillet, cook bacon in batches. Drain bacon in paper towels, crumble, and set aside. Remove all but 2 tablespoons bacon drippings from skillet. Add butter.

2. Cook onions and garlic in skillet until crisp-tender, about 5 minutes. Remove with slotted spoon and place in large bowl.

3. Add sausage and beef to skillet in batches and cook until almost browned. Remove meat with slotted spoon and place in large bowl. Add flour, salt, pepper, and paprika to skillet; cook and stir until bubbly.

4. Add 1 box of beef stock and the vinegar to the skillet, and bring to a simmer. Combine carrots, mushrooms, and potatoes in two 6- or 7-quart slow cookers. Add bacon, onions, garlic, and meat on top of vegetables.

5. Pour skillet mixture into both slow cookers and top with remaining box of beef stock. Cover and cook on low for 8–9 hours or until vegetables are tender and goulash has thickened. Serve over hot cooked noodles.

Best Pot Roast

SERVES 36

Pot roast cooks to perfection in the slow cooker. The vegetables give great flavor and texture to the gravy. Yum!

3 (4-pound) tri-tip beef roasts

¾ cup flour

1 tablespoon salt

2 tablespoons paprika

2 teaspoons pepper

6 tablespoons butter

6 onions, chopped

1 head garlic, peeled and minced

9 carrots, sliced

3 (8-ounce) cans tomato sauce

2 (6-ounce) cans tomato paste

2 cups beef broth

2 tablespoons sugar

1. Trim excess fat from roasts. On cookie sheet, combine flour, salt, paprika, and pepper. Dredge roasts in this mixture.
2. In large skillet, melt 2 tablespoons butter. Add one roast; brown on all sides, about 6–7 minutes. Remove from heat. Add 2 more tablespoons butter and brown second roast; repeat with third roast.
3. Add 2 onions to skillet; cook and stir until crisp-tender, stirring to loosen pan drippings.
4. Divide remaining onions, garlic, and carrots among three 6- or 7-quart slow cookers. Top each with one browned roast. Pour one can tomato sauce over each roast.
5. Add tomato paste and beef broth to skillet; add sugar and bring to a boil, stirring to dissolve tomato paste. Divide among slow cookers.
6. Cover slow cookers and cook on low for 8–9 hours or until beef is very tender. Remove roasts from slow cookers; cover to keep warm. Turn off slow cookers; using an immersion blender, blend vegetables in the slow cookers to make a sauce. Serve with beef.

Now the manna was like coriander seed, and its color was like the color of gum resin. The people went around and gathered it, ground it in mills or beat it in mortars, then boiled it in pots and made cakes of it; and the taste of it was like the taste of cakes baked with oil.

—NUMBERS 11:7–8

Chicken à la King over Seasoned Wild Rice Pilaf

SERVES 24
This concept, of making food in two slow cookers and serving one dish over another, saves time and makes feeding a crowd simple.

12 chopped raw chicken breasts

3 onions, chopped

2 (8-ounce) packages fresh mushrooms, chopped

2 (16-ounce) jars Alfredo sauce

2 (10-ounce) cans condensed cream of chicken soup

2 cups whole milk

2 teaspoons dried thyme leaves

1 teaspoon dried sage leaves

½ teaspoon white pepper

1 (16-ounce) bag frozen baby peas

1 recipe Seasoned Wild Rice Pilaf (page 206)

1. In two 5-quart slow cookers, combine chicken, onions, and mushrooms; stir to mix. Divide Alfredo sauce, soup, milk, thyme, sage, and pepper between the slow cookers; do not stir.
2. Cover and cook on low for 7–8 hours or until chicken is cooked. Have the Wild Rice Pilaf cooking at the same time the chicken is cooking.
3. When chicken is done, stir in the frozen peas. Uncover and cook on high for 20–30 minutes or until peas are hot and tender.
4. Serve the chicken mixture on the Seasoned Wild Rice Pilaf.

Chicken Barley Casserole

SERVES 30–34
This recipe uses two large slow cookers to feed a crowd. With such a large quantity, it's important to stir once during cooking time so the food cooks evenly.

2 (16-ounce) boxes medium pearl barley, rinsed

2 (32-ounce) boxes chicken broth

2 cups water

4 onions, chopped

2 (16-ounce) bags baby carrots

2 (8-ounce) packages sliced fresh mushrooms

14 chicken breasts, chopped

2 teaspoons seasoned salt

½ teaspoon pepper

2 teaspoons dried thyme leaves

4 cups shredded Havarti cheese

1. Drain barley and place one box in each 6-quart slow cooker; add half of chicken broth and water to each. Divide onions, carrots, and mushrooms among slow cookers.
2. Chop chicken into 1" pieces and sprinkle with seasoned salt, pepper, and thyme. Add to slow cookers. Cover and cook on low for 7–9 hours or until barley is tender and chicken is thoroughly cooked, stirring twice during cooking time.
3. Stir cheese into the slow cookers until melted, then serve.

Simmered Beef over Potatoes

SERVES 24

Apple juice adds a wonderful slightly sweet taste to this savory recipe. It can also be served over cooked pasta or four recipes of the Herbed Brown Rice Pilaf (page 146) rather than the potatoes.

5 pounds beef chuck roast
3 onions, chopped
2 (16-ounce) bags baby carrots
1 head garlic, peeled and chopped
1 (32-ounce) box beef broth
2 cups apple juice
2 (6-ounce) cans tomato paste
2 teaspoons salt
½ teaspoon pepper
1 recipe Rich and Creamy Potatoes (page 207)

1. Cut the roast into 6" pieces and trim off excess fat. Place onions, carrots, and garlic into two 6-quart slow cookers. Place beef on top. Pour half of beef broth into each slow cooker.
2. In large bowl, combine apple juice with tomato paste, salt, and pepper; stir with wire whisk until tomato paste dissolves and mixture is smooth. Divide among slow cookers.
3. Cover and cook on low for 8–9 hours or until beef and vegetables are tender. Have the Rich and Creamy Potatoes cooking at the same time. Serve the beef mixture over Rich and Creamy Potatoes, hot cooked pasta, or rice pilaf.

Seasoned Wild Rice Pilaf

SERVES 24

This simple side dish can be served under a meat mixture, or all by itself as a side dish. You could substitute sliced carrots or mushrooms for the onions if you'd like.

4 cups wild rice, rinsed and drained
3 onions, chopped
12 cups chicken or vegetable broth
¼ cup butter
2 teaspoons seasoned salt
1 teaspoon dried marjoram
1 teaspoon dried oregano
½ teaspoon pepper

1. Combine all ingredients in a 6-quart slow cooker. Cover and cook on low for 7–8 hours or until wild rice is tender. Stir and serve.

If your enemy is hungry, give him bread to eat; and if he is thirsty, give him water to drink.

—PROVERBS 25:21

Rich and Creamy Potatoes

SERVES 24

Frozen hash brown potatoes are a fabulous timesaver when you're serving a crowd. There are several types; this recipe uses the potatoes cut into small dice.

2 (32-ounce) bags southern-style hash brown potatoes, thawed

4 onions, chopped

12 cloves garlic, chopped

2 (10-ounce) cans cream of potato soup

1 (16-ounce) jar four-cheese Alfredo sauce

2 cups whole milk

½ teaspoon white pepper

1 teaspoon dried basil leaves

1 teaspoon dried thyme leaves

1. In 7-quart slow cooker, combine potatoes with onions and garlic. In large bowl, combine soup, Alfredo sauce, milk, and seasonings; stir until blended.
2. Pour soup mixture into slow cooker and gently stir. Cover and cook on low for 6–8 hours or until potatoes are tender, stirring twice during cooking time.

Slow Cooker Fruity Chocolate Drops

YIELDS 72 PIECES

Making candy in the slow cooker is an efficient way to produce a big batch. And you won't heat up the kitchen!

2 tablespoons butter, melted

2 cups salted cashew pieces

1 (12-ounce) package semisweet chocolate chips

1 (11.5-ounce) package milk chocolate chips

1 (8-ounce) package dark chocolate bar, chopped

1 (12-ounce) package white chocolate chips

1 cup dried blueberries

1 cup dried sweetened cranberries

1. Place butter and nuts in bottom of 4-quart slow cooker; stir to coat. Top with all of the chocolate. Cover and cook on low for 1½ to 2 hours or until chocolate melts.
2. Stir thoroughly to combine. Stir in dried fruit. Drop by tablespoons onto waxed paper or parchment paper. Let stand until firm. Store covered at room temperature.

Apple Chutney

YIELDS 10 CUPS

If ladies in your church know how to can food, you can make this delicious recipe and sell it at a fundraiser. Make sure you follow your local extension agent's instructions for safe canning.

¼ cup butter
9 cups chopped, peeled and cored apple
2 onions, chopped
¼ cup water
¼ cup lemon juice
¼ cup apple cider vinegar
½ cup brown sugar
1 cup golden raisins
1 cup dark raisins
1 cup dried cranberries
2 teaspoons cinnamon
¼ teaspoon cardamom
1 teaspoon salt

1. In 4- or 5-quart slow cooker, combine all ingredients and mix well. Cover and cook on low for 6–7 hours, stirring once during cooking time, until apples start to fall apart and mixture has thickened.
2. Spoon into sterilized jars and seal. These should be processed in a hot water bath for long-term storage. The chutney can also be frozen in freezer containers, or refrigerated and used within 1 week.

Poached Chicken Breasts and Broth

YIELDS 24 BREASTS

Sometimes you need a lot of cooked chicken, perhaps for a salad or a casserole or just sandwiches. This is an excellent way to cook a bunch with almost no work.

4 onions, chopped
5 carrots, chopped
4 stalks celery, chopped
24 boneless, skinless chicken breasts
8 cups chicken broth
2 teaspoons dried thyme leaves
¼ teaspoon pepper

1. Layer onions, carrots, and celery with chicken breasts in two 6- or 7-quart slow cookers. Pour half of chicken broth over each and sprinkle with thyme and pepper.
2. Cover and cook on low for 5–7 hours or until chicken is thoroughly cooked. Refrigerate chicken until ready to use. Strain and freeze the broth for another use.

On this mountain the Lord of hosts will make for all peoples a feast of rich food, a feast of well-aged wines, of rich food filled with marrow, of well-aged wines strained clear.

—ISAIAH 25:6

Beef Tacos

Tacos are easy to make and eat. Set out a couple of batches along with all the taco fixings you like, and stand back!

3 pounds ground beef

2 onions, chopped

6 cloves garlic, minced

2 jalapeño peppers, minced

1 teaspoon salt

½ teaspoon pepper

8 plum tomatoes, chopped

2 (15-ounce) cans kidney beans, drained

2 tablespoons chili powder

2 (15-ounce) cans refried beans

18–20 taco shells

3 cups lettuce

2 cups sour cream

4 cups shredded Cheddar cheese

4 avocados

¼ cup lime juice

1. In large skillet, cook beef until almost done, stirring to break up meat. Drain thoroughly.
2. In 6- or 7-quart slow cooker, combine beef with onions, garlic, jalapeño peppers, salt, pepper, plum tomatoes, kidney beans, chili powder, and refried beans. Cover and cook on low for 7–8 hours.
3. Heat taco shells as directed on package. Peel and chop the avocados and sprinkle with lime juice; place in bowl. Arrange a buffet with the hot filling, the taco shells, and remaining ingredients. Let people assemble their own tacos.

Then the king gave a great banquet to all his officials and ministers, "Esther's banquet." He also granted a holiday to the provinces, and gave gifts with royal liberality.

—ESTHER 2:18

Classic Slow Cooker Stuffing

SERVES 12–14

Adding condensed soup to stuffing makes it a bit creamy as well as moist. Be sure to stir the stuffing very well before you put it in the slow cooker. Have three or four of these slow cookers going at once to feed a crowd.

14 cups cubed whole wheat bread

½ cup butter

3 tablespoons olive oil

3 onions, chopped

6 cloves garlic, minced

2 (8-ounce) packages sliced fresh mushrooms

1 (10-ounce) can golden cream of mushroom soup

2 cups chicken broth

2 eggs, beaten

1 tablespoon chopped fresh sage

1 tablespoon chopped fresh thyme

1 teaspoon celery salt

½ teaspoon seasoned salt

¼ teaspoon pepper

1. Preheat oven to 300°F. Place the bread cubes on two cookie sheets. Bake for 20–30 minutes or until the bread cubes are very dry and slightly toasted. Let cool.
2. In large skillet melt butter with olive oil over medium heat. Add onions and garlic; cook and stir for 5 minutes. Add mushrooms; cook and stir for another 5–7 minutes until vegetables are tender. Set aside.
3. In very large bowl, combine soup, broth, eggs, sage, thyme, celery salt, seasoned salt, and pepper; mix well. Stir in onion mixture. Then add bread cubes, 3 cups at a time, stirring well to incorporate everything.
4. Spray two 4-quart or one 7-quart slow cooker with nonstick cooking spray. Add the stuffing mixture, cover, and cook on low for 5–7 hours, stirring once during cooking time.

Roasted Root Vegetables

SERVES 24–26

Roast root vegetables in one slow cooker, and cook Roasted Tender Vegetables (page 212) in another so they all cook to perfection. After they're done, you can mix them, or serve them separately as a choice in a buffet line.

8 potatoes, peeled and cubed
3 sweet potatoes, peeled and cubed
8 carrots, cut into chunks
2 parsnips, peeled and cubed
3 onions, chopped
6 cloves garlic, minced
2 cups vegetable broth
2 teaspoons salt
½ teaspoon pepper
1 teaspoon dried oregano leaves
½ teaspoon dry mustard powder

1. In 6- or 7-quart slow cooker, combine all ingredients and mix well. Cover and cook on low for 7–9 hours or until vegetables are tender when pierced with a fork.
2. Stir gently to combine, then serve, or hold on low heat for 2 hours, stirring occasionally.

Super Simple Mashed Potatoes

SERVES 14–18

Dried potato flakes are actually made from real potatoes. When reconstituted in this recipe, they are rich and creamy, with hardly any work.

½ cup butter
1 onion, finely chopped
3 cloves garlic, minced
2 cups water
2½ cups milk
1¼ cups ricotta cheese
⅓ cup grated Parmesan cheese
½ teaspoon seasoned salt
4½ cups dried potato flakes
Pinch nutmeg

1. In medium skillet, melt butter over medium heat. Add onion and garlic; cook and stir until tender, about 6 minutes. Add water; bring to a boil.
2. Pour into 4- or 5-quart slow cooker. Add remaining ingredients, mixing well. Cover and cook on low for 1 hour, then stir potatoes. Cover and cook for 30–40 minutes longer, until potatoes are hot and thick. Can be kept on low for 2 hours, stirring occasionally to maintain texture.

He has filled the hungry with good things and sent the rich away empty.

—LUKE 1:53

Roasted Tender Vegetables

SERVES 24–26
These delicate vegetables turn sweet when they cook. They do not cook for a very long time, so stagger your cooking times accordingly to be sure everything finishes at the same time.

4 green bell peppers, sliced

4 red bell peppers, sliced

2 (8-ounce) packages whole fresh mushrooms

2 (8-ounce) packages sliced fresh mushrooms

3 onions, chopped

6 cloves garlic, minced

2 cups vegetable broth

2 teaspoons seasoned salt

½ teaspoon pepper

2 teaspoons dried thyme leaves

In 5- or 6-quart slow cooker, combine all ingredients and mix well. Cover and cook on low heat for 3–5 hours or until vegetables are tender.

Chocolate Caramel Drops

YIELDS 120 CANDIES
Making candy in the slow cooker is a great way to streamline the process. The candy stays soft until you want to use it, so there's no reheating.

1 pound white almond bark, chopped

2 (12-ounce) packages semisweet chocolate chips

1 (11-ounce) package milk chocolate chips

1 (11-ounce) package white chocolate chips

2 (1-ounce) squares unsweetened baking chocolate, chopped

1 (14-ounce) bag caramels, unwrapped and chopped

5 cups small pecan halves

1. Combine almond bark, all the chocolate chips, and unsweetened chocolate in 5-quart slow cooker. Cover and cook on low for 2–3 hours, stirring occasionally, or until chocolate melts and mixture is smooth.
2. Stir in the caramels and pecan halves. Immediately drop candies by tablespoons onto waxed paper. Let stand until set. Store in airtight container at room temperature.

He who gives to the poor will never want, but he who shuts his eyes will have many curses.

—PROVERBS 28:27

Index